1994

Democracy in
the Russian School

Democracy in the Russian School

The Reform Movement in Education Since 1984

EDITED BY

Ben Eklof and Edward Dneprov

Westview Press

BOULDER • SAN FRANCISCO • OXFORD

Copyright © 1993 by Westview Press, Inc.

Published in 1993 in the United States of America by Westview Press, Inc., 5500 Central Avenue, Boulder, Colorado 80301-2877, and in the United Kingdom by Westview Press, 36 Lonsdale Road, Summertown, Oxford OX2 7EW

Library of Congress Cataloging-in-Publication Data
Democracy in the Russian school : The reform movement in education
   since 1984 / edited by Ben Eklof and Edward Dneprov.
      p.   cm.
   Includes index.
   ISBN 0-8133-1349-X
   1. Education—Russian S.F.S.R.—History—20th century.
2. Educational change—Russian S.R.S.R.—History—20th century.
I. Eklof, Ben, 1946–   . II. Dneprov, E. D.
LA583.R88D46   1993
370'.947—dc20   92-5888
                                                                    CIP

Printed and bound in the United States of America

The paper used in this publication meets the requirements
of the American National Standard for Permanence of Paper
for Printed Library Materials Z39.48-1984.

10   9   8   7   6   5   4   3   2   1

Contents

PART THREE
The Opposition in Power

Tables and Figures

The Peredelkino Conference, October 18, 1986, where the "pedagogy of cooperation" was formulated. *From left to right:* Sh. Amonashvili, L. Nikitina, S. Soloveichik, S. Lysenkova, V. Matveev, B. Nikitin, V. Shatalov, V. Karakovsky, I. Volkov, A. Adamsky, G. Aleshkina, and E. Il'in. (Photo by Yuri Vladimirov; provided courtesy of Stephen Kerr and Simon Soloveichik.)

1

Democracy in the Russian School: Educational Reform Since 1984

Amidst the turmoil and excitement of events of recent years in the former Soviet Union, changes in education have, perhaps understandably, attracted little attention in the West. As important as education is, most would consider it an issue for the "day after," once more pressing issues of economic and political stabilization have been resolved. Lenin once remarked caustically of the liberal enthusiasts in the Committee for Literacy in St. Petersburg at the turn of the century: "If they think they can change the world, let them try!" Lenin's skepticism about the capacity of schools to affect social change, and cynicism about those who try, has a modern ring, more so than the ameliorationist, Enlightenment-driven views of nineteenth-century Russian reformers, who believed that schools could be used to dispel the darkness of popular ignorance, to promote science and a modern cast of mind--to *transform* society. Today, schools seem mired in the woes of society, incapable of holding up against powerful currents increasingly marginalizing formal education, or subverted by poverty, crime, declining attention to the printed word, and the seeming irrelevance of the curriculum. Schools do a better job of *replicating* society than of changing it.

Yet today in the Russian Federation a team of militant reformers has come to power in the restructured Ministry of Education. They are determined not only to redesign the school system, but also to use the new schools to create a different society, one peopled by individuals capable of taking initiative and responsibility and of building a participatory democracy.

The Minister of Education, Edward D. Dneprov, is an historian by training, steeped in the issues, perspectives, and even rhetoric of the period of Russia's Great Reforms during the 1860s, but also a *shestidesiatnik* (or "man of the sixties") in that he came to political maturity in the era of the Twentieth Party

1

Congress and Khrushchevian reforms. Dneprov was responsible for putting together in 1988 a team of sociologists, psychologists, philosophers and innovators in education. This team was joined under the umbrella of *VNIK-shkola*, or, roughly, "Ad Hoc/Temporary Research Committee on the Schools" which in turn produced a set of *kontsteptii* (concept papers or guidelines) for reforming teacher training, overhauling the general education school, implementing continuing education, and restructuring pre-school education. The ideology of this movement stems from the "pedagogy of cooperation" which was first articulated in 1986,[1] but which has deeper roots in the developmental psychology of Lev Vygotsky,[2] the pre-revolutionary and early Soviet progressive education tradition, and diverse Western currents which have long influenced Russian pedagogy.

It is the task of this brief introduction to outline the history of the current reform movement in Russian education, to summarize its program, and to comment briefly upon the current status of the schools in the context of the current situation in Russia as a whole.

I am not a fully detached observer of these events. Trained as a social historian, I first met Dneprov in the archives, and a close professional and personal relationship developed around our mutual interest in the history of Russian education. In the summer of 1989 Dneprov attended a conference held in Philadelphia on the Great Reforms in Russian History; by then it had become obvious that his energies were elsewhere. As his prominence rose in the reform movement, so my own attention was diverted to current concerns in education, at least partially to understand why my colleague had become a public figure, what his program was and what its prospects for success were, and last, but not least of all, what perspective his training as a historian of pre-revolutionary Russia had contributed to his current activities. I admire and respect Dneprov and the team which came together under VNIK. This does not mean that I do not have an independent perspective, or that I am entirely unskeptical of certain components of the program or elements of the ideology. Yet it would be dishonest to conceal the personal connection that exists.

Moreover, having received my training as a social historian, I have developed a profound wariness of what Marx called the "illusion of politics," i.e., the belief that changes in society flow from the pens of legislators, or that there is any direct relationship between the beliefs and programs of politicians and what actually happens in schools. Instead, I see schools as arenas of "contestation," in which the diverse agendas of children, parents, teachers, administrators and the community at large are negotiated and the outcomes are unpredictable. I am ill at ease looking at schools "top down," but this is exactly what this volume is about. The reader is cautioned that I know more about what is happening in the corridors of the ministry than in the corridors of the schoolroom, where indeed the situation today seems to be remarkably diverse, volatile and--perhaps more than at any other time in the twentieth century--quite independent of ministerial control. There is no question in my mind that the "pedagogy of cooperation" and the VNIK program are eminently worthy of attention; for here many of the rich strands making up *obshchestvennost'*, or public consciousness in Russia today, can be studied, and the often contradictory relationship between these strands investigated. I am also certain that there is no way to fully understand Russian education today without reading the documents emanating from the ministry. The massive survey research conducted by VNIK and the formerly secret materials now released by the ministry provide us with extremely valuable information on conditions in the schools as well as on attitudes of key actors (pupils, parents, teachers). Nevertheless, this is primarily a study of the *prescriptive* rather than the *descriptive*; let the reader be forewarned.

Soviet Education Before 1985

The Soviet school emerged in stages and drew its inspiration from a variety of sources. The school system in Imperial Russia had been built from the top down, beginning with research institutions and universities, turning later to secondary schools, and only in the second half of the nineteenth century extending to primary education. It was structured along continental lines, and was especially heavily influenced by German pedagogy and administrative practices. At the same time, alternative approaches enjoyed considerable appeal among educators; particularly important were the preachings of Lev Tolstoy and, after 1905 the writings of John Dewey on education. The first Soviet school legislation (1918) and early approaches to education during the NEP period (1921-1929) reflected the profound influence of progressive theories and practice, both Russian and Western.[3]

The Soviet system of education which developed under Stalin and was elaborated, rather than dismantled, under his successors, uprooted the progressive, inquiries-oriented and democratic tradition of NEP.[4] As it emerged, the Stalinist school was an integral part of what the ideology of perestroika labelled the "administrative-command" system. Like the system as a whole, education was characterized by a "top-down" approach: vertical lines of authority extended downward from the ministries through the regional and district authorities (*ronos, goronos*) to the directors of schools, teachers, and ultimately the pupils. There were ways directors could exert a measure of independence, and differences in teaching style certainly created diverse climates in the classroom.[5] Under Brezhnev, as belief in communism evaporated and opportunities to advance in society narrowed--leaving many youth "warehoused" in vocational schools or indifferent to grades--alienation spread and disciplinary problems became serious in many areas. Nevertheless, the system remained characterized by authoritarian approaches, uniforms, homework, rote learning in large classrooms, and a uniform and tightly controlled curriculum. The Communist Party maintained tight control over definitions of historical truth and interpretations of current reality, even as Soviet literature increasingly portrayed a reality at odds with such interpretations and as young people gained more and more access to alternative sources of information.[6] Funding was rigidly controlled by the central authorities, and directors of schools were left virtually no discretion in allocating revenues.[7] At the same time, the proportion of national income devoted to education was steadily declining, and calculations of outlays per capita placed the Soviet Union far behind most developed countries in expenditures on education.[8] Teachers worked extraordinarily long hours[9] and had virtually no autonomy in the classroom or representation outside it; the official teachers' union served largely as a "transmission belt" or company union to convey directives from above. As for research in education, it was dominated by the Academy of Pedagogical Sciences, first founded in 1944 and employing (in 1985) 1,700 specialists in 15 (22 by 1991) various institutions. Although the Academy included talented and dedicated people, it tended to stifle competition (in fact there was no procedure for competition for grants in research), and it was held in low regard, both at home and abroad (in daily speech, it was distinguished from the "Big Academy" or the Academy of Sciences).

Reformers today argue that the Stalinist school suppressed individual identity formation (*lichnost'*), and worked instead to produce "cogs" (*vintiki*--a word borrowed from a famous utterance by Stalin). The contrast may be too stark, but there can be no doubt that the Soviet school encouraged conformity and political docility, and generally suppressed initiative as well as independent thought. The perceived needs of the economy and the state were put above those of the individual. On the other hand, because over time more and more subjects were added to the curriculum (creating, incidentally, the problem of *mnogopredmetnost'*, subject overloading) less and less attention could be devoted to socialization, or upbringing (*vospitanie*). By the 1970's the central goal of education had become imparting "ZUNY," which was the educator's derogatory shorthand for the Russian language equivalents of "knowledge, habits, and skills."

By the time of Brezhnev's death, problems had mounted, as had frustration with the seeming inability of in-house approaches to address these problems. According to the Soviet press at the time, education suffered from "overloaded syllabuses, textbooks, and pupils," from a shortage of qualified preschool and school-level personnel, from inadequate school buildings and equipment. According to official data, as late as 1988 21 percent of all students attended schools in buildings without central heating, 30 percent were in schools lacking indoor plumbing, 40 percent studied in schools lacking a sewer system, and forty percent (more in rural districts) had no access to sports facilities. More than a quarter of all children attended school in second or even third shifts.[10]

The content of the syllabuses and textbooks was "conceptually overexacting," though "taught by the same old methods." Formalism in assessment procedures was accompanied by widespread abuse--the notorious *protsentomania*, whereby virtually all students were passed on to the next grade, regardless of genuine level of achievement.[11] In short, overworked teachers, whose status in society was rapidly declining, were being required to teach an overloaded curriculum to an increasingly unmotivated student body in crowded classrooms, with inadequate facilities and few amenities, and using antiquated methods.[12]

Official Reform Before 1985

Despite the rigid control exerted over education by the Communist Party and the Academy of Pedagogical Sciences, it would be a mistake to overlook the waves of reform which broke over the Soviet school in the decades preceding Gorbachev's rise to power. Reformers divided into two more or less distinct camps: those who urged more equality, more uniformity and more applied, especially vocational, training; and a more disparate group urging diversity, decentralization and a range of experimental, individualized approaches--a *differentiated* education which its opponents would call elitist.[13] It would be wrong to label the former the official camp, and the latter the opposition, for debate took place *within* official circles and in the official press, and there is no *necessary* link between egalitarianism and centralization (indeed, NEP educational policy was egalitarian and placed great emphasis upon local school boards, while the Stalinist school was highly centralized, authoritarian and differentiated--in that it practiced streaming). Nevertheless, it is generally true that the egalitarian strain was linked with a belief in centralized hierarchy, conservative patriotism and an authoritarian classroom. It dominated the Central Committee, the ministry and the Academy of Pedagogical Sciences. Similarly, the drive for differentiation tended to be located at the margins of the official educational community, but was supported by the burgeoning middle classes and scientific community, which had little interest in programs forcing their offspring to work in factories or the fields and were inclined to oppose "levelling." This strain was transmitted in informal seminars within the educational community, by innovative approaches introduced in "marginal" subjects such as art and music,[14] through experiments in isolated schools (often repressed after intervention by the Academy of Pedagogical Sciences), and by a small number of committed reformers within the APN, protected by psychologist Vasily Davydov, whose international reputation gave him a measure of inviolability.[15] Within the reform movement today, the names of V. Sukhomlinsky, V. Shatalov, and S. Lysenkova, all teachers who suffered in the 1970s from the heavy hand of the Academy, are revered.

Under Khrushchev, a major reform was launched in 1958, in an attempt to make access to secondary schooling and the universities more democratic, and to force children of white-collar families to receive training in manual labor (thereby gaining respect for the more lowly trades). Khrushchev's drive to "polytechnize" the schools met with fervid resistance, and proved to be "administratively impracticable, socially unacceptable, and inadequately financed."[16] Nevertheless, a simultaneous drive to increase the amount and quality of foreign language instruction in the ordinary schools made progress, and special schools were opened in language, art, music and the sciences.[17]

Perhaps the most interesting set of reforms were those launched in 1966 and implemented throughout the 1970's--which came to be known as the (L. V.) Zankov reforms. These reforms rolled back the effort to "polytechnize" education and reemphasized the importance of a general education over labor training. In this, and in the implicit rejection of Khrushchev's efforts to enhance the prestige of manual labor, they were "conservative." But they also sought to revive aspects of the progressive tradition by introducing "developmental instruction" (*razvivaiushchee obuchenie*) as well as the new math and a social science curriculum which would incorporate new teaching approaches and contrasting perspectives (in order to combat the growing influx of information from Western sources; still, however, leading students to *correct* answers). What is particularly interesting about these reforms is that they legitimated the developmental and (through electives and the expansion of special-profile schools) differentiation components of the progressive tradition, making them part of the official reform effort.[18] These reforms did make some headway. However they ultimately foundered on the fundamental contradiction inherent in efforts to reinvigorate society from above, in efforts to enlist society's energies in the service of goals set by the state. This contradiction was a fatal flaw in Khrushchev's reforms. In fact, it has roots in Russian policy formation extending back as far as the Great Reforms under Alexander II (1855-1881).[19] Moreover, these efforts demonstrated the growing difficulty of devising measures that would satisfy the diverse constituencies represented in the school and the society as a whole.

Thus, there was some evolutionary change (particularly curriculum modification, and increasing length of schooling) and there were departures from the monolithic model of the general secondary school.[20] Paradoxically, many of these reforms ultimately contributed to the sense of crisis in education by the early eighties. Curriculum overloading was a way of avoiding fundamental change, and reflected processes occurring in the political environment as a whole. Interest group negotiations had become the way by which the Brezhnev leadership integrated all powerful sectors into the system. As long as the pie (the economy) continued to grow, each group could be mollified with a small increment from year to year. Similarly, in education, various groups (the scientific community, ideologists, industrial managers) all pointed to the exponentially growing volume of knowledge in the world and demanded time to impart more information. But the potential of the economy, like that of the school-day, was finally exhausted. To borrow the terminology of Soviet economists, the *extensive* approach to economic growth, whereby abundant resources were thrown at problems with little concern for cost or efficiency, was now bankrupt. Life, both inside and outside the classroom, was now a *zero-sum game*--my loss is your gain, and vice versa--unless the entire system, both school and economy, could be restructured to function according to *intensive* principles. What this meant in economic terms was relatively clear, or became so under Gorbachev: privatization, marketization, dismantling of the old command structures, and reliance upon individual initiative--the so-called *human factor*. But what did this mean for the schools? What traditions and what rhetoric could reformers in education call upon? Essentially, it meant that the old method of imparting an ever-growing body of information by means of traditional, "frontal," techniques (in Russian, the equivalent is roughly "the informational-explanatory method") had to be discarded, and the old, pre-revolutionary dream of helping students "learn how to learn" revived, now through methods built around developmental psychology.

In fact, one more attempt was made to square the circle, and to find a solution to the mounting problems of the school through incremental reforms which left the system fundamentally intact. The 1984 reform, initiated under Andropov, then Chernenko, but with the active participation of then-Politburo member Michael Gorbachev,[21] pursued several goals: to substantially increase funding (especially capital inputs and teachers' salaries); to encourage more children to pursue vocational rather than general education curricula after the eighth grade (surveys conducted at the time showed that most parents thought this was a wonderful idea, but not for their own children); to lower the age of entry from seven to six (thereby giving children an extra year of formal schooling and diminishing overloading, but also taking children out of the hands of incompetent kindergarten teachers, where child-care had been largely reduced to custodial functions); and, once again, to revise the general curriculum, improve teaching training and rewrite textbooks. The draft reform was published with great fanfare in early 1984, a huge, orchestrated "public discussion" ensued, and the final legislation emerged virtually unchanged three months later.[22] In January, 1985, a plan was issued for introducing computer education, and in April new rules were issued to govern teacher-pupil relations.

Gorbachev, Glasnost', Perestroika, and Education

But soon the law was a dead letter, overcome by events in the world outside, and labelled a typical product of the "era of stagnation" (the ritualistic, and quite inaccurate, phrase used to describe the late Brezhnev period in contrast to the period of "renewal" under Gorbachev--such simplified descriptors and polarities were, ironically, one of the most characteristic features of Soviet political culture).[23]

Indeed, since 1984 the Soviet Union has experienced a seemingly endless series of tumultuous events. Chernobyl, the Armenian earthquake and revelations of environmental devastation as well as "human degradation"[24] fought for headlines with the remarkable political changes which led to the first free elections in the Russian Empire since 1917, the establishment of the People's Congress of Deputies and, finally, to an end to the Communist Party monopoly over political power. In 1988 a powerful movement for political independence emerged on the empire's borders; in 1989 Eastern Europe won its political independence, and at the close of 1991, the Soviet Union itself disintegrated, leaving Russia aligned with most of the former republics in a fragile commonwealth (the CIS). The very scale and excitement of the momentous changes underway obscured, for the moment, the failure to develop or implement vitally necessary economic reforms.

Framing all of these events was the dismantling of censorship and elimination of police controls over the thought and behavior of the citizenry. Education has always been an issue of genuine and immediate concern to important segments of the Soviet population.[25] In a climate in which the national history, the economy, environment and political structures were all examined and found critically deficient, it was only natural that education would undergo particularly harsh critical scrutiny, and be labelled yet one more example of *katastroika* (the catastrophe wrought by perestroika). There is a universal tendency toward hyperbolic rhetoric, and especially the rhetoric of catastrophe, in education; this global perception of crisis in education, then, reinforced the national sense that everything was wrong, but that the schools were in particularly deplorable condition.[26]

After the famous April 1985 Plenum, in which the newly installed General Secretary of the Communist Party, Michael Gorbachev, called for serious change in the country, educators began to express dissatisfaction with the 1984 reform.[27] The newspaper *Teachers' Gazette*, under the editorial leadership of Vladimir Matveev, became a muckraking instrument of reform, as well as an organizational core for the innovation movement. Under its aegis, a group of innovative educators met at the writers' colony of Peredelkino in October, 1986. Claiming that working in isolation in different schools over a span of twenty-five to forty years, they had all come up with a common philosophy and similar approaches to the classroom, they issued a Manifesto under the rubric of "The Pedagogy of Cooperation." Over the course of the next two years, three other manifestos were issued, putting forth the philosophy of the "New Pedagogical Thought," which called for more humane relations between teacher and pupil, a "dialogue of cultures," an "open school," greater respect for the autonomy of childhood and for the role of play in learning, and for freedom of choice as well as self-government. Its proponents called the Pedagogy of Cooperation an "open-ended approach" and welcomed diversity in the classroom. They recognized that much of what they advocated was not original; what was different now was that the time was ripe, the environment more conducive, to establish a more democratic classroom, and make the school "an outpost of perestroika." At the same time, these educators went beyond abstractions to suggest ways to bring about a more democratic and humane environment in the classroom, as well as to promote effective learning. These included approaches which had been developed and tested, often in less than optimal conditions, by innovators such as I. Volkov, D. El'konin, B. Nikitin, Sh. Amonashvili, V. Sukhomlinsky, E. Il'in, S. Lysenkova, D. Ogorodnov, V. Shatalov, and M. Shchetinin. *Teachers' Gazette* also sponsored Eureka societies of reform-minded educators.[28] Like other "informal" groups springing up throughout the country, these societies mushroomed--there were some 500 by 1989.[29] In January, 1987, when a new Statute of General Secondary Education was promulgated, it was immediately attacked by *Teachers' Gazette* as contradicting the call for democratization of society issued at the January Plenum of the Central Committee of the Communist Party and as a virtual carbon copy of the earlier, 1970 Statute.

In one sense, the reform movement was a local embodiment of high politics, taking its cue from the general directions of reform under Gorbachev, and especially glasnost and democratization. But it also represented the renewal, or legitimation, of long marginalized or even repressed perspectives in education, the triumph of the progressive (used as a descriptive rather than a normative term) tradition against the educational establishment--the ministries, the Academy of Pedagogical Sciences and the official Teachers' Union. And the increasing official emphasis upon "the human factor" privileged education in the rhetoric of perestroika, for if the success of reform depended, in the long term, upon fostering qualities of initiative, independence and responsibility, what could be more logical than to begin with the schools? Thus, the period 1985-1987 witnessed the emergence of a campaign for greater teacher autonomy in the classroom and for new approaches to the child. At the same time, in the press criticism was widespread of special profile schools catering to the elite. Thus, the wave of criticism of the schools comprised elements of egalitarianism as well as support for differentiation.[30]

Unsurprisingly, there was bureaucratic resistance to reform, and the Academy of Pedagogical Sciences launched a fierce campaign (especially at an in-house gathering in December, 1986) to discredit both the reform movement in education and its most prominent proponents. The Ministry of Enlightenment in Moscow dragged its heels, and (except in Estonia, Kazakhstan and Georgia--see Chapter 5), the outlying regions continued to perform ritual obeisances while maintaining traditional practices.[31] But by mid-1987 Gorbachev's sweeping personnel changes were beginning to have an impact on both the Party and the ministries.

In February, 1987, a group of educators, including several representatives of the APN, met with a writers' group at the House of Literature in Moscow to discuss the theme "school and society." Several of the APN representatives criticized the pedagogy of cooperation movement but one of this group, Dneprov, offered his support, and called for a "revival of the public education movement" of the late nineteenth century as well as for the "destatization" (*razgosudarstvlenie*) of the schools. Matveev, who attended the meeting, published the text of Dneprov's speech (Chapter 6). A day later Yegor Ligachev, second to Gorbachev in the Politburo, but a staunch conservative as well, addressed the APN, and mockingly criticized Dneprov for erring as an historian by 150 years (there had been, he asserted, no official school in Russia since the reign of Nicholas I). But on April 17, Gorbachev addressed the Twentieth Congress of the Komsomol (Young Communist League), and sharply criticized the educational community for *probuksovka*, or stalling on reform.[32] What was causing the delay? Here is Dneprov's explanation:

> As with other reforms, educational reform has encountered a series of obstacles and barriers during its conception and promulgation. At the first and second stages of school reform--the period of preparation and adoption--the primary obstacles were ideological. During those years when the reforms languished, and during the first, "pre-market" period of implementation, political and societal barriers came to the fore. Today, the greatest dangers are associated with economic barriers. We emphasize that economic barriers have only recently become pre-eminent, rather than earlier, as others assert, perhaps to defend their failure to act, or even simply to sabotage the reform.
>
> An understanding of the nature of the obstacle course encountered by the school reform was essential not merely to adopt the correct tactics of maneuver, but also for devising a general strategy for development and implementation. That this was so was evident even at the initial stages of the reform to the proponents of school reform and to many others, but not to the architects and captains (*proraby*) of perestroika, for whom the light dawned only much later.
>
> At the onset of perestroika its initiators believed that the only way to overcome the inexorably approaching crisis was via *acceleration* of the economic machine. But adoption of the slogan *uskorenie* led to traditional, short-sighted extensive measures, which were simply dangerous in this context. After all, we were proposing to accelerate movement which was hurtling us into an abyss. The same could be said of the schools, where the ongoing crisis was only exacerbated by the 1984 reforms.

It soon became clear that the old economic wagon had built-in limits to the speed it could achieve--it could never become an airplane, nor even a steamship. For that, an entirely new design was called for. This put radical economic reform on the agenda. But it, like the effort then underway to reform the school reforms, could not take place without the larger context of overall societal and economic transformation. And so, reform of the political system was put on the agenda. But here it was suddenly "discovered" that at the end of the reformers' tunnel loomed the greatest obstacle: the pillars of outdated ideological nostrums, holding back economic, political, and social--including school--reforms.

The fact that this chief obstacle loomed large from the start gave a bitter ideological coloration to the project of school reform from its early days. And this fact prompted an equally bitter and protracted struggle against school reform. This struggle was "personally" directed by the Science and Education Section of the Central Committee of the Communist Party of the Soviet Union, which mobilized the army of official educators, well-nourished by the CC, into waves of frontal and flank attacks.[33]

An All-Russian Congress of Educators was scheduled to be convened in order to discuss ways to improve implementation of the 1984 reform. But it was to be packed with the old guard and was unlikely to produce a coherent agenda. On the eve of the Russian Teachers' Congress Dneprov published another article in *Pravda*, ("Faith in the Teacher") in which he proposed postponing the nation-wide congress. The article was heavily censored (particularly passages criticizing the 1984 reform) but nevertheless, in line with similar calls being made by leading reformers like Shalva Amonashvili and V. F. Shatalov, brought into currency the phrase "reform of the reform" and linked Gorbachev's recent criticism of the slow pace of perestroika to the lack of change in education. A day after the article appeared, on June 2, then Minister of Enlightenment of the USSR, S. G. Shcherbatsky, announced that the scheduled nation-wide conference had been postponed.

In July, new First Deputy Minister of Education A. A. Korobeinikov sent a note (co-signed by leading child psychologist, Anton Petrovsky--today the head of the reconstituted Russian Academy of Pedagogical Sciences) to the Central Committee of the Communist Party calling for additional funding for education, the establishment of a working group to draw up a package of reform proposals, and a conference of the Central Committee on educational concerns.[34] The note reached Ligachev, who in place of a conference (*soveshchanie*) proposed a more weighty plenum.

Frustrated by his inability to make progress, Dneprov withdrew from the working group brought together in the APN to propose reform, and travelled to Estonia in July and August in order to make contact with a reformist group in the Estonian Ministry of Education working on a radical set of measures for education. But in the Fall, he had several meetings with Yegor Iakovlev, Gorbachev's closest ally and the intellectual architect of perestroika as well as Politburo man responsible for education and ideology. At the encouragement of Iakovlev and Ligachev (who was bidding to replace Iakovlev in these spheres), a small group of five to seven individuals came together to work out a set of proposals to present to the Central Committee. This group, the embryo of *VNIK-shkola*, submitted its "platform" on December 31, 1987. A month earlier Dneprov, with behind-the-scenes assistance in dealing with the censor from powerful figures in the CC, managed to publish yet another article (Chapter 5) which included much material deleted from his previous article. This was followed, on February 13, 1988, by another piece (Chapter 3) calling for a major overhaul of the way education was administered and for elected school boards and, on March 1, by proposals to overhaul the Academy of Pedagogical Sciences (Chapter 7).

Dneprov has repeatedly called 1988 a major turning point in the history of Russian education, a year in which genuine reform "from below" was initiated, replacing the stage-managed efforts of previous years. This argument has much in favor of it; but there can also be little doubt that the trigger of this new reform from below was the speech "from above" by Yegor Ligachev on education to the Central Committee Plenum which convened on February 17, 1988, and that the subsequent Plenum resolution on education for the first time empowered teacher-innovators, until then waging an unequal struggle against the superior forces of the APN. In this speech Ligachev listed the woes plaguing Soviet education, lambasted the bureaucracy, and called for greater autonomy for the teacher, self-government of the schools, including election of principals, the establishment of elected school boards, a new curriculum for the schools, encouragement of diversity (to be sure, within the *unitary* system of education) and a new generation of textbooks. He also endorsed a restructuring of the APN, calling for "a genuinely new academy, with a new charter, new election procedures and, possibly, periodical recall of its members."[35]

In an interview, Minister Dneprov told me that of the proposals put forward to the CC by the working group, Ligachev's speech reflected most closely the concern to restructure educational governance, for democratization was the major concern of the Party leadership at the time. Other key proposals, including scaling down the official goal of achieving a universal eleven-year mandatory general education (Chapter 11), for making the school a joint state-societal enterprise (see Chapter 9), and for introducing *variativnost'* and *alternativnost'* were either ignored or met with a lukewarm response (the Plenum did endorse the notion of a *bazovaia shkola* or core curriculum, leaving more time for electives, individualized instruction and special-profiling of schools).

Events followed rapidly (see Chapter 8). On March 8, 1988, the three ministry-level structures controlling the schools (the Committee of Vocational-Professional Education, the Ministry of Enlightenment, and the Ministry of Specialized Secondary and Higher Education) were eliminated, or combined into the State Committee of Education, headed by Gennady Iagodin. Initially, Iagodin turned to the APN for help, but then, becoming frustrated, he contacted the group preparing the materials for the Plenum, instructing them to continuing preparing a package of reforms and to establish an independent organization. *VNIK-shkola* came into being on June 1, 1988.[36]

VNIK and the New Program for Education[37]

Wasting no time, the organizational bureau of the fledgling organization retreated to Lastochki, a Pioneer Camp near Sochi on the Black Sea, for a four-day conference.[38] The sessions, or *organizatsionno-deiatel'nostnye igry*, involved one hundred participants interacting in teams for up to fourteen hours a day over four days, in order to develop an ethos and strategy for *VNIK-shkola*, which soon grew from its core of twenty to over two hundred full or part-time members in eighteen so-called laboratories or workshops. When the group returned from Sochi[39] on July 26 (during the historic Nineteenth Party Conference) it had prepared "*concept papers (kontseptsii)*" on general education, restructuring the system of educational governance, and on reforming the Academy of Pedagogical Sciences, as well as a Draft Statute for the School. The concept papers were submitted to the Collegium of the State Committee of Education where, despite fierce, hostile, lobbying from the APN, they received tentative approval. Revised editions of all the concept papers were completed by August 25 (see Chapter 9) and published in *Teachers' Gazette*. Over the next half year, *VNIK-shkola* churned out an astonishing variety of documents, ranging from experimental syllabi for all aspects of the curriculum, to proposals for restructuring pre-school education, vocational education, teacher training, special education, as well as conducting numerous sociological surveys of public opinion and other matters related to education. In addition, it set up branches or "experimental laboratories" in Kalinin and Pervomaisk regions in Moscow, in the city of Urai in Tiumen region, in Krasnoiarsk and in Krasnodar region as well as in Sochi.[40]

By now the APN was running scared. *VNIK-shkola* represented the first challenge it had ever faced to its monopoly over the curriculum (although several of the founders of *VNIK-shkola* were themselves in the APN), and criticism of the APN, relentless since 1986, had intensified in 1988.[41] The State Committee of Education had appointed a special commission under First Deputy Minister Vladimir Shadrikov to reorganize the APN. In August, the

APN submitted its own *Concept Papers*.   Over the next several months an intense public debate raged in the newspapers[42]. The long-awaited Congress of Educators convened on December 20, 1988 and the outcome, after a protracted debate, was a resounding vote in favor of the *VNIK-shkola* proposals over the APN platform.[43]

Thus, by early 1989, victory seemed to be at hand for the reform movement. After a bitter struggle the previous year, the bureaucracy's hold over the schools had been shaken and the ministries themselves reorganized; the monopoly of the APN (though not the APN itself) had been smashed, a new teachers' organization established, and a sweeping program of change devised, discussed, and endorsed. As Dneprov frequently observes, all reforms must go through three stages: development, passage and implementation. Now, reformers looked forward to implementing change in short order.

And yet, today, in retrospect, Dneprov labels the period between January, 1989 and July, 1990, one in which reforms were "suspended in the air."

The next year and a half, when the fate of the reforms hung by a thread, were, at first glance, yet another, typical bureaucratic anomaly: the reform is dead, long live the reform! But, the seeming anomaly is but an apparition. Our habit of blaming the bureaucracy is highly superficial. In fact, the bureaucracy is a highly sensitive barometer, instantaneously registering the slightest changes in the political atmosphere. With a political standoff in society, the powers that be made a point of keeping the arrow on the barometer between the readings of "overcast" and "changing" weather.

The chameleon became the symbol of the authorities during the period of perestroika. It reflected perennial vacillation, a stultifying flood of verbiage accompanied by a no less stultifying inertia. The champions of perestroika created merely the semblance of reform, in the realm of education as elsewhere. Half a year transpired before the new Statute on the Schools, adopted by the Congress, was finally passed under enormous pressure from below. The *Concept* approved by this same Congress got lost in the political labyrinth and never saw the light of day. No one even discussed the need to devise a concrete program for promulgating this reform.

In short, the reform was essentially blocked. As a director of a school in Krasnoyarsk said, "the teacher picked up his foot but didn't know where to put it down"; i.e., whether to move forward or march in place. This condition of maddening indecision, with the reform hanging in the balance and teachers uncertain how to proceed, continued for a year and a half, until the new leaders of the Russian Federation committed themselves to an independent and consistent endeavor to implement the reforms.

In this period there were in fact some significant victories. One was confirmation by the State Committee for Education of four provisional statutes: for the secondary school (essentially embodying the key notions in *Concept Paper*), vocational education, the secondary specialized school, and higher education.[44] The Creative Teachers' Union held its first conference.[45] Iagodin created a National Council of Education and local elected school boards to allow more public input as well as local autonomy.[46] But the reform movement lost its most articulate voice when early in 1989 *Teachers' Gazette* was turned into a weekly, removed from the Russian Ministry of Education and turned over to the Central Committee, and Matveev was forced out as editor (he died in October that year). Elections to the Presidium of the APN produced mixed results, and reorganization of that institution was successfully blocked.[47] Indeed, when the first Congress of People's Deputies met, the APN was given *ex officio* several seats. The fledgling Creative Teachers' Union soon foundered. The National Council of Education, first convened on March 16, 1988, turned out to be a highly conservative organization. It pointedly ignored the *Concept Paper* endorsed at the Congress; this key document was approved only in December, 1989, and then five months later by the Collegium of the State Committee of Education (Chapter 8). The fate of *VNIK-shkola* itself hung in the balance. Established as an ad hoc committee, it initially had virtually no permanent staff, and almost all of the prominent psychologists, sociologists, historians, philosophers and teachers who contributed to its extraordinary efforts did so on a voluntary basis, outside their regular working hours. *VNIK-shkola* was given an additional lease on life early in 1989,[48] but its long term prospects remained murky.

As always, the fate of educational reform was closely linked to the general political and economic changes, or lack of them, in the country; from this perspective, the period beginning early 1989 was indeed one of increasing polarization and drift (Chapter 10). The stunning disintegration of the monopoly of political power exerted by the Communist Party and central government was accompanied by the failure of the 1987 economic reforms to take root and the growing revolt of the country's borderlands. Russia too, which those on the periphery of the country see as the *tsentr*, proclaimed its virtual independence in early 1990. As Boris Yeltsin came to power and the new Russian Parliament began to act, a new era began. It was now, in July, 1990 that Edward Dneprov was appointed Minister of Education of the Russian Federation by Prime Minister Silaev. The opposition had come to power.

By this time, the group around Dneprov had developed a "platform" of ten central goals--five concerning the "external affairs" of the school, and five concerning "internal" affairs (Chapter 12). These oft-repeated principles include, in the first group: democratization (promotion of personal autonomy, self-government, and cooperative practices); an end to the state monopoly over schooling, decentralization of administrative practices; multiplicity, variability,

and alternativnost' (legitimization of alternative forms of schooling); regionalization (the right, indeed obligation, of each region to devise and implement its
own program of educational growth; the right to national self-determination in
education (roughly, "multi-culturalism"); openness (the internationalization of
education, depoliticization and deideologization of the school, as well as
integration into the world educational system).   In general, the ambition
(described in Chapter 8) was to convert the schools from exclusively state-run
or state-dominated institutions to partnerships involving parents, students, the
community and officialdom.

As for the "internal" principles, they are: humanization (a child-centered
education, in opposition to the prevailing "childless" pedagogy in which the
teacher and lesson are central); differentiation (by inclination, interest, and
ability); lifelong education; and finally, a developmental education (emphasizing
inquiry and activization).   The unifying principle was that of *operezhenie*: the
school should be in advance of society; and the classroom should be in
"advance" of the child in that it should provide a challenging environment
facilitating growth.

The Opposition in Power[49]

But Dneprov has had to struggle to advance this agenda of reform.   Since
his initial appointment as Minister of Education, he has had to run the
confirmation gauntlet two additional times.   In addition, as Dneprov pointed out
in a speech in Sochi in September, 1991, the kind of reforms in education he
envisioned were bound to fail unless changes took place simultaneously in the
legal system, property rights, and the political process.   For that reason, and in
order to increase the relative weight of the Ministry of Education in the political
system, Dneprov has devoted much of his energy to the political struggle at the
top.   His critics, nevertheless, have bitterly attacked him for neglecting the
school in favor of "Big Politics" and, by implication, for pursuing his own
career ambitions.[50]

At the same time, he launched an ambitious, multi-pronged effort to
restructure the ministry, to put legislation in place to undergird reform, and to
line up financial support for his policies.   A broad-based strategy of reform to
bring the school system through the period of political and economic transition
was presented to the Conference of Educators in March, 1991, where it won
approval.   Within the ministry, many top advisors were brought in from VNIK,
and the ministry itself was restructured (see Chapter 20).   Among other
noteworthy changes were the establishment of an Institute of Childhood, an
Institute for the Study of Nationality Problems in Education (along with a
Council on Nationality Education) and the creation of a Council of Rectors of
Pedagogical Institutes to oversee a reform of teacher training, as well as a

Sociological Bureau directly under the ministry but with local branches under pedagogical institutes and institutes for inservice training (IUUs).[51]

In February, 1991, after considerable delay and frustration, seven different statutes on education (temporary statutes on higher education, on general secondary education, on specialized secondary education, on vocational education, on pre-school education, on institutions for orphans and wards of the state, and on extramural education) were approved by the Council of Ministers of the Russian Federation, thereby making these statutes (largely derived from the draft statutes approved by the Congress of Educators in late 1988) binding upon all institutions of government rather than upon institutions of the Ministry of Education alone. And on June 11, 1991, newly elected President Boris Yeltsin declared education a priority sector (Decree Number 1).

But along with these advances, resistance to reform continued, even heightened after Minister Dneprov prohibited pre-military training, political propaganda, or religious instruction in the schools. From Dneprov's perspective, this opposition was formidable indeed:

> Opposition to the school reforms did not abate at the political or the societal level; indeed the tempo of opposition increased as implementation began. It was not merely that each concrete step in the direction of reform met with corresponding resistance. Underpinning this reform was the overall activization of those forces determined to undercut the course of reform in Russia in general. These were the same forces which disemboweled the (Shatalin Plan) 500 Days Reform in November, 1990, and two months later provoked military clashes in the Baltic, and yet two months later, put troops on the streets in Moscow. The penultimate and final acts of this scenario are well known: the "(Valentin) Pavlov uprising" in June and the attempted coup in August.
>
> Opposition to school reform in the initial period of implementation was especially visible in two areas: that of demilitarizing the schools and of depoliticizing education. The future military leaders of the coup, Marshall Moiseev and General Varenikov, tried almost literally to wipe off the face of the earth the leadership of the Ministry of Education for its decision to eliminate obligatory military training and its order to remove all weapons from the schools. This seemingly internal issue, raised by the ministry in October, 1990, turned out to be a trial by fire of sorts. Over and over again and in various settings, intimidating generals hurled thunder bolts at the ministry, demanding that the order be rescinded. On three different occasions the question was examined--with different outcomes--by the Council of Ministers of the Russian Federation. It was only in May of 1991 that this august body finally came down resolutely in support of the initiative of the ministry.

And the events were no less dramatic surrounding the decision taken in January, 1991 by the Collegium of the Ministry of Education to depoliticize education and remove political parties from the schools. The leadership of the Russian Communist Party, hand in hand with *Pravda*, with the State Committee of Education of the USSR and the Academy of Pedagogical Sciences of the USSR, did not delay in unleashing a massive campaign against this decision. The ministry was accused of every conceivable mortal sin leading to the ultimate collapse of the school system. More traditional approaches were also brought to bear: threats of summons before the Politburo and exclusion "from the ranks" (of the Party). But such threats no longer held much conviction; the ranks of the faithful had dwindled. Moreover, the ranks of the Russian Communist Party were of the kind from which it was better to keep one's distance.

There were five basic barriers to educational reform during the initial period of implementation. Three represented traditional forces: the party structure, official pedagogy, and the aggrieved old *apparat*. Two were not so traditional: the army leadership and the incipient "shadow economy" in education, hastening to profit by trading in the property and resources of the educational system in the prevailing economic and legal chaos. Twice in one year these forces tried to paralyze the reforms and simultaneously to decapitate the overly independent ministry. And on both occasions, to repeat a phrase employed by *Izvestiia* ("A New Era?"), they managed to prevent the school from entering a new era.

Postscript: After the Coup

On the morning of the ill-fated coup attempt of August 19 (coincidentally, only a day or so after his latest confirmation in office), Minister Dneprov sent a circular to all local offices of education stating unambiguously that the coup was illegal and that the ministry recognized only the authority of the Russian government.[52] After the failure of the coup, the ministry enjoyed an interval of roughly four months in which it had unprecedented freedom to pursue its agenda: the State Committee of Education was abolished in November, the Academy of Pedagogical Sciences finally disbanded in December, and the belief spread that now, finally, real change could begin. In May, 1992, the minister also won approval for his long-advocated (see Chapter 18) Statute on Non-Government Educational Institutions--essentially a charter for private schools.

But since the end of 1991, optimism has rapidly eroded. The collapse of the economy has exacerbated already severe shortages in the schools. Teachers' wages are no longer sufficient to maintain even the most spartan of existences, and alienation among the rank-and-file has reached threatening proportions, as a strike movement repeatedly threatened to spread from health workers to teachers (in December 1990, November, 1991, and May, 1992).[53] A crippling struggle between the executive and legislative branches of government in the Russian Federation has contributed to the paralysis: several members of the Commission on Science and Education of the Congress of People's Deputies, headed by V. Shorin, have regrouped the forces formerly concentrated around the APN[54] and have led a vendetta against the minister, forcing him to divert yet more energies to "Big Politics." At this writing, the Law on Education, having undergone at least three drafts, was still being deliberated by the Supreme Soviet, and the minister was highly dissatisfied with the changes that had been introduced to the version he had drawn up (the first version was published in *Teachers' Gazette* in July 1991, and is translated in Chapter 21; the third version was published in the same newspaper on January 14, 1992).[55] As Russian nationalism, fed by resentment and confusion over the collapse of the Soviet Union, by deteriorating economic conditions, and by the harsh terms imposed by the IMF, has spread, Dneprov's critics have attacked him for spending too much time on international projects[56] and too little on the schools.[57]

As for the financial status of the schools, Dneprov managed to achieve a significant pay increase for teachers early in 1991,[58] and a commitment to increase the share given to education from the budget, but these hard-won gains were all but wiped out by inflation. At this writing, teachers were joining medical workers across the country in forming strike committees, and the ministry was once again seeking funds to provide a minimum wage for teachers of three thousand rubles. At the same time, the ministry essentially lost control over the purse strings: by 1992 it was responsible for funding teacher training, vocational education and educational research; the schools themselves were now funded (when at all) by local resources. This, in turn, has significantly augmented the authority of municipal and *oblast'*-level educational authorities. On the one hand, this was a direct fulfillment of the minister's ambition of eliminating the vertical controls which had so stifled initiative and diversity in education, and of turning the ministry into a consultative rather than a supervisory organ. On the other hand, by empowering local authorities who were often tied in with the old networks of power, it presented a significant roadblock to reform.

To make matters even more difficult, the ministry has relinquished the right to confirm appointments of local educational officials (see Chapter 15). Dneprov himself has consistently supported a position (first advanced at the turn of this century by liberal Russian educators) which, in the words of a Western observer, "finds a new, less authoritarian role for the Ministry of Education, namely that of providing expert advice and consultation." This is an approach which may now be "gaining widening support,"[59] but which also puts the ministry in a highly vulnerable position. As centrifugal tendencies increase throughout the country, pressure mounts for firmer controls from the center; as conditions in the schools deteriorate and teachers' wages evaporate in the face of inflation, parents and educators angrily call for the minister to "do something." And in many areas decentralization turns power over to regional level authorities or even teachers, a large proportion of whom are "convinced communists who find it hard to abandon. . . the beliefs they cherished for many years of their lives."[60]

Dneprov is an intellectual in politics, but his writings convey a sense of self-confidence, a determination to find practical solutions, to devise applications for the rich variety of innovative strategies put forward by educators, and an impatience with the opposition to reform which borders on militance. This militance, I believe, stems partly from personal biography--a long history of frustrating altercations with the conservative old guard in the Academy of Pedagogical Sciences in particular.[61] It stems as well from temperament; Dneprov drives those who work with him nearly as hard as he drives himself. It stems, finally, from a profoundly historical sense of the moment, a feeling that opportunities such as those presented today occur rarely, and simply must not be lost to the notorious Oblomovism of Russian intellectual life. It might seem that the militant tone of much of his writing (indeed, not only militant, but military: training in the navy as well as immersion in official Soviet culture resulted in an abundance of military metaphors and analogies in his writing) indicates a budding authoritarian in this *demokrat*. Nothing could be further from the truth. In an interview translated in Chapter 12, Dneprov's interlocutor points out that the minister "has taken on some difficult tasks," and asks if he thinks "he can pull it all off." Dneprov replies affirmatively, but adds: "not in the old way of orders from above." When pressed to describe how he plans "to go about breaking the existing practice of governing through decrees," he replies: "I wouldn't even employ the word **breaking**. . . instead the basic principle should be 'don't even think of issuing commands. . . .'" Elsewhere he argues that the ministry must be turned from a "general staff" into a "general contractor," and that the bureaucracy should administer processes, not people; its role must be to stimulate and negotiate, not command. In fact Dneprov has presided over a dismantling of the hierarchical structure of authoritarian controls in education unprecedented in Russian history. He has encouraged diversity; he has actively promoted the emergence of a system of private education to present a viable alternative to the official schools. His impatience with his opposition in the old guard is with their ability to appropriate the rhetoric and ideology of the reform movement in order to arrest change, or at least to protect their own status and privileges as change occurs. But he has emphasized that in his policies he would be "firm, not punitive."[62]

It is entirely possible that the radical changes underway in education will be diluted, even swept aside or reversed, should Dneprov's formidable opposition have its way and force him out of office, or should the country's precipitous economic decline--far worse than the West suffered during the Great Depression--not be arrested or political stalemate broken. There is, in fact, an inherent contradiction in what the old *VNIK-Shkola* group set out to do: use schools to change society. After all, Dneprov himself has stated that he was drawn into high politics by the recognition first, that the fate of education reform hinged upon economic change, and then that the outcome of the proposed economic reforms depended upon political change and, specifically, upon the survival of a national leadership committed to comprehensive reform. The social ills associated with poverty cannot be addressed in isolation by school programs, no matter how well designed. Thus, it may well be that Dneprov's program will slide into obscurity, like that of one of his most illustrious predecessors, Pavel Ignatiev, whose much admired overhaul of the Tsarist education system (1915-1916) was wiped out by war and revolution.[63] Or perhaps Dneprov will share the fate of Anatoly Lunacharsky, Commissar of Enlightenment during the early Soviet period, whose efforts to introduce a progressive, child-centered school system failed in the face of mounting unemployment, juvenile delinquency and other social problems, underfunding, and political upheaval.

But historical parallels have their limits, and the tendency to see Russian national character as immutable (and tragic), or its history as cyclical, is problematic at best. Despite the imposing difficulties facing the reformers, the environment (both foreign and domestic) is far different than it was earlier this century or during the Great Reforms of the 1860s. The country has enormous resources (human and material), a relatively skilled and highly sophisticated population, and continued potential for growth and evolution.[64] Ironically, perhaps the single most important factor instilling hope in the future must be traced back to the very educational system Dneprov and his group want, rightfully, to change. With all its flaws, the Soviet school has help create a demanding, critical and discerning population which now insists upon a better future, and a better education for its children. Dneprov's perspective, expressed in "The Fourth Reform," serves as a fitting conclusion here, in that it emphasizes the open-ended nature of the project he has undertaken:

> . . . [T]he 1988 reform merely laid the foundation for a genuine restructuring of the school. Its structure is only now being elaborated. And this process is hard going, with setbacks. But, after all, the criterion of success for any reform is its growth potential. We recognize that many of the ideas and positions we earlier adopted are in need of significant reassessment. Only then will it be possible for the school--finally--to keep pace with life.

A Word About the Text:

Edward Dneprov has been a prominent leader of the reform movement, and this volume is dedicated to writings by or about him. Yet he would be the last to claim that he alone originated the momentous changes which have taken place in recent years. Dneprov has often pointed out that the uniqueness of the educational reforms of 1988 resides in their origins in the public education *movement* rather than in official circles, or in the efforts of any individual or organization, no matter how important their role in defining goals or channeling public sentiment.[65] One could equally devote entire studies to the efforts of Shalva Amonashvili,[66] V. Matveev[67] and Simon Soloveichik, Vasily Davydov, Sofia Lysenkova, or many others.

The articles translated below were not originally intended to be a unified text or a comprehensive guide to the reform movent in education. Written at different times and addressed to diverse audiences, they range from what are essentially transcriptions of oral speech to a greatly detailed study of the state of the schools and to highly formal legal documents. Some were put together under the beady eye of the censor and employ euphemisms, circumlocutions, and obligatory obeisances to the Leninist tradition. Others were deliberately phrased to be provocative and polemical, even combative. Although Dneprov's training as an historian is evident both in his frequent attempts to draw parallels with the past and in his concern for the legacy his ministry will leave, the rapid unfolding of events between 1985 and the present have left little time for the kind of reflection and contemplation required for serious historical scholarship, and the proximity to events is too immediate to permit a detached perspective. Thus, the text should be read for what it is: a collection of articles of varying length written largely by or about Dneprov, and laying out in broad strokes the strategy for reform, but without the type of overarching framework or tightly integrated structure that we might expect in a scholarly piece. Roughly speaking, the articles fall into three groups: the first (three through seven) consist of Dneprov's early critiques of education; the second (eight through sixteen) consist of the *VNIK-shkola* program, and materials generated during or soon after Dneprov's appointment in 1990; and the last group (except Yeltsin's decree) were produced by the ministry.

By training Dneprov is a specialist in the history of the public educational movement of the second half of the nineteenth century, the structure of the educational system and policy formation. As minister, his daily work routines focus upon similar concerns. As director of VNIK, he was author or co-author of most of the concept papers produced in 1988, and as minister he also drew up or worked closely with those writing the various statutes or draft laws concerning every aspect of education. Nevertheless, this volume does not do adequate service to many essential components of the radical reform movement, or to many glaring problems in Russian education. Higher education, except for teacher training institutions, is outside the domain of the Ministry of Education. In some areas (such as teacher training), the original *concept papers* had many deficiencies, and are still under revision.[68] In the area of pre-school reform, the pertinent *Concept Paper* has been translated elsewhere.[69] Nationality education remains a central issue; even with the break-up of the Soviet Union, the Russian school system must deal with dozens of languages and cultures. Moreover, the issue of facilitating Russian-language instruction for the more than twenty million Russians remaining in the former Soviet republics is a serious concern for the ministry.[70] The health of school-age children is an urgent concern of the ministry (Chapter 19), and Dneprov has devoted much time to attempts to guarantee that children are adequately fed.[71] In the pivotal area of rural schooling, interesting efforts are underway to restore the earlier condemned "dwarf school" (*malokomplektnaia shkola*), to use it as a cultural hearth to revive the village in general, and even to experiment with approaches eliminating age segregation in the classroom.[72] Special education remains a central concern of the ministry.[73] This is true of vocational education as well. There are some 70 new curricula (*programmy*) in the ministry awaiting circulation, discussion, implementation. There are also 81 new textbooks received by the ministry and looking for a publisher.[74] Finally, the fate of organizations such as the Komsomol and Young Pioneers, and developments in extra-mural education as well as youth culture as a whole are urgent matters.[75] Each of these topics is discussed in the book (see especially Chapter 19). But each merits more comprehensive treatment. Gender and sex-role stereotyping are, lamentably, not issues adequately dealt with by the reform movement in Russia today.

Finally, it must be emphasized that although Dneprov actively collaborated in putting together this text, the selections (in particular of the articles about the minister) and translation are mine, as is the structure of the book. The introduction is also wholly my own interpretation. There were many difficult passages to translate; the texts contain numerous references to contemporary or historical events, and are sprinkled with a vocabulary reflecting the complex hybrid of political cultures making up current discourse in Russia. To make matters worse, the Russian educational tradition has developed its own jargon. At times it seemed to make sense to find exact, current equivalences in order to enhance the familiarity of the discussion to a Western ear. But at other times, particularly when the debate concerned ethnic issues or special education, using current Western terms (themselves often rapidly changing, imprecisely used, or loaded with hidden understandings) would have introduced a spurious, deceptive familiarity; for better or worse, such issues are understood in different ways in Russia today. So, at times I clung rather doggedly to the literal meaning of a sentence or paragraph, at others I took great liberties in freely rendering passages. Given the pressure of deadlines and my own deficiencies in Russian, I am sure many errors crept in. I alone am responsible for these errors.

I have incurred many debts in producing this manuscript. In Russia, Sergei Sosinsky provided first drafts of three of the articles included here. At Indiana University Eli Weinerman served ably as a research assistant; Greg Dudsic, Suzanne Mullin and Scott Presti provided invaluable assistance in preparing the text for production. I am especially grateful to Janet Sayre, who contributed her expertise in making the manuscript ready for publication and spent long hours rendering the text suitable for camera-ready copy. Helen Borovikova and Helen Lenskaia of the Ministry of Education helped locate materials and contributed their intimate understanding of the Russian educational system as well as of ongoing changes to improve the text. Howard Mehlinger, Director of the Center for Excellence at Indiana University also lent his expertise in a critical reading of the text; his personal friendship and encouragement has been equally important. Research and Graduate Development at Indiana University provided funding for a trip to Russia to collect materials. The Office of Research and Development of the School of Education at Indiana University has provided essential support for the Institute for the Study of Soviet Education (ISSE), under whose auspices this volume was written.

Notes

1. For the "pedagogy of cooperation" see the materials collected and translated in the journal *Soviet Education*, Vol. 30, numbers 2-3, 1988; and *Novoe Pedagogicheskoe Myshlenie*, ed. by A. Petrovsky (Moscow, 1989).

2. Vygotsky is a well-known figure in Western education circles, and exerted a powerful influence on Soviet education, and particularly special education, after the death of Stalin. On Vygotsky, see especially James V. Wertsch, *Vygotsky and the Social Formation of Mind* (Cambridge, Mass., 1985).

3. A concise history and description of the Soviet school system can be found in the entry by Friedrich Kuebart in *World Education Encyclopedia*, Vol. 3 (New York, 1988), pp. 1294-1320. See also John Dunstan, *Paths to Excellence and the Soviet School* (Windsor, England, 1978), esp. pp. 17-58. A convenient, if incomplete guide to the literature is William W. Brickman and John T. Zepper, *Russian and Soviet Education 1731-1989: A Multilingual Annotated Bibliography* (New York, 1992). The *Soviet Education Study Bulletin* regularly publishes bibliographic surveys of recent literature on education in the C.I.S. countries. A Russian-language source is *Narodnoe obrazovanie. Pedagogicheskie Nauki: Annotirovannyi Ukazatel' Otechestvennykh Bibliograficheskikh Posobii Na Russkom Iazyke, Opublikovannykh s Serediny XIX Veka Po 1978 God* (Moscow, 1981).

4. On the early Soviet school, see the valuable work by Larry E. Holmes, *The Kremlin and the Schoolhouse: Reforming Education in Soviet Russia, 1917-1931* (Bloomington, Indiana, 1992).

5. See *Inside Soviet Schools*, by Susan Jacoby (New York, 1975).

6. On this, see Ben Eklof, *Soviet Briefing: Gorbachev and the Reform Period* (Boulder, Co., 1989), p. 44; S. Frederick Starr, "Soviet Union: A Civil Society," *Foreign Policy*, No. 70 (Spring, 1988), pp. 31-33.

7. The central bureaucracy provided directives detailing precisely how each ruble was to be spent. But, because of chronic shortages in goods, needed equipment, furniture, or classroom materials could often not be purchased. Yet, funds left unspent at the end of the budget year could not be spent on other needs or carried over into the next year. Instead it was returned to the Ministry, which in turned had to surrender the unspent revenue.

8. According to Yegor Ligachev, in his speech to the Communist Party Plenum in February, 1988, the share of education expenditures in the state budget declined from 11 percent in 1970 to 8 percent in 1986: see *Teachers' Gazette*, February 18, 1988, pp. 1-4.

9. According to one study conducted in Sverdlovsk, teachers spent between nineteen (in urban schools) and twenty three (in rural schools) hours giving lessons each week. If preparation, marking, meetings and other social duties are included, the work week was fifty five and fifty eight hours respectively: Mervyn Matthews, *Education in the Soviet Union* (London, 1982), pp. 62-63.

10. *Soviet Education*, Vol. 31, No. 4 (April, 1989) p. 35.

11. As a result of grade inflation, many of those newly matriculated in institutions of higher education were ill-prepared. A survey of 27,000 new entrants in VUZy at the beginning of the 1987-1988 school year concluded that twenty five percent could not satisfactorily answer test problems designed to measure achievement equivalent to a high school education. Forty five percent of those entering *technicums* could not pass the test. At the Ivanov Engineering Institute, seventy percent could not pass the mathematics test: see *Soviet Education*, Vol. 31, No. 4 (April, 1989), p. 20.

12. A concise summary of the problems and issues facing the Soviet education system can be found in John Dunstan, "Soviet Education: Some Issues of the Eighties," *NASSP (National Association of Secondary School Principals) Bulletin*, Vol. 66, no. 454 (May, 1982), pp. 30-44. See also David L. Williams, "Preparing Future Generations," pp. 105-107.

152, 144

13. Williams, "Preparing Future Generations," p. 11; see also the polemical article by the director of an experimental school in Krasnoyarsk, Sergei Kurganov, entitled (in Russian) "Will Washington Teach Us Russian...Or How Russia Differs From Mozambique," *Teachers' Gazette*, No. 41, 1991.

14. On this, see Muckle, *Portrait of a Soviet School Under Glasnost* (New York, 1990), pp. 109-110. It is revealing that renowned educator, Shalva Amonashvili points out that a turning point in his own professional life was when he attended a presentation at the APN by Dmitri Kabalevsky, whose approaches to early music instruction are recognized throughout the world: see *Novoe Pedagogicheskoe Myshlenie*, p. 157.

15. The history of this experimental movement in the post-Stalin era remains to be written. For one example of the rough-shod tactics used by conservatives to repress any experimentation not sanctioned by the APN, see the case of Vasily Davydov, described in *Moscow News*, No. 21, 1988. A censored survey of experimentation in the schools before 1985 can be found in A. M. Tirul'nikov, *Pedagogika, Rozhdennaia Zhizn'iu* (Moscow, 1988). See also Sh. A. Amonashvili, "*Osnovaniia Pedagogiki Sotrudnichestva*," and M. Sikora "*Pedagogi-Novatory v SSSR: 'Krizis' Academicheskoi Pedagogiki?*" in *Novoe Pedagogicheskoe Myshlenie*, pp. 144-177 and 178-190.

16. Mervyn Matthews, *Education in the Soviet Union* (London, 1982), p. 32.

17. Matthews, *Education in the Soviet Union*, p. 28; John Dunstan, *Paths to Excellence and the Soviet School* (Windsor, England, 1978).

18. The commission appointed to devise a reform was appointed in October, 1964, and the decree laying out the basic terms of the reform issued on November 10, 1966. The Zankov reforms were a complex and contradictory set of measures, the details of which are too complicated to adequately treat here: see Matthews, *Education in the Soviet Union*, pp. 46-57.

19. Alfred J. Rieber, "Alexander II: A Revisionist View," *Journal of Modern History*, Vol. 43, no. 1 (1971), pp. 42-58.

20. Dunstan, *Paths to Excellence*, p. 29.

21. Gorbachev was initially a member of the Politburo commission overseeing the reform and the, after Chernenko's promotion, succeeded to the position of chairman of the commission. When Gorbachev became General Secretary, Yegor Ligachev was placed in charge of the reform effort in education. Note that it was the Communist Party Central Committee, rather than the Ministry of Enlightenment, which stage-managed the process: Williams, "Preparing Future Generations," p. 109.

22. On the 1984 reform, see Beatrice Beach Szekely, "The New Soviet Educational Reform," *Comparative Education Review*, Vol. 30, no. 3 (August, 1986), pp. 321-343; John Dunstan, "Soviet Education Beyond 1984: a commentary on the reform guidelines," *Compare*, Vol. 14, no. 2, 1985, pp. 161-187; Joseph Zajda, "Recent Educational Reforms in the USSR: Their Significance for Policy Development, " *Comparative Education*, Vol. 20, no. 3 (1984), pp. 405-420.

23. In fact, one respected Western observer, James Muckle, has argued that the 1984 Guidelines had several important features and might have had far-reaching effects, in that they called for sweeping changes in aesthetic education and called for teachers to develop creative attitudes in children: *Portrait of a Soviet School Under Glasnost*, p. 73.

24. In a celebrated article written in 1987, political commentator Nikolai Shmelev decried "rampant apathy, indifference, theft and lack of respect for honest work...signs of an almost physical degradation of the Soviet people as the result of drunkenness and sloth." See "Advances and Debts," *Novyi Mir*, No. 6 (June, 1987), p. 145. Similarly, below Dneprov refers to the biological decline of the *genotype* (or gene-pool) as a result both of Stalin's murderous policies and Soviet economic and social policies as a whole.

25. David L. Williams, "Preparing Future Generations: Recent Changes in Soviet Educational Policy," in *The Gorbachev Generation*, ed. by Judith S. Zacek (New York, 1989), p. 109.

26. The following description of events is based upon materials, including several unpublished manuscripts of articles, provided by Minister Dneprov, as well as upon accounts in the periodical press. Two commendable English-language accounts can be found in *Soviet Education Study Bulletin*, Vol. 7, No. 1, 1989: A. Suddaby, "Perestroika in Soviet Education," pp. 14-21, and J. Sutherland, "Soviet Education Since 1984, the School Reform, the Innovators, and the APN," pp. 21-33.

27. See the October 24, 1986 article by prominent sociologist M. Rutkevich, "Is the School Reform a Mistake," translated in *Current Digest of the Soviet Press*, Vol. 38, No. 47, 1986.

28. For brief descriptions of these approaches, see *Pedagogika Sotrudnichestva: Otchety Vstrech Pedagogov-Eksperimentatorov* (Ministerstvo Narodnogo Obrazovaniia Gruzinskoi SSR: Tbilisi, 1988), esp. pp. 29-42. The same materials are in *Teachers' Gazette*, October 18, 1986; February 10, 1987; October 17, 1987; March 19, 1988, and October 18, 1988. See also below, "The State of Education".

29. The *Evrika* societies formed the core of the Creative Union of Teachers, which formed in 1988 and held its first national congress in May, 1989.

30. *VNIK-shkola* sociological research of public opinion showed that in 1988 roughly fifteen percent of teachers could be described as favoring radical innovation in the schools and that parents' demands on the school were quite diverse. For example, a survey of (generally well-heeled, and disproportionately women) parents from Kalinin district in Moscow showed that thirty one percent expected the schools to develop a broad range of capabilities, thirty one percent wanted a "firm basis of knowledge," twenty-one percent hoped that schools would provide their children the foundations for making independent choices in life, thirteen percent were looking for the schools to implant "a high level of culture," nine percent wanted primarily firm preparation for enrolling in the university, seven percent "conditions for self-realization," and four percent "adequate professional training." See V.S. Sobkin, et. al., *Otnoshenie k Obrazovanie: Sotsiologicheskii Ekspress-Analyz* (Moscow, 1989), p. 22; as well as a survey by the same title of teachers, parents and schoolchildren in Rostov-on-the-Don (Moscow, 1989).

31. See the criticism of education in the Armenian SSSR expressed at a gathering of the commissions on public education of the USSR Supreme Soviet on January 20, 1988, summarized in *Teachers' Gazette*, January 23, 1988. For the changes in Estonia, which preceded the groundswell of reform in Russia, see the article by E. Grechkina, "On the Road to Renewal," in *Soviet Education*, Vol. 31, No. 3 (March, 1989), pp. 73-95, and the original, Russian version, in *Narodnoe Obrazovanie*, No. 8, 1987, pp. 11-17; also: *Platforma Narodnogo Obrazovaniia Estonskoi SSR i Programma Perestroiki Narodnogo Obrazovaniia Estonskoi SSR: Proekty* (Komitet po Narodnomu Obrazovaniiu Estonskoi SSR: Tallin, 1988); E. R. Grechkina et al., *Na Puti k Novoi Shkole: Opyt Perestroiki Narodnogo Obrazovaniia v Estonskoi SSR* (Moscow, 1988).

32. See the translation in *Current Digest of the Soviet Press*, Vol. 39, No. 16 (May 20, 1987), p. 12.

33. This, and the following direct quotations are from an unpublished text entitled "Obstacles to Reform" provided the author by Minister Dneprov.

34. On this see *Teachers' Gazette*, July 14, 1987.

35. The text of the speech was reproduced in *Teachers' Gazette*, January 23, 1988, and is translated in *Soviet Education*, Vol 31, No. 4 (April, 1989), pp. 6-67.

36. Decree (*Prikaz*) Number 99 of the State Committee of the USSR of Education: May 31, 1988: Appendix Number 3 to this document provides a full list of original participants, including eleven school directors and fourteen practicing teachers, as well as three full members of the APN.

37. Much of the following material, including the direct quotations, is taken, with permission of the author, from "Reform of Russian Education," a draft of an article to be published in *The Russian Revolution in Education*, (forthcoming: edited by Per Dalin and Edward Dneprov), from the unpublished stenogram of a speech given at the

Conference on Russian Education in the Transition Period (March 26, 1991), and from the draft of a speech given to a Conference on Reform in Education, held at Sochi, September 6, 1991.

38. On the formation of *VNIK-shkola*, see *Teachers' Gazette*, June 14, 1988. The initial group included, besides its director Dneprov, B. Bim-Bad, Vasily Davydov, Artur Petrovsky, A. M. Abramov, O.S. Gazman, V.I. Slobodchikov (who now directs the Center for Pedagogical Innovation--as *VNIK-shkola* was later renamed). A full list of the original members is in *Vremennyi Nauchno-issledovatel'skii Kollektiv "Shkola" (VNIK)* (Moscow, 1989), a collection of articles from the press in preparation for the Congress of Educators which met in December, 1988.

39. On the Sochi conference, see *Sovetskaia Kuban'*, August 3, 1988, and *Chernomorskaia Zdravitsa* (August 31, 1988).

40. See *VNIK-shkola: Bibliografiia Osnovnykh Rabot* (Moscow, 1989). For a survey of its work up to February, 1990, and a description of its internal structure, see *Vnik-shkola: Promezhutochnye Rezul'taty Raboty* (Moscow, 1990).

41. For a collection of newspaper articles from 1988 criticizing the APN see *VNIK-shkola, Kakoi Byt' APN SSSR (po materialam pressy)* (Moscow, 1988). The two individuals singled out most frequently for criticism for their active suppression of innovative teachers and scholarship were Boris Likhachev and Zoya Malkova (the latter was in charge of the Institute of General Pedagogy, which exerted a monopoly over curriculum development); see, for example, the vitriolic article by Irina Khankhasaeva in *Rossiiskaia Gazeta* (December, 1991, entitled *"Akademicheskii Teatr Pedagogicheskoi Dramy"*). The most cogent defense of the APN was put forward by Boris Gershunksy: *"Kakoi byt' nauke o narodnom obrazovanii (tezisy kontseptsii)"* (report to the general convocation of the APN: Moscow, 1991); *"Eto li Doroga k Khramu?"* *Sovetskaia Pedagogika* (No. 1, 1990), pp. 98-102. Gershunsky later came out in support of reform of the APN: see *"Pedagogicheskaia Poema: Kakoi byt' nauke ob obrazovanii," Teachers' Gazette*, October 22, 1991.

42. Some of the materials produced by this debate are in the *VNIK-shkola*-produced volumes *Vremennyi Nauchno-Issledovatel'skii Kollektiv "Shkola (VNIK)* (Moscow, 1988) pp. 1-214; and *Moia Rech' Na Pedagogicheskom S"ezde (po materialam pressy)* (Moscow, 1988).

43. For a brief discussion of the competing proposals see Muckle, *Portrait of a Soviet School Under Glasnost*, pp. 76-81. Dneprov's speech to the Congress is in *Teachers' Gazette*, December 24, 1988.

44. The original *VNIK-shkola* version of the Statute is in *Teachers' Gazette*, No. 97, August 16, 1988, p. 2. The slightly amended version approved by the 1988 Congress of Educators and promulgated by the State Committee is in *Teachers' Gazette*, No. 85,

July 18, 1989, pp. 1-2; a brief analysis of the Statute can be found in Muckle, *Portrait of a Soviet School Under Glasnost*, pp. 82-83.

45. For materials on the Creative Teachers' Union, see the collection of newspaper articles assembled by *VNIK-shkola* entitled *Tvorcheskii Soiuz Uchitelei SSSR* (Moscow, 1989).

46. See *Teachers' Gazette*, August 24, 1989 (Decree of August 15, 1989, No. 667, in accordance with the resolution of the Supreme Soviet of the USSR date October 10, 1988: *Polozhenie o sovete srednei obshcheobrazovatel'noi shkoly*). It is instructive, from the perspective of 1992, in reviewing this radical document, to read (Article 3.2): "School boards will work in close contact with the administrative, party...Komsomol and Pioneer organizations."

47. S. Knizhnik, *"Sumerki pedagogiki (pod svodami khrama vospitaniia),"* *Nedelia*, No. 39, 1989.

48. Decree of the State Committee of the USSR for Education, Number 2, January 2, 1989 and was finally given permanent status as a research institute with a new name: The Center for Pedagogical Innovation. After his appointment as Minister, Dneprov remained nominally in charge, but psychologist Viktor Slobodchikov became, for all practical purposes, its acting director.

49. For a brief treatment of Dneprov's activities as Minister, see the article by Herbert Buchsbaum, "Coming in From the Cold," *Agenda*, (Winter, 1992), pp. 54-57.

50. See, for example, the highly critical article by Irina Khankhasaeva in *Rossiiskaia gazeta*, June 6, 1992, entitled "An Exam for the Minister of Education."

51. A survey of ongoing activities is in a brochure put out by the Ministry of Education entitled: *O deiatiatel'nosti Ministerstva obrazovaniia Rossii v 1991-1992 godu* (Moscow, 1992).

52. For an account of the activities of the Ministry of Education see *Teachers' Gazette*, Nos. 34-35, August 20-September 3, 1991, pp. 1-2.

53. See *Rossiiskaia gazeta*, June 6, 1992: page 2. As the author of this article correctly points out, although wages are an important issue, teachers also feel "betrayed." However, the sense of betrayal is not directed exclusively at the Minister, as she implies. Teachers have lost control of the classroom, have seen their authority undercut, and have been blamed for lying about Soviet history: see William B. Husband, "Secondary School History Texts in the USSR: Revising the Soviet Past, 1985-1989," *The Russian Review*, Vol. 50 (October, 1991), pp. 458-480. On May 6, 1992 *Nezavisimaia Gazeta* published an "open letter" from Dneprov to Yeltsin (written April 21), calling once again for significant wage increases for teachers. In this letter, Dneprov points out that increases granted in December, 1991 increased wages more than twofold, but that the average

teacher's salary in Russia (756 rubles) remained significantly lower than in other CIS states, and that between that date and March, 1992, teacher's salaries dropped from 63% to 21% of the average wage in industry. With a promised increase to 1,360 rubles, this will now rise to 53 percent of the average industrial wage.

54. As Irina Khankhasaeva wrote in December, 1991 in *Rossiiskaia Gazeta*, "...It will not do to think that the APN, now 'former,' will quietly leave the stage. This is a clever, devious, battle-hardened opponent, with whom it does not pay to flirt with, or to seek compromises. If you give them the slightest opening, the APN will be reborn again; no matter how thorough the reorganization, how complete the perestroika. We cannot underestimate the adaptability of...those leading lights of the old APN, such as Korotov, Kondatov, Bodalev, B. Likhachev, Malkova, Razumovsky, Filonov, Batyshev, Protchenko...."

55. A version of the law was, apparently, finally adopted by the Congress of People's Deputies on May 22, 1992 (private communication with Professor Gerald Read).

56. For a spirited defense of Dneprov, and argument that the campaign against him is an indirect attack against Yeltsin, see Leonid Radzikhovsky, "The School of Politics and the Politics of the School," in *Nezavisimaia Gazeta*, June 11, 1992. This argument gains credence if we consider that Dneprov is a close ally of Foreign Minister Andrei Kozyrev, who has also been under attack for pursuing a policy regarded as too accommodating to the United States, and for resisting calls for military intervention in the Caucasus and Moldava. Radzikhovsky observes that Dneprov's opponents from the old Ministry and the APN has joined in the parliamentary commission on education in an effort to oust him. See also articles in *Moskovskie Novosti* (June 21, 1992); *Moskovskii Komsomolets* (May 14, 1992, and June 12, 1992); *Izvestiia* (May 13, 1992); *Komsomol'skaia Pravda* (June 11, 1992).

57. For a list of the international projects now underway, see Ministry of Education of the Russian Federation, *Mezhdunarodnaia deiatel'nost' Ministerstva obrazovaniia Rossii* (Moscow, 1992).

58. For the decree (Number 21, January 23, 1991), see *Vestnik Obrazovanii*, No. 3 (March), 1991, pp. 34-35.

59. J. J. Tomiak, "Education in the Baltic States, Ukraine, Belarus' and Russia," *Comparative Education*, Vol. 28, No. 1, 1992, p. 42.

60. Tomiak, "Education in the Baltic States," p. 40.

61. Dneprov's candidacy to full membership in the Academy was repeatedly blocked before and after 1985. His own personal biography was attacked, notably by one Ruvinsky, who established *Pedagogicheskii Vestnik* and a largely fictional teachers' organization claiming to represent one hundred thousand teachers and, thereby, to merit a seat in the Supreme Soviet. Ruvinsky wrote several scurrilous articles accusing

Dneprov of "draft dodging" as well as various financial peculations. Within the educational community, there was considerable speculation that Ruvinsky himself was being financed by "other sources". My information on Ruvinsky comes from Oleg Matiatin, a well-regarded writer on education for *Pravda*. See also Chapter 16.

62. It is noteworthy that one of Dneprov's most vociferous and persistent critics, Boris Gershunsky, who wrote numerous articles defending the old Academy of Pedagogical Sciences, has now repented and offered his services to the Ministry and has been welcomed with open arms by Dneprov. For a biographical sketch of Gershunksy, see M. Potashnik, "Neizvestnyi Gershunskii," *Narodnoe obrazovanie*, No. 9 (September), 1991, pp. 64-71.

63. In an interview I asked Dneprov whom, among past ministers of education of Russia he most admired; his response was Alexandr Golovnin (1861-1866), rather than Pavel Ignatiev (who served during World War I), with whom he was flatteringly compared in a lengthy article in the press in 1990 (*Teachers' Gazette*, No. 29, July, 1990). Dneprov's perspective was that whereas Ignatiev merely codified proposals for reform which had long been advanced by the educated public, Golovnin had to introduce radical measures in advance of the time and of public opinion. Dneprov's early academic writings concentrated on the navy journal *Morskoi Sbornik* which, under the Grand Duke Konstantin's tutelage, became an advocate of radical educational reform in the late 1850s.

64. For the changes in Soviet society since 1917 (and especially, urbanization, education, and the emergence of a civil society) see especially Moshe Lewin, *The Gorbachev Phenomenon: An Historical Interpretation* (Berkeley, 1988); for an expanded version of my own perspective, see *Soviet Briefing*, esp. pp. 1-13 and 172-187.

65. As James Muckle astutely notes, "It has never been true that Soviet teachers sat around waiting to be told what to do, and previous reforms of the system have either emerged from movements of opinion in the profession and in society, or else have failed because they did not have support among educators. All the present ideas about reforming teaching methods and considering the child as a first priority rather than asking how much information can conceivably be thrust down his neck have been around in the Soviet Union for many years now. Pressure for them has been gathering momentum among teachers and parents. They did not suddenly appear when Gorbachev announced the policy of glasnost." *Portrait of a Soviet School Under Glasnost*, p. 74. Shalva Amonashvili repeatedly makes this point about the "pedagogy of cooperation": there is nothing new in the *ideas*; what is new is the *movement*.

66. Amonashvili, a prominent figure in the Congress of People's Deputies and close personal friend of Dneprov, was renowned even before 1985 for his child-centered approaches to teaching. His highly personal manuals (published in 1983 and 1986 in print runs of 400,000 and 500,000 respectively), sold old immediately in the stores: James Muckle, *Portrait of a Soviet School Under Glasnost*, pp. 75-76. The two works are entitled *Zdravstvuite, deti!* (Moscow, 1983) and *Kak Zhivete, Deti?* (Moscow, 1986).

The former has been translated, with a brief biographical introduction by Beatrice Beach Szekely, in *Soviet Education*, Vol. 30, Nos. 4-5 (April and May, 1988).

67. Steven Kerr of the University of Washington is collecting materials for a biography of Matveev, whose sixtieth birthday is being observed by gatherings in Moscow in the Fall of 1992.

68. On teacher training, see the essay by Victor Bolotov in *ISSE Newsletter*, Vol. 1, no. 1 (November, 1991); and the articles in *Soviet Education*, Vol. 33, no. 3 (March, 1991).

69. See "A Conception of Preschool Upbringing," in *Russian Education and Society* (formerly *Soviet Education*), Vol. 34, no. 5, 5-39.

70. See also the article by Mikhail Kuzmin, "The Rebirth of the National School in Russia," *Soviet Education Study Bulletin*, Vol. 10, no. 1 (Spring, 1992) pp. 17-23; as well as the article "*O kontseptsii natsional'noi shkoly RSFSR, nauchnykh i organizatsion- nykh mekhanizmakh ee realizatsii*," in *Vestnik Obrazovanii*, No. 3 (March), 1991, pp. 25-35. (This material will be translated in Vol. 2, no. 1 of the *ISSE Newsletter* [Fall, 1992].) For a brief introduction to language issues in the Soviet schools, see Williams, "Preparing Future Generations," pp. 126-130, and Glyn Lewis, "Bilingualism as Language Planning in the Soviet Union," and Wolfgang Mitter, "Bilingual and Intercultural Education in Soviet Schools," in *Western Perspectives on Soviet Education in the 1980s*, ed. by J.J. Tomiak (New York, 1986), pp. 75-96 and 97-122.

71. See the valuable study produced by the Soviet Children's Fund, *Polozhenie Detei v SSSR 1990 God: Sostoianie, Problemy, Perspektiva* (Moscow, 1990), as well as the useful material provided in Landon Pearson, *Children of Glasnost*, 231-262.

72. See the round table discussion reprinted in *Teachers' Gazette* on December 9, 1988, and the pamphlet jointly published by the State Committee on Education and *Vnik-shkola*: *Sel'skaia Shkola: Problemy i Perspektivy Razvitiia* (Moscow, 1989).

73. See Landon Pearson, *Children of Glasnost*, pp. 173-206; William O. McCagg and Lewis Siegelbaum, eds., *The Disabled in the Soviet Union* (Pittsburgh, 1989); and the many articles devoted to "special needs education" in *Soviet Education*, Vol. 32, no. 10 (October, 1990).

74. *Rossiiskaia Gazeta*, June 6, 1992.

75. On the Komsomol up to roughly 1987, see Jim Riordan, "The Komsomol," in *Soviet Youth Culture*, ed. by Jim Riordan (Bloomington, In., 1989), pp. 16-44. For a brief discussion of the dissolution of the Komsomol and of new children's organizations, see the note by Andrei Tiuliubaev of the Russian Federation of Children's and Youth Organizations, in *ISSE Newsletter*, Vol. 1, No. 2 (July, 1992).

2

Here's Wishing You Well, Comrade Minister!

On July 13, 1988, at the first session of the Supreme Soviet of the RSFSR, the delegates selected Edward Dmitrievich Dneprov to the post of minister of education. Dneprov is an educator, scholar and public activist, whose articles on educational issues have been published in *Teachers' Gazette* in recent years.

Edward Dneprov was born in Moscow in 1936 to a military family. In 1954 he graduated from the Nakhimov (Naval) Academy in Leningrad and in 1958 from the Frunze Naval Institute. He served as an officer with the Baltic and Black sea fleets. He joined the Communist Party in 1958. In 1971 because of health problems he was demobilized from the navy. While serving as an officer he graduated from the Department of Journalism of Leningrad State University, and in 1967 received his *kandidat* degree in history. He worked in the sector of the history of pedagogy of the Scientific Research Institute of General Pedagogy under the APN (Academy of Pedagogical Sciences of the USSR), was the director of the advisory board with Pedagogika for republishing classic works in education, and then became general editor of that publishing house. In 1976 he returned to the Institute of General Pedagogy and became first the director of the sector of scholarly-pedagogical information, and then of the Laboratory for the History of Schools and Pedagogy in pre-revolutionary Russia.

Edward Dneprov was a leader in initiating and organizing the perestroika of public education and pedagogy. *VNIK-shkola*, which he founded and directed, drew up critical documents setting forth a strategy for renewal of the schools, new principles for organizing and financing education. This platform was approved by the All-Union Congress of Educators (December, 1988). Since June of this year Dneprov has served as director of the Center for Pedagogical

Innovation (as *VNIK-shkola* was renamed). In addition, Dneprov is the author of more than 160 scholarly works published abroad as well as at home. In response to questioning from delegates from the Supreme Soviet, Dneprov responded in part:

> I would like to see each nationality, each region, develop its own educational platform (*kontseptsiia*) and its own program of reform in accordance with local conditions. The mission of the ministry must be, above all, not to unify, but rather to stimulate in all possible ways the expeditious development of such programs. As far as minority (*natsional'nye*) schools are concerned, the ministry must re-establish the high-level Soviet (Council) on Nationality Education which existed under (Commissar of Education) Lunacharsky in the 1920s.

Teachers' Gazette
July 1990 (No. 29)

PART ONE

The Educational System Under Fire

3

Bureaucratic Tyranny
(Must Be Eliminated
from the School)

Even as we are undergoing profound experiences today, we find it impossible not to think about the future at the same time. And just as inconceivable not to be concerned about those who will be the workers and citizens of the future--our children. This is why there is such heightened public interest in the schools. The stalemated reform of the schools is causing increasing public anxiety.

We can discern three fundamental reasons for the lack of progress: the extreme conservativism of the educational bureaucracy and of pedagogical science; the profoundly undemocratic nature of the schools themselves; and the inertia regnant in educational theory and academic pedagogy.

Preserving the Status Quo

The root evil of the existing system of educational governance is its bureaucratic nature, which precludes any chance for the population to play any role in running the schools. The present structure of governance is a highly articulated hierarchical system of bureaucratic institutions which functions more to serve its own needs than those of the schools or of society. It stands for the absolute tyranny of the educational bureaucracy (*narobraz*) over more than sixty million "enserfed" schoolchildren and their parents, who share the unfortunate fate of their own offspring. It is difficult to think of any other branch of the bureaucracy wielding such untrammeled and unchallenged power over such a large number of hapless subjects.

It isn't only schoolchildren and their parents who have fallen under the sway of the bureaucracy of enlightenment. The ministry has also managed to usurp the powers of the local soviets, turning these territorial units of school administration into instruments of the educational bureaucracy. As a result, we have a cumbersome bureaucratic structure resting on the emaciated shoulders of the schools, an army of supervisors who continue, as in the past to squeeze the life out of the school under the guise of governing.

It is only with enormous reservations that one can call the existing multi-tiered ministerial system one of educational governance. For the employees of this system the very term "educational governance" is a highly abstract one. During a survey taken not long ago of three hundred administrators at various levels none could explain coherently what was meant by governance or what should be the focus of their efforts to administer education. Most of those surveyed felt that supervision (*kontrol'*) was their central mission. And this was manifest in the financial, surveillance and control-oriented directions of the current organization by which education is administered.

At the same time, proper educational governance is, above all, facilitating growth, the goal-oriented nurturing the seeds of the future, and building structures which embody long-term potential. On the other hand *kontrol'* implies nothing more than preservation of the status quo, warding off and suppressing any and all deviations, including those pointing to the future. Since we were not interested in genuine growth in education, nor in analyzing which roads were promising and which were dead-ends, we had no need of authentic structures of governance. Instead, what we needed, and had, was a system of surveillance and control which we are still inclined to label one of governance.

In such a model of bureaucratization the fundamental "system generating" factor inevitably becomes, on the one hand, the stream of circulars from above and, on the other, of statistical accounting and form-filling from below. Is it then surprising that the almighty statistic, the sacred percentage, becomes the be all and end all in such a system--the only "reliable" indicator of one's self-importance? Thus, in an environment already conducive to a mania for percentages, the educational ministry itself encourages, nay makes inevitable, ubiquitous grade-inflation.

Like Carbon Copies

The paradox of the given bureaucratic system consists, however, in the fact that in duplicating the system of local soviets, the educational bureaucracy remains entirely free of any societal element--the very heart of the soviet system. Yet at the dawn of era of the socialist school system its founders envisioned a most active role for the public in running the schools.

Signed by Vladimir Lenin, the Statute on Organizing Education in the Russian Socialist Soviet Republic" (Council of People's Commissars, June 18, 1918) established, along with local administrative branches, organs of public governance--boards (*sovety*) of education, entrusted with the broadest powers. All segments of the population were included in these boards in the same proportions as they were represented on local soviets. Nadezhda Krupskaia often emphasized the enormous significance of these boards for the future of socialist education. "We are profoundly convinced," she wrote, "that education must be in the hands of the people." The mission of the boards was to "organize the self-activity of the masses in school affairs, to draw the populace into planned efforts to properly advanced education." The work of the boards demonstrably embodied Lenin's principles of administrative organization. Clarifying these principles, Krupskaia commented that "the issue of the school boards is closely interwoven with that of soviet democracy as a whole."

Later, as Lenin's principles of governance were progressively abandoned and centralization and bureaucratization of the system came to prevail, in education as elsewhere, the school boards were liquidated. As the population was excluded from having a say in school affairs, the system lost its joint state-societal nature and was transformed into an run-of-the-mill state institution. The ministerial bureaucracy assumed all power in education.

Even today we cannot overcome the stereotypes of "institutional" thinking, as we continue, under the sway of a powerful inertia, to think of the schools as exclusively official institutions.

It was precisely democratization that was the fulcrum of the Leninist conception of the socialist school, of a combined state-and-society system of governance of education. Restoration of this vision as an organic part of the Leninist vision of socialism as a whole is fundamental to the success of the perestroika of the schools now on the agenda.

The contemporary meaning of the Leninist notion of school governance is to be found in replacing the rigid mechanism of bureaucratic *kontrol'* by a more flexible system of state and societal governance, of administrative methods of management by methods using economic, societal and pedagogical criteria. We must overcome stereotypes dictating a necessary uniformity, and monolithic nature to this system, and adopt a position encouraging variation in accordance with local conditions. The drive towards uniformity which still prevails in determining strategies of school governance is no less than an outgrowth of the old bureaucratic ways of thinking.

A Regimen of Trust

Restructuring the ways the schools are run will require a whole series of integrated, radical measures supported by legislation, by which a new quality of governance can be ensured at all levels of the system.

First of all, we have in mind autonomy at the level of the school itself. Two principles must be put in place here: a regimen of trust and the maximum expansion of the right of the school to determine its own path--in curricula and upbringing, in selecting textbooks and approaches, in working out its own, individual (lit.: "authorial" or *avtorskaia*) guidelines or design. To bring these principles into reality we need above all to have elected top school officials, the establishment of broad-based school boards along the lines of those existing in the twenties, not of the closed pedagogical boards of recent times (these broad-based school boards were established by the Statute on the Unified Labor School of September 30, 1918). Such earlier boards included in their membership all school employees, representatives of the public, of parents, and of schoolchildren at least twelve years old. Finally, we need a comprehensive strategy to develop student self-government.

It would be expedient to consider establishing school-development boards (drawing upon the Bulgarian experience with school curators) which would include, through elections, political, party, scientific, scholarly, economic, cultural, educational leaders. These boards would comprise an activist core for the schools, and could play a role in planning, in mobilizing public support, and in seeking out financial and manpower resources.

The second level of school governance is the territorial. Here it would make sense to re-establish Lenin's boards of education (*sovety po narodnomu obrazovaniiu*) and to fundamentally alter the nature, role and functions of the educational departments (*otdely*) now in existence.

The departments of education, if subordinated to the local soviets rather than to the Ministry of Enlightenment, should be responsible for ensuring the adequacy of resources, for the material and technological side, and for organizational issues pertaining to the school--and not merely for pre-school, the general education school and extra-mural programs, but for all components of the regional system of lifelong education. Functioning in this manner, they will no longer be mere appendages of the education bureaucracy. Responsibility for direct supervision over this system will then be transferred to elective, representative institutions: boards of education as well as the inservice training programs and methods groups under such boards. The boards as well as organizations under them must structure their activities in a non-bureaucratic (or non-sectorial) fashion (*na vnevedomstvennoi osnove*). The board should include a group of advisors selected from among the most experienced methods specialists to work directly with the schools. The inspectorate, long ago converted into the primary instrument for subjugating the schools, will henceforth be eliminated.

The boards of education offer the potential of significantly expanding and enrichening public input in local soviet politics as a whole. They can flesh out and supplement the activities of commissions made up of soviet deputies; at present, such commissions function primarily to control rather than to organize (stimulate) and work essentially at the behest of the local executive committee (*ispolkom*) rather than of the school.

And finally, we come to the pinnacle of the structure of governance in education. We have in mind a model that we believe offers considerable long-term promise. The supreme organ of governance over the entire system at all levels will be an all-union and--at the level of the republic--all-republic, congress of education, to be summoned once every five years (This was the name given to the first such congress, which V. I. Lenin addressed on August 28, 1918). The congress will elect a public council of education (*sovet po prosveshcheniiu*) which will include in its ranks prominent teachers, scientists, writers, business managers, etc. In the intervals between congresses, the council will set priorities, direct and supervise the activities of the bureaucracy in education, and ensure that all decisions made in this sphere are democratic and publicly vetted.

To facilitate the development and implementation of a united official strategy in education, to eliminate lack of coordination and outright fragmentation of the various components of the school system (the general education school, vocational and professional training, higher education), we must give careful thought to establishing a single headquarters in education, a unified system of administration. This would release or dismantle the barriers existing between the various branches, and facilitate going over to more systematic policies and programs at the all-union and regional levels. It would provide for combining fiscal, manpower, and other resources and for more rational utilization of physical plant and other material assets. This, in turn, will prompt accelerated growth (of education as a whole). The core of such a unified system of governance could be a combined state inspectorate of education. Even today this service is among the most efficient and useful; in the new environment it would gain added authority--that of *gospriemka* (roughly "state requisitioning").

The fundamental purpose of the administrative structure outlined above is the resurrection and promotion of societal instruments of governance. Here it is of utmost importance that the stress is placed precisely upon the right words. Emphasis should be given not to the establishment of public *kontrol'* in education, but to the creation of fully-empowered societal institutions of educational governance. Such institutions (lit. *organy*) will have as their mission: to open up the school to the public, to underscore the importance of public initiative, and to emancipate teachers from the smothering weight of the bureaucracy, thereby eliminating this profession from its condition of profound apathy. The establishment of public structures of governance spells emancipation from bureaucratic tyranny and opens the way to the comprehensive democratization of our schools.

Pravda
February 13, 1988

4

Faith in the Teacher:
The Energy of Renewal
for the School

It is obvious to anyone who has been closely watching school life lately that the course of the school reform is unsatisfactory. But it took Gorbachev's acerbic comment that reform was on the skids for education officials to become aware of the obvious.

Are they really aware of it however? Or is it only a matter of rhetoric? Not one official in the field has yet explained why the reform has failed. Neither was the answer furnished by the annual general meeting of the Academy of Pedagogical Sciences, although the notion that school reform had failed was accepted by many who spoke at the meeting. The academy meeting had more important matters to attend to: the central concern was self-protection from criticism in the press.

Is it possible to avoid failure of the reform without discovering the causes of its failure? And will narrow sectarian rhetoric yield much concerning restructuring if the purpose is a facelift--changing the signs on research institutes, enlarge and split up the institutes, propose another variant of school curricula, etc.? Without claiming to make a comprehensive analysis of the causes of the unsatisfactory course of the reform, I would like to voice certain considerations.

Obviously, in the context of the fundamental changes which began after the April (1985) Plenary Meeting of the Communist Party and the 27th Congress of that party, the school reform should be reshaped to a certain extent. References to the prior public discussions are hardly valid. Moreover, the author of these lines could list dozens of comments made in the course of this

42

debate that were not taken into account. But that is not the most important point. The most important thing is that the level of public awareness is already far advanced from what it was several years ago. Perestroika has changed it radically.

A candid appraisal of the state of affairs and a willingness to overcome the fear of thinking will provide the energy needed to get reform back on track. Isn't it time for us to look the truth in the eye? Isn't it time to accept obvious truths? Our primitive idea of universal secondary education arose at a time when the "educational wave" was part of an overall wave, when not only the economy but also the school moved along "extensive" lines.

Despite having rejected a number of unfounded assumptions of the 1958 school reform, the 1984 school reform largely repeated a basic concept judged unrealistic twenty years previously. Once again it attempted to combine general and vocational training within the framework of the general education secondary school, and at the same time, to shift onto the shoulders of the major industrial enterprises the burden of vocational training. It turned out that, in this case, enormous material outlays yielded a minimal economic and pedagogical effect.

On the whole, the system of economic delivery of public education underwent no serious changes in the course of the reform. That is why today we are actually suffering from residual principles of school financing and a lack of specificity in allocating responsibility for financing and provision among the various agencies involved in education.

The list of urgent issues could be considerably extended. But what is the sense? Isn't it time, I repeat, to provide an adequate appraisal without using the obvious successes of our school as a cover? Isn't it time to stop marking time and transfer the problem of restructuring the school and pedagogical science from the realm of talk into the sphere of action? There is still little action today. Yet there are ample examples of old-style bureaucratic activity; the most vivid instance was the secondary school draft charter drawn up by the Education Ministry of the USSR, which drew a sharply negative response from teachers and the entire education community.

According to the unanimous opinion of the staff meeting of the General Pedagogy Research Institute (Academy of Sciences of the USSR), even an improved version of this draft simply could not be accepted as the basis for an eventual charter. The draft reveals its authors' failure to grasp the social, legal and pedagogical significance of such documents (for example, the difference between the school charter and rules for pupils) and ways of restructuring education. It is undemocratic, not in line with the spirit of the time; it looks to the past and not the future. The draft demonstrates the futility of efforts to reform the school without restructuring it.

The drawing up of this particular draft charter for the school shows what we can expect from the old guard in this area. Recently, a high official of that ministry said at a discussion in the Literature Club that the principal reason for the poor performance of the school reform lies in the "teacher's ignorance" and "inability to do the job." This wily bureaucratic conclusion, which turns reality upside down, lies at the core of the draft school charter. It contains a theoretical "justification" of the education department's authoritarian style of work, the right to command the mass of teachers allegedly unable to do without a helmsman.

Is it possible that in some other field one might argue: everything is fine except the machine tool operators, foremen, and engineers are ignorant and aren't doing their job?

I would like to hope that no one will suspect me of idealizing teachers. Among them, as in any other large group, one undoubtedly finds ignorant people, lacking the necessary skills and refusing to work. But who does not understand that their failure to do their job is due above all to the boundless control exerted over the teacher, persistent harassment, ever increasing work loads (the lion's share of this work-time being spent on meaningless reports, satisfying the whims of the commissions which endlessly attack the schools, and fulfilling innumerable instructions and regulations). The Education Ministry of the Russian Federation alone annulled 10,000 (!) official papers which had descended upon schools in 1959-1985 from the depths of the bureaucracy. A veritable paper mill! In endlessly generating these reports, commissions and circular letters, the bureaucratic machinery is destroying the creative spirit and the physical and moral well-being of the teacher. And in the process, mediocrity is elevated to the status of an established norm for all teachers. How can all this be explained? Perhaps by the fact that officialdom is not accountable to the teacher?

The public education department is convinced that once the reins are slackened everything will collapse. My objection to this is: *the teacher has my faith*! I believe in the teacher's independence, initiative, ability to work creatively, and in his integrity! I have no doubts that, once freed from the bewildering stream of instructions, the teacher will come into force and decisively demonstrate his responsibility. *Pedagogical collaboration* will breathe new life into the school, rid the school of oldstanding vices and provide a powerful impetus for the teachers' creative efforts. In collaboration with society, science and the children, the teacher will restructure and renew the school.

There is only one road to the renewal of the school: its democratization, the decisive removal of all obstacles hindering the development of the country's educational potential. The first, necessary step along the way the is radical restructuring of the multiple mechanisms of education administration, a sharp reduction of excess links, the unification of general education and vocational training administration structures, the election of officials at all levels, the setting up of competent public bodies to supervise school affairs (similar in type to those early school boards set up by the decree on June 18, 1918, which served our school well in its time).

Renewal of the school poses serious tasks for educational science. In addition to those mentioned above, these tasks include overcoming dogmatic conceptions of schooling, and attempts to impose uniformity. They include, further, the promotion of differentiated schooling, and of schools with different structures in different regions of the country. We are faced with the task of working out a long-term concept of the content of education (without which we are doomed to the end of our days to efforts to patch up the existing curricula), of setting up an effective system which combines teaching with productive work, and with effective teaching of work habits.

Society today expects education to promote individual identity formation as the school's main strategic aim. It awaits fundamentally new content and organization of teaching and education in general, which will enable us to overcome the authoritarian relations in the school and to achieve a unity of instruction and education. This unity can be attained only provided instruction is organically embedded in the whole educational process and the school itself included in a single complex of social and pedagogical institutions. Only in that case would it be possible to achieve the transition from the current school as an establishment with purely instructional functions (afflicted by the illness of percentage mania) to fulfillment of its true role--that of a basic link in the general system of communist education.

A fundamental restructuring of pedagogy, and above all of the Academy of Pedagogical Sciences of the USSR, is necessary to solve the above problems and other burning issues of the day. Bringing an end to inertia, such restructuring would provide a strong impulse for the schools' development, combining pedagogical science with the environment that nourishes it--teaching and education practice--and the general body of the sciences of man and society.

The issue of the future place of the Academy of Pedagogical Sciences in the education system is by no means last in importance. The long-standing status of the academy under the Education Ministry of the USSR has proven to be a dead end. It would be, however, a gross mistake to attribute all the troubles of contemporary education research to this circumstance. But at the same time this situation makes pedagogy a priori an applied science in the worse sense of the word, i.e. a science responding only to directives from above, to interpreting and justifying them. Yesterday, for example, it was necessary to make the school curricula more complicated; today it must be simplified. Scholarship will inform us tomorrow what must be done tomorrow.

The optimal situation for the Academy of Pedagogical Sciences is for it to be independent of any agency, not only in function but also in substance, because it must encompass the full range of educational disciplines instead of restricting itself to pre-school and school pedagogy. The academy must be called upon to work out a comprehensive official strategy of education, which promotes growth of all links in the socialist system of education and upbringing, including higher learning and the sub-system of personnel retraining.

Built along the lines of Lenin's ideas and principles, the Soviet school has vital and fruitful traditions. We still have not appreciated them fully, have not learned to take advantage of the rich experience gained by many generations of Soviet teachers and carried on today by teacher innovators. Our foothold lies in these traditions and this experience, as well as in the public educational movement which always was a leading and decisive factor in the development of our national school and pedagogy, and which is now entering a new period of upsurge.

Pravda
June 1, 1987

5

Learning to Teach

Observing today's school with a sense of pain, I tend to think about my colleagues--future historians. How will they explain why in recent years our chronicle of societal renewal has been accompanied by continuing stagnation in the schools.

It is the fourth year of the school reform, perestroika is gaining momentum in the country, yet there are no changes in the schools. Gorbachev's biting words to the effect that reform was on the skids were uttered in April, more than half a year ago. Yet, not only doesn't one sense any renewal of the school, but there is an increasingly acute contrast between the dynamic economic transformations, the process of democratization and the stultified education machine. At the August educational conference in Elektrostal, Yegor Ligachev pointed out that the public was dissatisfied with the course of the reform and that the Education Ministry of the USSR was not playing an effective role.

These judgements by party leaders could be supplemented by equally pointed remarks in thousands of teachers' letters and hundreds of articles published in recent months in the central and local press. But take a look around. What has changed? The public education system and the Academy of Pedagogical Sciences serving it have become so ossified that they remain immune to all criticism. Neither thunder nor lightning are capable of moving them. It is indeed easy to understand the anger of those who propose to disband the academy, etc. But to destroy is not to build. Isn't it better to try once again to understand why the momentum for change has diminished, and how to get back on the right track again?

It would hardly seem useful to turn once again to an analysis of the 1984 school reform. Isn't everything clear already? No, not everything, and not to everyone.

The opinion of the rank-and-file was quite clearly expressed by a prominent teacher, B. Dynga: "Instead of the new school the teachers were dreaming of, we are seeing the old school newly patched up. We are patching up the school in places where the foundation must be changed, mending parts which need replacement. . . . The impression is that we are moving with our backs forward."

The opinion of the "upper echelons" concerning the 1984 reform was divided. At the Russian teachers congress, for example, the education minister of the Russian Federation, G. Veselov, referred only to altering a number of items in the reform documents, while chairman of the Vocational Training Committee of the Russian Federation, V. Kaznecheev, insisted on the need to introduce fundamental changes into them to bring them in line with the requirements of perestroika. One must agree that there are two different approaches here, two different standpoints: either continue to produce bureaucratic smokescreens or honestly and directly look reality in the eye. The present and future of the school depends on which of these views prevails among the leadership. In the final count, it is the country's fate which is at stake, because our future begins in the schools.

At a recent meeting in Ostankino, a distinguished teacher, I. Dubinin, said: "Everyone's asking: why is the reform failing? My view is: something that doesn't exist cannot fail." Isn't it time for all of us to admit the fact? And to answer the question: why has reform not taken hold?"

Elements of crisis in the school, reflecting in specific form stagnant tendencies in society, were felt long before the beginning of the reform. The root contradiction which gave rise to these phenomena consisted in the fact that all aspects of the school's functioning--pedagogical, organizational, administrative, legal and financial--by design excluded the possibility of normal development. The 1984 school reform adopted before the (crucial) April Plenary Meeting (1985) of the Communist Party (launching reform) made no attempt to do away with that contradiction. It was not preceded by a sober and critical analysis of the situation or scholarly consideration of urgent problems. The reform was laid out within the three coordinates of bureaucratic thinking: the evolutionary principle, i.e., further "improvement" of what has long outlived its time; the functional approach, i.e., patchwork instead of major system decisions, inevitably leading to loss of what is most crucial, and yielding little in terms of results; the sloganeering approach, i.e., to teach more and better, etc. . . . all instead of building real mechanisms for change.

In the slogan "To raise the quality of teaching," supposed to be one of the chief tasks of the reform, lies its central contradiction, its main self-deception. How was it possible to raise quality further if 99-100 percent of the pupils were achieving satisfactory marks according to official reports? Why reform a school that--according to the records--was functioning 100 percent satisfactorily? Or was the reform yet another example of self-deception? Actual results at school were at best 70-80 percent satisfactory. In many schools they were at best 40 or 50 percent satisfactory. Thus the result of fraud in education was on a level with the infamous "cotton scandals" (in Uzbekistan). But the harm done by the former was much greater in economic, ideological and moral terms. Since no measures were proposed to eliminate this fraud, the reform in effect legitimized global, disastrous deception in the schools.

Failure to provide a theoretical underpinning for reform is not as inoffensive as may seem at first glance: theoretical miscalculations inevitably result in practical mistakes. The attitude to theory characteristic of a former age has also had a telling effect, as the bureaucratic machine and official dogma are integrally and closely linked: only those assumptions having the force of administrative orders are "theoretically" justified.

Let us provide only one example: the loudly trumpeted idea of universal vocational training was provided neither with a conceptual basis nor a reliable practical mechanism for implementation. As a result, the general education school is just as ineffectual in solving vocational education problems as the vocational school is in tackling general educational tasks. But we have the same impressive figures in reports here: 70 percent of graduates obtain vocational ratings. And the same dim reality: slightly more than 10 percent actually took up work in their vocational field.

Adherence to established stereotypes, dogmatic thinking and authoritarian decisions are the decisive features of the school reform. That is precisely why bureaucracy's pet idea of a uniform and standardized school for the sake of a spuriously conceived unity and convenience of bureaucratic management has become the reform's keynote. The absence of a free and creative pedagogy and a view of the teacher as a cog in the machine--something a lot is being said and written about today--are the natural outcome of this pedagogical totalitarianism and arbitrariness.

In consequence the reform problem aggravated rather than solved the problem of the school, and led to a deterioration in school affairs. On the other hand, it confused and largely disoriented the teacher: "What is the reform? What does it consist in?" teachers from Gomel asked, for example. "We are reading between the lines, searching for some hidden meaning, but have been unable to see any reforms."

In its early stages, perestroika revealed many sore spots, including those in school affairs. The lack of socialism in the school became increasingly obvious; a system which alienated the school from society, the pupil from the school and the teacher from teaching took shape over decades. It is becoming increasingly clear that the order of the contemporary school is incompatible with ongoing changes in society's development and with democratization. Under the circumstances, it would seem that education leaders, displaying the political wisdom and boldness befitting their rank, would size up the situation, admit the reform's failure and focus their effort on elevating the school to the level called for by perestroika. However, a different position was adopted--that of shielding a reform still not in place, and moreover, of imposing strict proscriptions against attempts to revise it.

At the April annual meeting of the Academy of Pedagogical Sciences one of the highest ranking leaders of education averred that the draft reform had been discussed publicly and had won popular support. "I stress that it (the reforms) gained the support of all the people because in some quarters there is mounting doubt concerning these documents. They *were* widely discussed, and not a single comment was overlooked," said the leader.

However, different opinions were voiced in the press on this account. Here are some of them:

Zagorsk city party committee instructor S. Persiianov: "Isn't it a bit too much to claim that the reform represents a popular creative effort? Only three years after the reform was adopted, another public discussion of the reform is being carried out. What is this if not a public vote of non-confidence?"

Kiev city party committee instructor B. Zhebrovsky: "Let's recall how we discussed the draft reform. How many interesting and bold thoughts were expressed. They were conscientiously collected, carefully screened, but only those thoughts which fitted the prescribed script were retained."

District education board inspector from Altai Territory Y. Yevseiev: "No one pinned any hopes on the reform, because all sensible proposals were rejected at the district level."

Chairman of State Vocational Training of the Russian Federation V. Zaznacheiev: "The possibility of combining general secondary and vocational education in the vocational school provoked doubts even when the draft was being discussed. . . . Unfortunately, those doubts were not taken into account at the time, and no one pays heed today either. The result is self-deception."

Such statements could be multiplied. It is also possible to list dozens of remarks made concerning the draft reform by staff members of academic institutes on the draft reform. How were all these remarks taken into account during preparations for the reform? Arguing that the reform was the result of public discussion is spurious. But illusions are detrimental for policy, including school policy.

Finally, mention must be made of two more important circumstances predetermining the failure of the school reform. These circumstances are described in the following fundamental conclusions. Speaking in Elektrostal, Yegor Ligachev said that "genuine school reform is possible only in the context of deep-going social change". And the second conclusion: "The principal lesson," Gorbachev noted in late September, "consists in the fact that the processes starting in the past and the reforms attempted. . . were not backed up by expansion and development of democracy and involvement of the working people themselves and all of society in these processes through the mechanism of democracy. Therein lies the main cause of failures in the past."

Education leaders must closely consider this unusual lesson in order to reshape their usual ways, to cast off the stereotype of reforms "from above" and learn to organize and carry them through "from below." This has not yet occurred. The nascent attempt to reform the school has been proceeding along old, narrow, bureaucratic lines: people isolated from the school drawing up secret documents behind closed doors in which once again there can be no fresh ideas. The only possibility of avoiding past mistakes is to forsake the traditional secrecy of school reform and involve the entire community in restructuring the school.

The public education bureaucracy is merely one bastion in the fortress of stagnation firmly entrenched against the changes advancing against it. The confrontation between renewal and stagnation in school matters, the confrontation between the new pedagogical thinking and old dogmas will, most probably, continue for some time to come. The length of that period largely depends on two factors: who directs changes in the school and how active society proves to be. All of us are only now growing accustomed to the democratization process and to a large extent underestimate our own capacities. Yet the (recent) postponement of the National Teacher Congress showed that these possibilities were sufficiently large.

The recent Communist Party resolution on ways of eliminating shortcomings in our treatment of orphans is a direct call to pay more attention to the younger generation. The resolution calls for "the broadest public initiative and diverse activities of educational agencies. . . " and for supporting undertakings by the Soviet people which enhance the environment for bringing up our children.

Such undertakings are necessary. The time has come to unite the forces of the public movement in education and to channel them into the organizational mainstream. This could be done by the Teachers' Union or an Educational Union, i.e. with an organ of democratic self-government serving as an equal partner with officialdom at all levels. This union could be directed by a voluntary education council including in its membership the best teachers, scholars, cultural figures and managers. That council would take upon itself those functions which are fulfilled today haphazardly or not at all: articulating society's needs in terms of the school, serving as a watchdog over the bureaucracy, offering democratic solutions to school problems, providing support for creative efforts and innovation, facilitating involvement of the community in renewing and developing the school. . . . It is necessary to step up preparations for the National Educators' Conference, which could also serve as the founder of the proposed union. It is necessary to collect and generalize all the best and most constructive proposals in the press on restructuring the schools, to proclaim an open contest for the best concepts and programs for that restructuring. Finally, it is necessary to make preparations for the National Teachers' Congress a popular cause.

Without waiting for the reorganization of the Academy of Pedagogical Sciences, which is marking time, ways must be sought now for rallying the country's best intellectual forces to solve top-priority problems in school affairs, consolidating them in a provisional research task force which would take upon itself the task of working out the methods, theory and organization of school renewal today.

I firmly believe that this extremely important public task will be actively supported by the creative unions and the Academy of Sciences of the USSR. This is attested to by the activities pursued by the journalistic club "Attitude," undertakings launched by D. Kabalevsky, B. Nemensky and (prominent film director) R. Bykov, by the energetic research group on educational issues headed by vice president of the Academy Y. Velikhov, by the readiness of the Economics Ministry headed by Abel Aganbegyan to render comprehensive assistance in solving school problems.

Progressive teachers are ready for school renewal--witness the rising prestige of the innovation movement. Ideas of school renewal are increasingly supported locally: the school experiment in Estonia has been launched on a republican scale and the broad public movement there supported by the republican ministry. The Communist Party of Kazakhstan has sponsored a program of education renewal. In Tbilisi recently the Communist Party of Georgia helped hold a meeting of education innovators. In recent years the press and TV have contributed greatly to drawing public attention to schools and to the increase of pedagogical initiative "from below."

Thus, substantial forces have been mustered. The problem is to unite them. That problem must be solved without delay. If the school is not aroused from its slumber, this failure will soon have a detrimental impact on the overall process of regenerating our society.

Soviet Culture
November 14, 1987

6

The Yardstick of History

The ability to orient oneself historically shapes the outcome of one's thoughts and determines how realistic one's orientation is. The ability to draw conclusions from history is also critical. The great historian Vassily Kliu-chevsky wrote: "History is not a schoolmistress but. . . a tutoress; it does not teach, but only punishes the pupil for not knowing his lessons."

Knowing history is above all being aware of patterns in historical develop-ment. In our case they are historical-pedagogical patterns. This knowledge cannot be derived from contemporary problems. It would be naive to believe in the possibility of building the modern school properly while ignoring the lessons of the past and failing to take into account general patterns in the historical development of pedagogy. Even today some fail to realize that progress in the school is determined by its links with social movements for change, that the viability of pedagogical science depends on its in-depth relations with social thinking, and that discoveries in pedagogy do not take place in the study alone.

Let us take a look at the role of the public movement for educational change in the development of the country's education capability. Emerging during "the first democratic upsurge in Russia" (according to Lenin), the movement became the leading force in the founding of primary school, female, vocational, technical education, teacher training and kindergartens. Despite the resistance of the education ministry, the progressive-minded Russian public opened the doors of the school to advanced approaches in education, both foreign and domestic. This remarkable phenomenon--the public movement for educational change--has not been studied in terms either of its history or of its insights into education.

53

Historians of the Soviet school and pedagogy did not investigate this movement as it appeared in its new socialist garb (after 1919). This, however, does not mean that it did not continue to exist. Suffice it to recall the founding of the socialist school, the struggle against illiteracy, the work carried out by the Down with Illiteracy Society set up on September 1923, or the national culture campaign launched in 1928. This powerful public movement was headed by the People's Commissariat for Education of the Russian Federation, the center of all educational innovation in those years.

Today we are witnessing the beginning of the second upsurge in the social-pedagogical movement in the last thirty years. It largely depends on us whether this upsurge will be short-lived, as was the case under Khrushchev, or whether it will make a significant and long-term contribution to perestroika and renewal of the school.

The January, 1987 Plenary Meeting of the Communist Party pointed out that we have paid a high price for having abandoned Lenin's principles and methods of building the new society, violating democratic norms, making voluntaristic mistakes, displaying dogmatism in thinking and inertia in practical matters. We have a tendency to accept such criticism in its most general form, without relating it to our own activity. Apparently we believe that we are not individually to blame.

Let us consider more carefully the road travelled by the Soviet school, in particular its relationship with society in recent decades. It is not difficult to see deviations from Lenin's principles and methods of building the school, violations of democratic norms, voluntarism, dogmatism and inertia. In effect, following the demise of the public education councils (school boards) as instruments of public control over school development set up by Lenin's decree of June 18, 1918, the public was isolated from school affairs. The school increasingly became a purely state institution. Since the state was reluctant to avail itself of society's services, the school proved equally reluctant to avail itself of these services.

This gap between school and society is particularly apparent today, when the people have been called upon by the Communist Party to take part in running the state. Unfortunately it is increasingly obvious that the school remains a bulwark--one of the strongest--of the statist vision of society, of the dogmatic-bureaucratic way of devising policy.

Even now, when the Communist Party has irreversibly adopted a course of expanding socialist democracy, when, in Gorbachev's words, "it is either democratization or inertia and conservatism in society: there is no third way," we are still reluctant to take the smallest step towards democratization of school affairs. We still refuse to comprehend a simple but important truth: democratization of the school is inevitable due to the democratization of public life; but at the same time, the transformation of public life is impossible without the transformation of the school, which now serves as an institution for the reproduction of society. Or perhaps, on the contrary, we are well aware of this and for that reason are in no hurry to reconstruct school affairs? This is unlikely. Most likely, we are simply being held captive by the force of inertia and are unable to embark upon any project going beyond the usual, convenient and well-trodden paths.

Several years ago the public diagnosed three prolonged illnesses characterizing Soviet pedagogical theory: its incompetence, its societal and, largely, for the most part, scholarly worthlessness. Open criticism of these illnesses in the press has been stepped up recently, provoking a response in the form of a counterattack. Public engagement in education is treated in academic circles as embedded in the quotidian, lacking theoretical structures. Such a response reflects not merely elitism, but also historical and scholarly illiteracy.

We often use concepts without having a clear idea of their essential meaning--a practice which does not contribute to rigorous thinking. Among such vague notions which nevertheless play a key part in pedagogy is the expression "pedagogical thought," absent from all pedagogical dictionaries. Yet an understanding of the meaning of that expression and of its connection with the notion of pedagogical science vividly demonstrates the sterility of the above thesis concerning everyday consciousness.

Pedagogical thought is the sum total of public ideas concerning upbringing and education, while *pedagogical science* is a system of knowledge concerning these social phenomena and the pedagogical process. Once it emerged as a distinct discipline, pedagogical science joined the broad stream as the cutting edge of pedagogical knowledge. The future advance of the two realms is inseparably linked, involving mutual influence and connection. Pedagogical thought serves as a kind of transmitter between social thought and pedagogical science, providing the latter with new social ideas. The science of education and teaching, in turn, introduces a theoretical understanding of pedagogical phenomena and processes into pedagogical, and at the same time social, thought.

For a long time pedagogical thought in Russia occupied a more impressive place in social consciousness than educational science did in scientific thought as a whole. This reflected, on the one hand, the social importance of upbringing and education, and on the other, the insufficient development of pedagogical theory. In these circumstances, social thought assumed a decisive role in educational policy, through the filter of pedagogical thought. That role, in particular, was assumed in the first twenty-five years of the 19th century by Decembrist thought, in the mid-19th century by revolutionary-democratic thought, and at the turn of the 20th century, by Marxist pedagogical thought, within which the beginning of Marxist educational theory appeared at the time. In each period official pedagogics defended its domain from the encroachments of popular thought, declaring it to be "unscientific."

We often accuse certain individuals of deliberately obstructing progress in society or education, and such people do exist. But the situation should not be over-simplified; let us instead attempt to understand what nourishes the confrontation.

Pedagogy is dual in nature. At its core are two conflicting elements--standards and the creative approach--education is as impossible without standards as it is without their creative overcoming. Constituting a visible dialectical unity of opposites, each of these elements is, however, capable of generating its own system of pedagogical thought. At all times (in the Soviet experience) official pedagogy served in effect as a monolithic system in which the standard always functioned as dogma and to limit or repress creative initiative.

This should not be read to imply that different, creative systems of pedagogical thought are built by categorically rejecting standards. On the contrary, standards here retain their positive role. But as distinct from the advocates of standardized pedagogy, creative pedagogy does not make a fetish of standards. Rather, it regards them as a way station, not the terminal of the educational process.

Thus, the prevalence of (fixed) standards in pedagogy goes far to explain the fact that educational thought is usually in the second or third tier of progress in society. Some people twist standards for their own ends, and such people must be discredited. Yet today the problem does not lie in them alone; rank-and-file teacher consciousness must be shifted from the standard to the creative approach.

This shift is both particularly difficult and necessary, because, for a long time, teachers' consciousness was shaped by an inert and dogmatic system which denied all creative endeavor and all attempts to apply realistic categories to problems of education. To destroy this obstructive system is the first, imperative step on the road to restructuring the school and pedagogical science.

Like any malaise emerging in the academic body, the gap between pedagogical theory and practice in recent years could not do without dressing up in theory, and even history. Here is one such instance. The following appeared in the journal *Sovetskaia pedagogika* (1977, No. 3, page 54): "All the great teacher innovators were basically scholars and builders, and not observers." "In constructing their theories" they "proceeded from seminal, fundamental ideas, relying only marginally upon detailed empirical studies. They began their activity by rejecting existing pedagogical practice and constructing their ideal pedagogical system."

These historical and theoretical considerations fail to stand up to historical verification. In addition, even in terms of elementary logic, they lack credibility. Undoubtedly, all the great teacher innovators proceeded from "seminal and fundamental ideas", but they could not reject existing practices out of hand without first studying them at great length (one has only to take the trouble of glancing at their writings to see this). It was a profound knowledge of school practice and a desire for change, driven by new ideas, that made them great teacher innovators.

All prominent scholars in the history of our national pedagogy drew inspiration from practice. One would have to be historically myopic not to recognize this and to oppose theory-builders to empiricists who, according to the above logic, do not belong to the scholarly community. It is according to such reductionist logic that we today attempt to place (the early Soviet educator) A. S. Makarenko[1] outside pedagogical theory, banish him from "the officer corps of science" and place him in "the pedagogical infantry," with gifted practical teachers (*Sovetskaia pedagogika*, 1987, No. 2, page 13). We justify our reluctance to understand the profound theoretical implications of his concept of education by maintaining that his experience was unique and unparalleled. But, as Konstantin Ushinsky explained in the middle of the nineteenth century, it is not experience that is repeated, but thoughts derived from experience. In modern parlance, the "algorithm" of experience is repeated--in particular the algorithm of educational techniques elaborated by Makarenko.

Assertions that Makarenko's experience could not be replicated are spurious, but do merit investigation--why are they made? We must analyze the precise social and pedagogical reasons why Makarenko's ideas were marginalized. Such analysis is particularly appropriate today as we learn to look the truth in the eyes.

Since Makarenko is no longer an authority in the field of theory, what can we say about contemporary teacher innovators? Here too, resort to history is used to deny the novelty or importance of their ideas.

However, we should not be too credulous. All "new" ideas in education have an historical lineage. But these ideas tend to germinate only when they fall on fertile soil and when public consciousness is prepared to accept them and introduce them into general practice. The idea that education must reject narrow specialization, proclaimed in 1856 by (the doctor and educational reformer) Nikolai Pirogov, was merely an elaboration of a similar argument set forth much earlier by (radical literary critic) Vissarion Belinsky. But it was only in a period of societal upheaval that the idea came to the fore and, once firmly associated with the name Pirogov, became a tenet of progressive Russian pedagogy. In much the same way the idea of popular education, also first put forward by Belinsky, was brought to the attention of Russian pedagogy by Ushinsky in the same period of upheaval, at a moment of rising Russian national awareness.

When treated more competently, history yields quite different lessons. And certainly, the time has come to discard the practice of using history for dubious, narrowly political aims.

Lately there has been talk that the new pedagogy of cooperation has elevated Soviet pedagogy to a new plane by rejecting the excrescences of authoritarianism as well as a straitjacketed understanding of the meaning of "pedagogical influence." But it would seem that the "notion of pedagogical equality in teacher-pupil relations" is but one of three dimensions of the pedagogy of cooperation. The others involve collaboration, first between pedagogical science and practice, and, second, between school and society.

The pedagogy of cooperation is modern not only in the timing of its appearance. At its very heart lies the idea of the democratization of "pedagogical relations" in the broad sense of the phrase--as a specific form of social relations activated in the sphere of education and socialization.

The school (like society) does not always develop in evolutionary fashion. The times frequently set up obstacles to progress that can be overcome only in a revolutionary way. Today such an obstacle stands in the way of growth in education. The school will be able to break through only by collaborating with scholarship and society and through collaboration between those who teach and those who learn.

Teachers' Gazette,
April 21 1987

Note

1. Makarenko worked to rehabilitate and educate homeless, delinquent and juvenile children in the Soviet Union. His controversial (and, Dneprov would argue, distorted) legacy can be investigated in a wide range of works both by and about him, in Russian and in Western languages. See the brief bibliographical note in a special issue of *Soviet Education* devoted to recent articles about him: Vol. 31, No. 11 (November, 1989) pp. 3-5.

7

Who Will Restructure the Academy of Pedagogical Sciences, and in What Direction?

In the documents of the February, 1988 Plenum of the Central Committee of the CPSU, it is unambiguously stated that the Academy of Pedagogical Sciences is in need of a fundamental reorganization. There one also finds the direction this reorganization must take, and the tasks it involves. But it is obvious that no such reorganization will be forthcoming if it is turned over to those very people who for many years have overseen the stagnation of our schools and educational sciences. The result will be the same as has taken place with the (1984) school reform. Must we once again surrender to illusions and entrust the cause of perestroika in education to the very people who bear direct responsibility for the crushing stagnation which has prevailed to this date?

The present leadership of the APN USSR has long ago made obvious to everyone its incompetence. Even in the context of perestroika it has been unable to redirect the Academy to new tasks. It has proven just as incapable of recognizing its new mission, of mobilizing the talent of the educational community and society at large, and of putting education at the forefront of change as it has of overcoming the inertia of stagnation, of facing public criticism, and of coming to grips with new processes and tendencies generated within the scholarly community or the school.

More precisely, the APN placed itself in opposition to these processes and tendencies. It engaged in a full-scale defensive operation to combat the encroaching changes, and labelled harmful or incompetent everything that didn't fit into the sarcophagus of its conventional understandings. Since the April 1985 Plenum the leaders of the Academy have not put forth a single constructive idea,

59

nor have they put together a program, nor have they moved an inch in the direction of renewing the school or education as a discipline. They haven't participated in even a single open forum. This is understandable for in such a forum it is easy to see that the Emperor has no clothes. But they have been busy filing complaints at "higher levels" against the press, against those who "wish to undercut the authority of science," etc. The Academy's leaders are fond of accusing the press of a low level of culture. But it is tempting to ask: Who ruined Sukhomlinsky? Who stamped out the experiments of Zankov and Davydov, who sought to repress Amonashvili? Who carried out a prolonged war against innovators and many other similar activities, and is this what you call a high level of culture? It would be better not to distort the meaning of words, for the educated public, thank God, has a good memory.

Blind obedience to authority, trailing behind events, talmudic splitting of hairs--such features explain the lethargy of the Academy's leadership, its inability to focus on the school's real needs, and its estrangement from the formation of school policy. And this is the source of dogmatic, myopic, conformist thinking, which in turn leads directly to paralysis. How in the world can we hope for the Academy to play the role of prognosticator, of serving as a cutting edge, if its people not only cannot take the reins of leadership in school change, but don't even know which way to turn? That this is true is crystal clear from the way the Academy has treated the movement of innovation in the schools: its stance has been one of aggressive hostility. This should be no mystery: aggressive behavior has always been a characteristic means of self-affirmation for those with a dogmatic cast of mind.

Today the Academy of Pedagogical Sciences is undergoing a profound crisis. In my opinion, this crisis has at least four fundamental causes: first, the devaluation of the scholasticism and pedantry on which official pedagogy has long rested; second, the long-standing rift between this official pedagogy and school practice; third, the manifestly outdated nature of the organization and activities of the Academy; and finally, the inability of the present leadership of the Academy to come to grips with the changing situation in society and education. Moreover, one of the fundamental paradoxes of this situation lies in the fact that the Academy, which always embodied (not in individuals, but as a whole) official pedagogy, is not merely not providing a program in line with perestroika, but is actually resisting it--and doing so quite stubbornly. Should we then be surprised that in the public mind we are the APN (b)--or former Academy of Pedagogical Sciences (this is a pun on the old title of the Communist Party of Bolsheviks, or CP (b)); or that a variety of facetious names have been constructed around the initials APN, including Academy of Declining Sciences, Academy of Dead Sciences, the Academy of Past Sciences, the Anti-Science Academy.

The leadership of the Academy made no contribution whatsoever to the preparations for the February Plenum. Whatever contribution the Academy did make was done on an individual level in terms of civic initiatives taken by its members. Far from supporting such initiatives, the leadership actively obstructed them. As a result, the public did not receive concept papers for general education, for universal vocational literacy, for school governance; nor did it receive other long-awaited proposals for the school.

To be fair, it must be noted that behind closed doors at Pogodin Street the top command made several attempts to hammer out a *Concept* of general education. At one point, during the summer last year, the author of these lines was called in to participate. But when I saw of what fabric and on what basis the reform was being prepared, I was compelled to decline a role in co-authoring this project.

Consider the estimate given the "improved variant" of the *Concept* last January by the initiators of the renowned Estonian experiment in education, which called for a comprehensive transformation of the schools: "to talk of the presence of a 'scholarly design'" in the APN document would be wrong, write the restrained Estonians. "It is also obvious that on the basis of the document in front of us there can be no hope for. . . a well-thought-out restructuring of the schools." The general education school is treated in "abstract, schematic fashion," and the approach adopted in general must be described as narrowly bureaucratic." It lacks such pivotal notions as that of "*development, individual identity, activization, labor, world views, goal-directed socialization, a functional approach to general education. . . .* Human needs are not accentuated in the consideration of content. . . ." "The guidelines before us," conclude the reviewers, "do not meet the standards set by modern Soviet philosophy, sociology, psychology and education."

The Estonian scholars also pointed out the inadequacy of the research agenda put forth by the APN document, and modestly reminded the APN leadership that "one must not design experiments. . . without first providing a conceptual foundation." As we can see, a mountain of effort gave rise to a molehill in terms of results.

Because the enormous strivings of the APN presidium have proven barren, the Central Committee of the Communist Party was forced, in the course of preparations for the February Plenum, to assume the burden of fundamental research on those problems pertaining to the present and future survival of the Soviet school. And the school finally received much of what it has waited for over a long, frustrating, sometimes seemingly hopeless interval. But, once again, its gains were won despite rather than because of this bankrupt (lit.: outdated) leadership.

The rudiments of military science (and of politics, for that matter) teach us that when, after a protracted defense, an army begins preparations for an offense, it is time to change the leadership, no matter what the winning qualities of the former commanders. A change in strategy calls for a new vision, new approaches, for preparedness and decisiveness. The present leadership possesses none of these qualities. Likewise, it displays absolutely no capacity for genuine leadership in education, despite its insistent claims to the contrary these many years past.

Nevertheless, it is difficult to imagine that this leadership might, as in the good old days, actually stand on its honor and collectively resign. To the contrary, it will dig in and fight for its inviolability.

The February Plenum brought to a close the epoch of academic stagnation and opened a new page in the history of the Academy. What will be written on this page, and whether public expectations will be fulfilled or once again dashed, depends entirely on who will be selected to head the Academy, who will take charge of its restructuring.

In order to carry out a fundamental restructuring of the APN USSR we need an entire set of large-scale measures, carried out in stages. First, as one presentation to the Plenum pointed out, a constituent body for a new Academy must be established with representatives of the ministries, the scientific establishment, public and creative organizations. Collectively, these representatives would serve as the founding members of a reorganized Academy. This should include: the Ministry of Enlightenment of the USSR, the State Committee on Vocational Education, the Ministry of Higher Education and the Ministry of Culture of the USSR, the Academy of Pedagogical Sciences of the USSR, the creative professional unions (writers', film, artists' and theater unions), the Lenin Soviet Children's Fund and the Soviet Cultural Fund, as well as the Council on Physical Culture.

The constituent organizations of the reformed APN would each nominate, according to a quota system, candidates to be founding members of the Academy. After an open public evaluation of the list of candidates conducted in the press, confirmation would follow at the level of the Council of Ministers, and those approved would become charter members. The active membership would select an organizational committee--the constituent organ of the new Academy. According to the precedent set when the RSFSR APN was converted in the APN USSR (i.e., from a republican-level entity to a union-level Academy), the USSR Council of Ministers would confirm the choice of president and vice-president, who would be in charge of the organizational committee. Alternately, a more direct path could be followed: direct public nomination (*vydvizhenie*) of the membership of the organizational committee.

In considering the composition of the organizational committee and its leadership--the future president of the APN--we must keep in mind that the issue of who will be president of the APN is one which greatly concerns the public. Testimony to this is in letters from teachers as well as in items in the press. Thus, the selection process must take heed of public expectations, of the manifest desire to see at this post a prominent figure from the world of education who combines the attributes of scholar, innovator in the schools, consistent and energetic proponent of perestroika of the schools and education as a whole, experienced administrator. Such a leader must enjoy the respect of teachers, of scholars and educators, and of the public as a whole. The new president of the Academy must enjoy the kind of prestige within the scholarly community and the public at large that will guarantee confidence in the Academy and in its ability to work productively.

This constituent organ of the Academy, the organizational committee, once created in a timely manner, will carry out the initial stages of reorganizing the APN USSR. The present presidium will surrender its functions. The organization committee will deal with the following fundamental tasks: announcing and conducting (on the basis of an open, public discussion) the first round of nominations to the Academy, working with quotas for each of the basic specialized disciplines and leaving fifty percent of the positions temporarily vacant; organizing elections to governing bodies (the presidium, the central bureau [*biuro otdelenii*]), preventing, in the process, anyone from occupying overlapping, multiple positions. The present-day leadership has usurped many posts in just such a way, thereby consolidating their monopoly and simultaneously retarding progress in scholarly research.

The organizational committee, jointly with the newly elected presidium, will create a new structure for the Academy and design a specific plan of reorganization. It will establish an inter-departmental, ad hoc research group to work full speed to prepare guidelines and curricula for a renewed school, to be presented at the (upcoming) congress of educators.

Once the new structure and plan for reorganizing the Academy are approved by the governing organs, the organizational committee will surrender its authority to the new presidium of the APN USSR.

At the second stage of perestroika of the Academy, which should occupy no more than a year and a half, the presidium will provide: dynamic implementation of the scheme for reorganizing the APN USSR; a list of candidates to head the Academy's new institutes, its scientific-research and development educational complexes, its regional and applied-research centers; the establishment and putting into operation of such institutes; the focusing of the energies and resources of the Academy around the key issues related to school reform at all levels. As this stage is brought to completion, the presidium will organize a second round of elections to fill half the remaining vacancies in the Academy in order to bring in those who have distinguished themselves in the process of restructuring the schools and educational sciences. The list of candidates must once again be subject to intense public scrutiny. At the same time, the customary annual gathering of the APN USSR will be used to analyze the results of these efforts to date, and to refine the mission of the Academy.

After another year has passed, a third round of elections should be held to fill all remaining vacancies in the APN USSR. The principle of selection should remain the same--public discussion of the contribution made by candidates to school reform.

Implementation of such a plan for reorganizing the APN USSR will ensure that its perestroika will be genuine, and will infuse it with forces which have demonstrated their effectiveness and ability to get reform moving. If, on the other hand, the key positions in the Academy are retained by the present leaders and by *their* leaders during the reorganization, this will only prolong stagnation in the Academy, while a one-shot, hasty replenishment of the ranks of all old and new command structures will merely serve to consolidate the social base of the forces of stagnation.

The conclusion to be drawn from what has been presented above should be obvious. If we want to use the APN USSR as a headquarters for a genuine renewal of the schools and of the educational disciplines, rather than as a citadel of stagnation, then we mustn't dally over the question of who is to reorganize the Academy of Pedagogical Sciences, and in what direction.

Teachers' Gazette
March, 1988

PART TWO

The VNIK Program

8

The Fourth Reform:
Polemical Notes on a History
of the Present

We know that our crisis, including the crisis in education, must be overcome in stages. Recognition of a crisis is a first stage not to be underestimated. Rejecting those educational policies which have brought ruin upon the school and devising a strategy of renewal is the second. Finally, implementation of this strategy is the decisive stage of overcoming the crisis. That is where we find ourselves now. The question of "how" is, to be sure, another problem, but not a crisis. Instead it points to recovery, however slow that might be. The critical point was passed more than a year ago.

Counterreform

When our group developed a *Concept* of general secondary education, we were intensely pressured to reduce its critical portions and even entirely to delete the word "crisis." In the end, we arrived at a compromise and talked of a "pre-crisis" situation in the schools. We agreed in order to retain those constructive ideas aimed precisely at overcoming the crisis in the schools.

The reasons for this crisis were also identified in the *Concept*: the totalitarian-style statization of the school; isolating the school from society and turning it into a closed, for all practical purposes, strict regime state institution; the "myth-making" nature of school policies, which burdened the school with global-scale goals--either quite unrealizable at the given stage of societal development (universal secondary education, an entry age of six, etc.), or entirely unsuitable for the general education school (universal vocational train-

65

ing); the prison camp atmosphere and routines of the school; the emphasis upon extreme unification and denationalization (i.e., exclusion of local cultures); the suppression of teacher initiative and creativity; the lethargy displayed by official pedagogy, and so forth. All of this was exacerbated by grossly inadequate financing and a sharp decline in the social status of education.

As a result we succeeded in transforming the school from a force for social change into a retarding factor, into a means of permanently purging local cultures (lit.: nations) through a general levelling and by tearing out the roots of local ethnic intellectual life.

The 1984 school reform, instead of alleviating, actually exacerbated the crisis in the schools. In reality it didn't merit the name reform because it was not preceded by a sober, critical analysis of the nation's schools, by research into the legal, pedagogical, economic, and organizational aspects of reform, or by study of the mechanisms of implementation. Instead, the schools were presented with a random assortment of what were essentially partial and cosmetic measures. Take for example, the proposed salary increases for teachers. Could they stop the flight from the school? Since the barracks-like atmosphere in the schools was not affected by the reforms, the best teachers, finding no outlet for their talents, continued to leave the profession.

Many of the goals proclaimed by the reform were simply misguided: the integration of general and vocational education; vocationalization (professional-ization) of the general education school (repeating the error made in 1958); a push for even greater uniformity in the schools--on this occasion by establishing a uniform type of vocational school (PTU).

When three years ago in *Pravda* I proposed a reform of the school reform, this was merely resorting to the euphemisms we traditionally employed. But, unfortunately, at that time there was no other choice. Neither official nor public opinion was ready yet to discard the 1984 reform. Now it is finally time to admit that this pseudo-reform was but third in a series (the other two were in 1958 and 1964), each of which only ended up in further disbalancing the school, compounding errors and exacerbating problems and in educational decline in general.

The real date for the start of the new, fourth, school reform is 1988. This reform was prepared in two stages. The political guidelines were provided by the February, 1988 Plenum of the Central Committee of the CPSU. The *Concept* and the basic reform documents, which were drawn up by specialists and leading educational reformers, were subjected to intensive public scrutiny and adopted by the All-Union Congress of Educators (in late 1988). This is what gives these documents genuine historical significance. I say this not merely because I was myself involved in putting together the reform package, but as an historian. Incidentally, many foreign historians of the Soviet school are of like mind. I am convinced that our own historians of education, who are beginning to come alive and shake off the bonds of official pedagogy, will sooner or later come to the same conclusion.

It is typical that almost the first to comprehend the significance of the new school reform were its most avid opponents, who labelled it a counterreform in relation to the 1984 reform. By such labels it was indeed a counterreform, but the only counterreform in our history to have a plus sign attached to it.

The 1988 school reform was conceived as part of a broader, more general reform of education. The package presented to the Congress of Educators included *Concepts* of pre-school education, of a general (secondary) education, of teacher training and of lifelong education, (draft) statutes for the general secondary school, for the PTU (the vocational school), for specialized secondary schools, for higher education, for school boards and many other aspects of education.

However, not all of these documents dealt as systematically with the fundamentals of the educational system and, notably, with the economic base, as did those on the school itself. Some were self-contradictory or proposed only traditional palliatives (for example, the *Concept* for teacher training). And not all were fully implemented in practice. Perhaps the most egregious example: it took the real threat of a strike by pre-school employees to force the bureaucracy under the State Committee of Education to give up its own, explicitly conservative draft statute on pre-school education in favor of that proposed a year earlier by VNIK.

What factors played a role in the conceptual formulation of the new school reform? At the outset of perestroika economic factors and the sense of an inexorably approaching crisis held sway. At first it seemed that this crisis could be overcome by accelerating social and economic development. But the proposed acceleration was understood only in quantitative (lit. extensive) terms, and held out little promise of success; after all, what was proposed was to accelerate movement towards an abyss. This fully applies to the school and to the implementation of the 1984 reform as well.

It soon became clear that the old economic wagon was simply not designed to move any faster; this wagon couldn't become an airplane, or even a steamship. Instead the entire economic mechanism itself had to be changed, and this called for a radical economic reform. But such a reform--and here we are talking about school reform as well as economic reform--was inconceivable without accompanying social and political changes on a large scale. And so political reform was put on the agenda.

And here, at the end of the reformer's tunnel, emerged the primary obstacles to renewal: antiquated ideological dogmas hindering political, social, economic and educational change.

The lessons learned at this time were the departure point for the perestroika which ensued, during the formulation of the *Concept* of general secondary education.

The central premises underlying the new school reform were the following:

First: Ordinarily, in preparing a reform, we have been taught to look for a central link in order to pull the entire chain. However this approach is a flawed one, as the experience of perestroika has shown. Specifically, in looking for that link in the economy, we first put our hopes upon the system of state orders (*gospriemka*), then on cost accounting (*khozraschet*), then on rents. But the truth is that any reform, school or other, can be effective only when it is systematic in nature, when it encompasses in an integrated manner the entire gamut of problems involved. In our case, this ranges from philosophical, economical and legal questions to issues of the techniques of upbringing and instruction.

Second: Reforms have real promise of success only when they include within them the prospect of growth, challenge (*operezhenie*). This characteristic of genuine reform is particularly irritating to its opponents, who are mired in the past and who accuse reformers of being out of contact with reality, with the contemporary situation. The validity of such a charge rests upon how one approaches the present day. It always contains something from the past and something of the future. And the issue of which of these polarities will undergird the reform will be decisive in determining whether reform will prod us forward or will itself be left by the wayside.

Third: One of the tried and true ways of trivializing and discrediting any reform is to accuse it of "jettisoning the legacy of the past." Here (our opponents) usually have in mind by "legacy" not that which was vital in our past, not those cultural traditions which have been torn up by the roots, but that stultifying legacy which has stamped out life-giving forces in our society. The new school reform has rejected that legacy left behind by socialism of the barracks, by the administrative-command system. It has rejected that legacy created by the inhumane, anti-democratic school, which spawned a fourfold type of alienation: of school from society, of the pupil from the school, of the teacher from the pupil, and of both teacher and pupil from educational activity.

An essential feature of the new school reform is its open-ended nature. Drawing upon both Russian and global experience at school reform, as well as upon the latest humanitarian, international trends in pedagogy and psychology it has also tapped into that which is new and progressive in Soviet pedagogy, both science and practice. This reform was discussed exhaustively and with considerable interest by the press, in seminars, at teachers' conferences and gatherings as well as local education boards--at the very heart of the world of education.

During the period of preparation there were many critical moments when the fate of the key ideas of the reform seemed to hang by a thread. The most dramatic moment was on the eve of the Congress of Educators; the hard-liners, backed up by former high ranking bureaucrats in the Science and Educator Sector of the Central Committee of the Communist Party, launched a massive campaign against the *Concept*. It was only through the support of the press and the perseverance of the leadership of the State Committee of Education of the USSR that the *Concept* survived the period leading up to the Congress. And at the Congress it was resoundingly approved.

And so the subsequent fate of this *Concept* seems all the more strange in the light of these events, a fact pointed out on several occasions to the readers of *Teachers' Gazette.*

The Missing Chapter

The misadventures of the *Concept* on general secondary education recall to mind the theme of "the missing document" in hackneyed mystery stories. At the session of the Congress dealing with issues concerning the secondary school, 925 voted for the *Concept* and three abstained. The Congress as a whole approved the *Concept* in its resolutions and moved to send it, after reworking, to the All-Union Council on Education. On January 15, 1989 we submitted the reworked *Concept* along with a draft Statute on Secondary Education to the State Committee of Education. When it met between March 16 and 18 that year the All-Union Council on Education ignored the expressed desires of the Congress and failed to consider the *Concept*. Soon in the bowels of the bureaucracy a new, "short version" of the *Concept* was undertaken, supposedly at the request of the Council of Ministers. Three months were spent on preparations, but then it turned out that the Council of Ministers needed something quite different--a program for implementing the reform. Nevertheless, in December, 1989, without the slightest hesitation, the Council put its stamp of approval precisely on this, the shorter version, rather than upon that approved by the Congress. Moreover, the decision by the Education Council took place after the fact, that is five months following approval of that version by the collegium of the State Committee of Education and after it had been sent out to local authorities. As for the *Concept* approved by the Congress, it remained under wraps, despite repeated public calls for its publication (consider, for example, the speech by Shalva Amonashvili at a session of the Supreme Soviet of the USSR in July, 1989).

Despite all the cheap detective story aspects to this tale, the *Concept* continued to exert an influence. Many of its principal tenets by now had gained a firm foothold in the public consciousness of the educational world. Even its former opponents now frequently make use of its basic tenets for their own purposes. And this, for sure, is one of its major victories.

As for the Statute on the School, in which the fundamental tenets of the *Concept* are embodied as norms, the delay in its publication/promulgation is also a mystery of sorts. After this Statute was approved by the Congress of

Educators, it took more than a half a year of bureaucratic negotiations before it finally saw the light of day. In the course of these negotiations, the original thrust of the Statute was attenuated. It took considerable effort by VNIK and the support of the deputy chair of the State Committee, Vladimir Shadrikov, to safeguard both letter and spirit of the Statute.

Today we hear much criticism of the Statute for the "hastiness" with which it was promulgated. But let's reconstruct the events. Work on the Statute began in a special commission in June, 1987, after the public picked apart the pitiable draft statute (*ukaz*) put forth by the former Ministry of Education. I was a member of this commission. A year later, preparation of the Statute was given over to VNIK. In August of 1988, the draft we had drawn up, after approval by the State Committee of Education, was circulated and extensively discussed. In December, 1988, the draft was approved by the Congress of Educators, and after yet another half year promulgated as the Temporary Statute on the General Secondary School. So, add it up: two years of work. And they call this haste? One wonders what they would call dallying!

However paradoxical it may seem, one of the first attempts to publish the (draft) Statute after its approval by the Congress of Educators was undertaken by the Education Council. At the previously mentioned March, 1989 gathering of the Council, an attempt was made to defer action, despite approval by the Congress, and once again to circulate it for discussion at the level of the school. It took three days of heated discussion before the Statute finally won approval.

At this point another question comes to mind, one quite rightly put forth in *Teachers' Gazette* in issue number 12 of this year (1990): "how much does the public really need such a public board (i.e., the Council) functioning under the aegis of the bureaucracy?"

I confess. It was I who put forward the idea of creating an All-Union public Council as the supreme authority in educational matters in *Soviet Culture* in November, 1987. But then we were talking not of a bureaucratic entity, but precisely of a public board which brought together the country's best people. Proposals for such a board were repeatedly aired at the Congress of Educators. But the Council was in fact created as a bureaucratic entity. And how was it created? In the old way, according to previously compiled lists, submitted to delegates at the Congress, with no choice provided. The delegates were not familiar with the names presented nor, and this is most important, the projected status, mission, and functions of this board.

In point of fact our group had prepared a draft statute for an all-union board of education. But neither this draft nor any other saw the light of day at the Congress. How was I to know (we learned only later from the published Statute on the Board of Education, in essence, copied from our proposal) that it had been. . . approved by the Congress of Educators!!

I have no doubt that in the All-Union Board of Education there are many business-like and energetic individuals dedicated to school reform. But they are doomed to inactivity or ineffectualness by the nebulous status of the Board which resembled more than anything else a STU, or bureaucratic working group. It may be than in and of itself this is not so bad--other ministries don't even have that. But is it enough? At the meeting of the Board which approved the "short" version of the *Concept* it was observed that the Board had still "not found its proper role;" (this a year after its founding!) that it occupied an ill-defined, intermediary space between the State Committee of Education and the Committee on Science, Education, Culture and Upbringing of the Supreme Soviet, that it was necessary to persuade itself as much as the nation that a new type of education was called for. Well, that's a worthy task for self-education!

The New Policies in Education

One of the core ideas underlying the *Concept*, that of a crisis in the schools, concerns above all a crisis in school policies. Accordingly, the path to resolution of this crisis involves first of all a changes in values and orientation when it comes to policies. In this context, special significance accrues today to the ideas put forth in the section on education in the Platform of the CC of the CPSU presented to the 28th Party Congress (July, 1990).

The basic merit of the draft Platform lies in the rejection of dogmatic conceptions of socialism and the striving to achieve socialism at any cost according to predetermined schemes, of the authoritarian regime which earlier prevailed and which was based upon (an interwoven structure of) state and party power of totalitarian statization of life, and--even more, I would say--of the party monopoly on power, of the dictatorship by any class, including the "apparatus," of Stalinist notions of a unified state. I am especially heartened by movement towards notions such as that of "societal self-government," (to be sure, we still don't dare call it by its proper name: "civil society"), and "the individual as the goal of history." We have finally gotten past the notion of the "human factor," a notion which was a product of our technocratic-state consciousness, in which the human being is but a means, a factor of production or of other state-determined goals. We have come to understand that the state and the production system should have human well-being as the only proper goal.

A primary merit of the Platform is the emphasis given to educational issues and other social problems. This is yet another step, following upon the 19th Party Conference (June 28-July 1, 1988) towards recognizing that education is a powerful lever for socio-economic and spiritual progress. To be sure, so far this recognition is visible more in declarations than in reality; after all, in the government program adopted by the Second Congress of People's Deputies, education, culture and science all, as earlier, take a back seat.

The Platform marks the opening of new opportunities for receiving public support for a new educational policy: one bearing the idea of democratic, humane socialism, founded upon universally recognized human values, characterized by realism and by a profound recognition of the significance of education and the laws governing its development.

The primary task of such a policy is to enhance the social status of education and the prestige of knowledge. Our people always held education in high esteem, but they have been convinced that it is to no purpose: is there any sense in studying for sixteen years in order to receive a low-status degree in engineering, education or medicine with a salary of 120 rubles a month or so?

No less important is the goal of overcoming the "sectoral" or provincial perspective on education. Each preceding reform in education was narrowly sectoral in definition. But education is not merely a sector (of the economy or society) but a pivotal sphere of public life, of acculturation, of restoring harmony and civilization to our way of life.

Taking as our point of departure the experience accumulated in recent years, particularly by our working group (VNIK), we can identify ten key principles of the ideology of renovation in education and, accordingly, of our new education policy. Five of these address the, so to speak, "external" side, the societal and pedagogical preconditions for assuring that the educational system be full-blooded and vital: these are democratization, multiplicity or diversity (lit.: "multi-layering": *mnogoukladnost'*), providing alternatives, guaranteeing openness, and *operezhenie*). Then there are five "internal," that is properly pedagogical, conditions: humanization, augmenting the humanities, differentiation, lifelong education and emphasizing the development direction/aspect of education. All of these principles are profoundly interconnected, but each offers its own distinctive frontier in education.

Virtually all of these principles have been adequately presented in the *Concept* approved by the Congress. Today they are an inseparable component of the new pedagogical thought. However, as we drew up the *Concept* we deliberately circumvented two central questions, which today have become highly acute: that of demonopolizing education as a decisive factor in its democratization; and that of establishing a system of alternative education. At the time, it was simply impossible to present such notions.

Types of Educational Systems

Any societal movement must take place in stages. Reform will inevitably fail if it extends far beyond the "zone of proximal development" of public consciousness. At the first stage, that of elaborating the ideology of school reform, the most important mission was to construct a new paradigm of the school, to break down the old stereotype of the school as a state institution and to restore its true essence as a societal institution, providing in equal measure for the needs of the individual, the society and the state.

When in April, 1987, I made the first attempt, on the pages of *Teachers' Gazette*, to talk of total statization as the fundamental shortcoming of our school system, this provoked a harsh reaction from purveyors of official pedagogy. One of the most consistent hardliners ominously proclaimed at a general gathering of the Academy of Pedagogical Sciences, that this historian of the pre-revolutionary school, Dneprov, was mistaken by at least one hundred years--we have no statization of the school, he declared, and we won't put up with libel!

Later, during the preparatory stages for the February, 1988 Plenum of the Central Committee of the CPSU, a group of colleagues from (that same) Academy, who will later serve as the core of VNIK, proposed establishing a (joint) state-public (or state-societal) education system with a corresponding administrative structure (or structure of governance). The idea was approved by the February Plenum and thereby gained the status of a political guideline (lit.: recommendation). And finally, when in August, 1988, the idea of a public-state education system was enunciated in our *Concept*, we once again encountered a wave of protest. The same hardliners now claimed that VNIK was revising the resolutions of the February Plenum by proposing, in place of a state-public system (which, naturally, after the Plenum, they have welcomed and endorsed), a public-state system.

We must give the leaders of conservative pedagogy their due. Their "class awareness," refined by many years of struggle, has not let them down; the inversion of words is by no means an issue of no import, this is not merely a question of semantics. In reality, the notion of education as a state-societal system presupposes that in the state rests ultimate sovereignty; it makes the laws and administers education in cooperation with society. But in so doing it has the final say in structuring this cooperation and it turns to society for expertise. A societal-state education system rests upon different foundations. It "deletes" the very notion of sovereignty, and bases itself upon an equal partnership between state and society in the sphere of education. Societal initiative is not kept within prescribed boundaries, but acts as an independent agent in promoting education, in setting strategies and programs of growth. With the regionalization and municipalization of education societal initiative becomes the decisive factor in the formation and evolution of the diverse levels of this system of education.

The "change of accent" in the *Concept* was brought about not only because earlier those who had formulated it had had to take into account the bureaucratic mentality and propose an intermediary formula in overcoming the primacy of state over society in education. The main impetus for the switch can be found in the changes which had taken place in society in the interval between the February Plenum and the Nineteenth Party Conference (that is, between February and June, 1988).

Today we have advanced even farther. For that reason the agenda now includes establishing an independent system of alternative schools run by society.

Our experience with perestroika, brief but laden with events as it has been, permits us to discern and conceptualize those four basic types of educational systems which have long existed across the globe: the state-run; the state-societal, the societal-state, and the societal (i.e., private). The key difference among them resides in the interrelationship of state and society in terms of initiative and proprietorial rights. These four types of educational systems are not necessarily mutually exclusive, but can and most often do coexist, with mutual ties, supplementing one another. This, in substance, is the meaning of pluralism in the world of education.

The Alternative School

At the February, 1990 Party Plenum Edward Shevardnadze spoke in terms which applied in full measure to education: "The monopoly on power has played a cruel joke on us. It has eradicated political life as a sphere of interaction among diverse political forces." Just so, monopoly has eliminated public life in the sphere of education, and this has reduced public interest in education, and ultimately undercut education itself.

The state monopoly on education is a variation on serfdom. It deprives the public of choice in education. All channels and ways of disseminating education, all methods of educational production are concentrated in the hands of the state, which constructs education in its own image and likeness, and uses it for its own goals. But, as our seventy-year experience has shown, the interests of state by no means always coincide with the public interest. Our people, however, had no alternatives, including educational alternatives. This was so, despite the fact that in proclaiming the public's right to an education, the Constitution of the USSR nowhere stipulates that it must be provided exclusively by the state.

The campaign against a state monopoly over education was always a primary thrust of the Russian public education movement. This campaign facilitated the formation of new, progressive types of schools and also markedly expanded the frontiers of the country's educational system (before the 1917 Revolution), permitting the reconstruction from top to bottom of its most important rungs: primary, vocational and technical, women's, extra-mural, pre-school, and private tertiary education. The public in the Russian Empire emerged as a powerful factor in educational growth, forcing the state to respond to stiff competition. And it is precisely the lack of such a factor in our times which has so contributed to creating a crisis in the schools.

The possibilities are growing for overcoming monopoly in all spheres of education. Even the Party no longer has any pretensions to a monopoly, and expresses its willingness to cooperation with diverse societal forces. What remains is to move the main Leviathan--the various bureaucracies. But they can be budged only through establishment of a market, that is, an educational free market. It would be even better if the bureaucracies themselves evinced a willingness to demonopolize and enter the market. As was stated at the Second Congress of People's Deputies of the USSR, the stance taken by the state and its ministries towards monopoly is a yardstick of their reformist commitment.

Under a free market system the educational bureaucracy will be forced to fundamentally reevaluate its activities, to become simultaneously a general staff and general contractor. Even in this context it will maintain control over a key lever: setting standards or establishing minimal competencies (with a built-in tendency for increasing rigor) and the right to direct supervision (of classroom practices).

The necessary first step in establishing a free market in education is the legalization of what V. Zhukov, in his article, "The School under House Arrest" (*Teachers' Gazette*, No. 8, 1990), deftly called "the shadow pedagogy" (by analogy with the informal economy, or black market). This shadow pedagogy must be decriminalized and allowed to evolve into a full system of alternative education. Above all this pertains to the semi-legal network of cooperative schools and to individual tutoring or instruction. Both of these are at present being exploited by the government as a type of field emergency hospital, where children are sent to be reanimated after their potential has been virtually extinguished in the official schools.

The author of this article has identified those distinctive features of alternative education now in place which, properly used, could play a major role in the effort to renew the mass school. In Russia at the turn of this century *obshchestvennye*, or societal (i.e., public, non-state) and private schools served just such a role. At that time there were also in existence so-called "clandestine schools," where instruction took place without reference to official practice. All official attempts to clamp down on such schools failed; as a result during the Revolution of 1905 the government was forced to accommodate their existence. In addition, experience has shown that schools of diverse ministries with a vested interest in education could serve as another type of alternative school. The military gymnasia of the 1860s to 1880s created by Minister of War Dmitri Miliutin, and the commercial schools established a bit later by Minister of Finance Sergei Witte were exemplars of the Russian secondary school which serve as alternatives to the reactionary policies pursued by the Ministry of Education.

Putting the issue of alternative schools on the agenda was one of the outstanding public services provided by *Teachers' Gazette*. And much depends on the future resolve the newspaper shows in this area. In particular, I have in mind the possibility of the government reconsidering its semi-legal decree imposing limits upon the cooperative movement under whose rubric fell the cooperative school as well.

At a round table organized by *Ogonyek* following the All-Union Congress of Educators VNIK proffered a harsh criticism of this decree and proposed creating a structure for alternative schools. But somehow, through official channels, this round table, scheduled to be published in January and already set for the printing presses, was suppressed. Once again we raised the issue in a draft bill entitled *Fundamental Laws on Education of the USSR and Union Republics*, which was approved at a plenum of the State Committee of Education in April last year. After revisions, this draft has now been circulated for discussion. The term "alternative schools" has been deleted, but the right of public and cooperative organizations to have their own schools has been retained.

The primary obstacle in the way to implementation of the goal of creating a system of alternative education is our levelling genotype. Over the decades this attitude has been implanted in our consciousness and remains one of the last and most obdurate of the barriers encountered by perestroika.

Levelling is a cheap surrogate for equality. If the vector of equality is always moving upwards, the vector of levelling inexorably moves downward. Likeness in poverty, including educational poverty, soothes our soul. And we cannot, or will not understand, that in an educational space where everything has been levelled, all differences eliminated, there can be no progress. Sooner or later we will have to search not for illusory, but for genuine ways to guarantee society equality in education.

One such way was proffered in the Temporary Statute on the School, in the form of the school providing supplementary, fee-based services. Such services have already been approved and are enjoying success in a number of regions. The fees charged for such services are quite modest, otherwise they would simply be unpayable.

Thus, the 1988 reform merely laid the foundation for a genuine restructuring of the school. Its structure is only now being elaborated. And this process is hard going, with setbacks. But, after all, the criterion of success for any reform is its growth potential. We recognize that many of the ideas and positions we earlier adopted are in need of significant reassessment. Only then will it be possible for the school--finally--to keep pace with life.

Teachers' Gazette
July, 1990 (No. 25-26)

9

A Concept of General
(Secondary) Education

The Plight of the Contemporary School

School and society are inseparable. How society lives and evolves is shaped by how it undertakes learning. And how it undertakes to learn is shaped by how it wants to live.

The path which our school has followed is almost identical to that pursued by our country as a whole. In hindsight, as we re-examine our own history, it is impossible to overlook not only the enormous achievements but also the hardships, the mistakes.

The negative phenomena which accumulated during the long period dominated by the administrative-command system and which were especially salient during the period of stagnation (i.e., under Brezhnev), resulted from departures from the Leninist conception of socialism. The pre-crisis conditions of the school, reflecting analogous conditions in society as a whole, had identical roots; namely, the deformation of the Leninist conception of the socialistic school as a societal institution ensuring the fulfillment of the educational needs of the individual, the society and the state.

Central to this process of deformation was the restructuring of the basic goals of the school (i.e., from the initial, progressive goals set forth during roughly the first decade of Soviet rule after 1917); it now focussed entirely upon the needs of the state. Transformation of the school into a state-dominated institution made it a closed, virtually strict-regime establishment. Gradually, the needs of the child and the interests of society were pushed out of the school.

An inevitable consequence of the transformation of the school into a state-run, bureaucratic institution was to create a dictatorial regime of uniformity in

77

thought, organization and inspiration. In carrying out the social-pedagogical mission imposed by the administrative-command system of turning out "cogs" the schools embarked upon the path of universal levelling. In so doing it deprived not only the individual, but the school system as well, of the opportunity to grow and develop, and this with time objectively undercut the intellectual foundations of the nation.

Replacing authentic progress with sloganeering, the dominant policy was to impose upon the school globalized tasks which either were unfulfillable at the given state of societal development (tasks such as universal general secondary education, beginning school at six years of age, etc.) or were entirely unsuitable for a general education school (mass vocational training). Such tasks, intended to be implemented across the board, had no foundation in scholarly research and were not backed up by the necessary resources in terms of personnel, financial and material support.

As a result, each successive reform or reorganization of the schools created further disbalances, compounded earlier mistakes, and exacerbated existing problems, leading to regression in the system of education as a whole. The situation was further complicated by a precipitous decline in the social prestige of education.

Perestroika is creating a living and resuscitative link between the school and the educational traditions of the 1920s and the 1980s. Through these vital threads are being reborn traditions which never fully disappeared, even in the worst years of our history. Simultaneously, perestroika provides a firm response to the question: "What part of our legacy are we now to discard?" We are to discard the legacy of the administrative-command system, which has little in common with genuine socialism. We are to discard that legacy which engendered a deficiency of socialism in the schools and shaped a threefold system of alienation: of the school from society, the pupil from the school and the teacher from the pupil.

The pivotal notions for renewing the Soviet school include those which put an emphasis upon development, democratization, humanization, and a realistic school policy. Such notions describe the profile of the new socialist school and, furthermore, serve as measures of the achievement of socialism in education.

A Developmental School, a Developing School

The notion of development is key to the ideology of the new school. There are three fundamental facets to this notion: the continuous evolution of education; the transformation of schooling into a tool for the development of individual personality; and making education a genuine factor in societal development.

The first aspect of the idea of development is that of the constantly evolving school. Such a school would eliminate many of the most egregious problems now facing us, such as the anomalous status of teachers' creative endeavors and of pedagogical innovation in general. In the constantly evolving school, creative quests (*poiski*) become an organic component and factor of accelerated development. The dynamism and diversity of the creative search are ensured by the provision of a wide network of experimental sites, ranging from *avtorskie* schools to entire districts and regions designated experimental.

Coordination and stimulation of experimental endeavors are implemented within the framework of a continuous renewal of the existing system of education. This framework is designed to be extremely receptive to new and promising directions in the schools, to serve as a prop for pedagogical experimentation, and a transmission belt facilitating the transfer of all that is new and progressive to the mass school. Such a system protects society and school from the traditionally "volcanic" nature of school reforms, and evens out the bends along the road of qualitative renewal of the school.

The second aspect of development concerns the decisive role the school plays in establishing and nurturing the individuality of the child.

The existing school, while proclaiming the goal of promoting the harmonious and comprehensive development of the individual, in reality excludes just such development through its authoritarian structure, its overly didactic content (*didaktotsentrism*), form, and methods. Intellectual development is replaced by mechanical assimilation of the notorious ZUNY (knowledge, habits, skills). Instead of affective development there is primitive, fragmented information about art. Instead of promoting a receptivity to labor and work capacities the school fosters an implacable alienation from work--the inevitable consequence of the arbitrary, unsystematic and pointless practices spuriously labelled "student labor." As for the results of physical education in the schools today, they are the subject of increasing concern in the medical community.

The zones of childhood development (a reference to child-psychologist Lev Vygotsky's zones of proximal development or ZPD) are increasingly constricted as a result of the artificially school-centristic (*shkolotsentrism*) nature of childhood and the striving to confine the entire life of the child within the four walls of the school, even to make the school a warehouse for children. The inevitable consequence of such forced servitude to the schools has been the large-scale establishment of unsanctioned youth peer groups (*neformaly*).

The first task of the new school is to eliminate obstacles retarding the development of the child, to construct a pedagogical system which can instead work entirely to stimulate such development.

Finally, the third aspect of development is to orient the school as a socio-cultural institution not in the direction of replicating ossified societal practices but rather of transforming society (lit.: promoting societal development).

So redirected, education and the school emerge as fundamental components of economic and societal progress as well as of spiritual renewal, spurring on dynamic, renewing societal processes of transformation and fostering an attitude according to which education is meaningful and ongoing, both in personal terms and on the level of society as a whole.

At present there is no mechanism capable of reorienting the school in a developmental direction, of promoting both personal and societal growth. Such a mechanism can be found only through the democratization and humanization of the school itself.

The Democratization of the School

Democratization is at once the goal, the means and the guarantee of the irreversibility of the perestroika of the school. It cannot be reduced merely to changes in the system of governance of the school, but permeates all aspects of school life, affecting its atmosphere as well as internal structure.

Democratization of the school offers a firm rebuff to the notion of *vintiki* ("seeing people as cogs") in favor of a conception of the person as the ultimate value of a socialist society. It involves a turning away from bureaucratic and careerist needs and interests in favor of those of the individual and the society as a whole. It implies overcoming the depersonalized, suffocating uniformity of school organization, of contents, form and methods, in favor of infinite diversity, variation, and polyphony (multi-voicedness). It means the emancipation of pedagogical relations, a transformation of their very essence, a departure from the system of subordination or antagonism in the direction of cooperation. It involves opening up the school (*otkrytost' shkoly*), attracting to it public energies and involving the public in its evolution.

Democratization of the school is what underlies the Leninist principles of the school, what made the Leninist school qualitatively new, and what was lost in the period of domination by the administrative-command system.

Democratization of the school, finally, is the most reliable way to make *vospitanie* a decisive factor in the democratization of society as a whole.

All attempts to "pedagogically adapt" democratization or to set the "degree of implementation" of democracy in the schools are no more than bureaucratic ruses of the pedagogy of stagnation. There cannot be too much democracy, just as there cannot be too much truth or justice. Instead, there can only be too much despotism (self-assumed power, *samoupravstvo*) or too much untruth.

Today the first step toward democratizing the schools is in overcoming the stereotypified state vision of the school, the stereotype that the school is a state institution. The school is not a state establishment, but a societal institution, or a societal-state system whose mission is to meet the needs of the state as well as of society as a whole and of the individual.

One of the fundamental laws of educational development is that such development is possible only in a context of cooperation between state and society. The interruption of such mutual interaction, as we have learned through direct national experience, leads to educational stagnation. The school as a societal-state institution cannot survive on state inspiration alone. Sooner or later it will suffer from "oxygen deprivation." And sooner or later society will have to intervene to resuscitate it.

The alienation of society from the school and school from society must be overcome, as must be the isolation of the school from ongoing societal processes and from the narrow, corporate nature of professional educators, from what Marx labelled "professional cretinism." Educators must recognize that they have no monopoly over upbringing, but are empowered only at the discretion of the people.

The school as a subsystem of society must be an open institution. Its forms and principles of co-organization (activity) must be extraordinarily variegated.

The Humanization of the School

The basic shortcoming of the contemporary school is its depersonalized nature. The command, administrative and bureaucratic spirit and structure of the school, its technocratic tendencies, resulted in losing sight, at virtually all stages of the educational process of precisely what is central to all forms of human activity--the human being. It was forgotten that "man is the measure of all things."

An approach which dealt with children as "objects" of instruction and socialization led ultimately to the child's alienation from the process of learning, turned the child into a goal and an instrument of the school. In the end, instruction lost its meaning for the child, and knowledge became something external to the child's real life. The teacher also became alienated from the process of education. He or she was deprived of the opportunity to independently set classroom goals, to select means and methods. Teachers lost sight of the human measure of their professional activity--the individual personality. In substance both teacher and pupil turned into cogs of different caliber of the educational machine.

Only through humanization of the school can the alienation of both teacher and pupil from the process of formal education be overcome. Humanization means turning the face of the school toward the child, it means respect for his or her individuality, dignity, it means trusting the child, receptivity toward his or her goals, needs and interests. It means orienting the school not merely towards preparing the child for the future, but also guaranteeing the fullness (the validity) of the present, of each of the stages of development, of childhood, adolescence and youth. It implies doing away with the present indifference to stages of childhood in present-day education, taking into account the unique physiological and psychological aspects of each developmental stage, of the distinctive sociological and cultural context of the life of the child, of the complexity and variegated meaning of the child's inner world. This implies an organic interweaving of the personal and the public, making societal concerns personally important for the child, helping him recognize that "the free development of the individual is the prerequisite of the free development of the community (of all)."

Humanization is a key element of the new pedagogical thought. It calls for a reexamination, a reevaluation, of all components of the educational process in terms of their capacity to mold human beings. It implies a radical alteration of the very essence of this process, placing the child at the center. Thus, the basic point of education becomes to promote child (pupil) development. Child development becomes the fundamental indicator of the quality of performance of the teacher, the school, the entire system of education.

In the ideology of the pedagogy of cooperation, which is the binding ingredient of the new educational thinking, and in cooperation between state and society, between society and school, between teacher and pupil, the dominant thrust is to bend all efforts to establish and promote the identity of the child.

Perestroika is the path to the new socialist school. Restructuring the school is the path:
- from dogmatic and voluntaristic school policies to a new approach based on realism and scholarly foundations;
- from a conformist and self-replicating school to a developing and developmental school;
- from an administrative, bureaucratic, closed and monolithic school to one that is open, democratic, multi-voiced and diverse;
- from an authoritarian, impersonal and technocratic school to a humane school.

Restructuring the Schools

The Goals of the General Education School

Education is both the process and the result of the development of *lichnost'* through both instruction and socialization. The substance and the goal of a general education reside in nurturing overall individual capacities and developing universally applicable types of activities *universal'nye sposoby deiatel'nosti*). A general secondary education is the foundation of all subsequent specialization, a key component of lifelong education. It creates the necessary conditions for personal self-definition and development on the part of the individual.

The central goal of the general secondary school is to facilitate the cognitive, moral, affective and physical development of the individual, to help discover creative potential, to shape a (communist) worldview based upon values common to all humankind, and to provide a diversified environment for the flowering of the child's individuality in line with developmental stages. The emphasis upon the personality development of the growing child gives a "human measure" to such school goals as establishing a civic consciousness, preparing for life, work and creative societal endeavors, participating in democratic self-government and sharing responsibility for the fate of our country and of civilization as a whole.

The dominant understanding of the goal of schooling merely as "preparation for life" isolates the child's school life from the real world, separates the school from life, and instruction and socialization from other aspects of child development. Such factors, like mass communications, the "street," the family milieu, and processes of self-education, are often more important than the school, especially during adolescence and youth.

The school has not achieved its goals if it has not provided for the full experiencing by the child of each developmental stage. Experiential fullness is an essential condition for the flowering of the individual personality.

The Structure of the School

The three fundamental developmental stages of the young person-- childhood, adolescence and youth--describe the three rungs of schooling: primary (I); basic (II); and senior (III). Pre-school instruction and socialization, of enormous independent value, enter here as the preparatory stage to primary education.

Such a structure is traditional. However, the goals, constructs and content at all levels are in need of reconceptualization. In the light of renewal of the school, such a re-conceptualization must incorporate the central notions of realism, development, humanization, and democratization.

The central task of the primary school is to establish the individual identity of the child, to uncover his or her capacities, to nurture the desire and ability to learn, to facilitate firm acquisition of literacy and numeracy, and to provide experience in interpersonal interaction and cooperation.

Instruction and socialization at the first level of schooling is built upon the unmediated curiosity of the child about the surrounding world and the self. Correspondingly, at this stage, subject instruction takes place as integrated courses providing elementary concepts about nature, society, humankind and labor. At the same time, even at this stage, instruction should include differentiating elements to take account of the child's inclinations and abilities. In the early years differentiation occurs through elective course-work, primarily in the spheres of aesthetics, physical culture and other activities (sports games, singing, music, recitations as well as art). At a later stage, such activities can include expanded study of native or foreign languages, math, technology, and home economics.

Another fundamental innovation in the approach to primary education is flexibility concerning the age of initial entry and the duration of elementary education.

The age of entry--six or seven years--is determined by the child's functional maturity for school, his or her objective readiness for classroom instruction. A medical-pedagogical commission as well as school psychologist evaluate the child's level of maturity at two points, upon the child's achieving five and six years of age. The length of primary education--three or four years--will be determined by the individual capacities of the child. Pupils who have not fully mastered the curriculum can be retained for an additional period and, if necessary, provided with an individualized program.

The second rung--that of the basic school--provides the foundations for the general education needed for subsequent learning as well as for meaningful participation in the life of a socialist society regardless of the individual's subsequent specialization.

The universal requirement that the basic school provide a basic secondary education by no means implies the complete *uniformity* of these schools. The mandatory curriculum, mastery of which guarantees fulfillment of the basic requirements for a general education, will take up seventy-five to eighty percent of the school day. The remainder of the time is left to supplementary subject matter at the discretion of the pupil, according to his or her inclinations and interests. In addition, as the student advances, the time allotted for such study increases. Finally, pursuit of one's interests and inclinations is also ensured by broad resort to elective courses, extramural learning, and a multi-levelled curriculum. The basic school is compulsory. Its graduates are offered the right to select the type and length of additional secondary education or, equally, to begin work with the option of continuing their education through correspondence or evening courses.

A fundamentally novel approach to the organization of the third rung of the educational ladder is that at this stage instruction is conducted on the basis of a broad and profound level of differentiation. Such differentiated instruction provides the best way to incorporate the interests and maximize the capacities of the individual student, and to facilitate professional self-definition.

At this stage as well mandatory course instruction is accompanied by electives. But at this level less time is devoted to compulsory subjects. The focus of such subjects also changes, with generalization given greater emphasis. In substance, these should be integrated courses, facilitating the establishment of a worldview by mastery of four cardinal spheres of life activity: the human being, humankind and society, humankind and nature, and humankind and the noesphere (a term widely used by the scholar Vladimir Vernadsky [1863-1945], a geologist who pioneered the concept of the biosphere, and whose writings enjoy considerable popularity in Russia today. Roughly speaking, the term refers to the sphere of the nous, or life of reason, into which the biosphere, under the impact of science and technology, is passing today).

Such a course of study, as just outlined, eliminates those negative centrifugal tendencies characteristic of a differentiated education throughout the world. At the same time, the general level of education is augmented by introducing genuine rather than illusory and spurious interdisciplinary instruction. The same goal is served by increasing the relative importance in the curriculum of creative tasks and self-directed student activity.

In order to provide for a more substantial degree of differentiation, schools of the third rung can establish a particular "profile" (humanitarian, matho-physics, chemical-biological, economic, technological, agricultural, art-oriented, etc), and can organize labor activities in line with this profile.

Each child shall have the right to enroll in any school; to transfer from one school to another during the school year at any level of education; to select an *individualized profile* (curriculum); to define the tempo or interval of mastery of the course curriculum, and to study externally any or all subjects. It is the responsibility of the school to provide compensatory programs for learning disabled children and accelerated instruction for the gifted and talented.

The structure of general secondary education presented here radically alters the organization, functions and nature of evening and external education. Evening and correspondence course schools can become branches of third level schools or may serve as equivalents. In such branch units students can receive a secondary education corresponding to their differentiated profile, or may supplement their education.

Thus, the structure and organization of the general secondary school are rendered sufficiently flexible and variegated, adapted to the interests, inclinations and capacities of the pupil, and are designed to create a favorable climate for individual development and to facilitate the realization of one's life aspirations.

Restructuring the Pedagogical Process

According to technocratic pedagogy, the pedagogical process is traditionally described as an intermediary and mediating link between a given content and the pupil, who "must master" this content. This "intermediary link" is ordinarily equipped with a variety of specialized pedagogical methods. But in this approach the most important links in the pedagogical chain--the pupil and the teacher--are eliminated. The inevitable result is a depersonalized and authoritari-an pedagogy.

The view of the pedagogical process as a technological conveyer belt is bolstered by a quite widespread technological (i.e., methodological) fetishism, a belief in the marvelous power of method independent of the personal qualities or goals of educators, and regardless of the inclinations, capacities or interests of the pupil. In this scheme of things, the ideal teacher is a kind of teaching machine. But in reality it is precisely the nature of individual contact between all those who participate in the process of education which decides the degree of success or failure of any given methodology, and of education in general. An education oriented towards promoting individual capacities and individual identity is possible only through joint efforts, through substantive cooperation.

It is impossible to restructure the educational process without reconceptualizing its very essence, its goals, its content and its organization. The pedagogical process involves joint efforts on the part of educators and pupils to achieve the goals of education. It involves effective organization of all the activities of the school. The new societal functions and educational tasks of the school must be embodied in real, daily pedagogical practice and, above all, in a new attitude on the part of teacher and pupil about working together. If at present this direction is, in substance, externally provided, and so not palpably connected with schoolwork and, therefore, not recognized by the pupils as a goal they helped set, then any reorientation of the educational process must provide a precise reconceptualization of goals.

The entire pedagogy of cooperation is based upon a consciousness of common goals. Cooperation represents the humanitarian notion of the joint developmental activity of children and adults, bound by mutual understanding, by mutual engagement in each other's inner world, and by collective assessment of the results of such activity.

The belief system and instrumentation of cooperation serve as the basis of an entire, systematic methodology of instruction and socialization, but also emerge as an important, integral component of the content of education. The pedagogy of cooperation is juxtaposed to the alienation and authoritarianism characteristic of (existing) relations between adults and children, to a system in which the rights of teachers and obligations of pupils predominate.

At the core of the strategy of cooperation is the idea that the educator stimulates and guides the cognitive and experiential/vital (*zhiznennykh*) interests of the child. This implies, in particular, that the teacher understand the pupil, acknowledge his or her right to err. It means that the teacher be open and, what is no less important, take personal responsibility for his or her judgements, evaluations, recommendations, demands and mistakes. Earning, in the course of such interaction, the respect and trust of the class, the teacher simultaneously and substantially promotes among the pupils the development of their capacity to understand themselves, their actions, their genuine goals, motives and the reasons for failure and success.

Relations of cooperation must be supplemented and continuously enriched by cultural content, which is embodied in the material of instruction and socialization, in forms and methods. These inseparable components of the educational process, despite the high specificity characteristic of each (to be considered below) make up a complete system. The principles underlying their restructuring are the same.

The Content, Forms, and Methods of Instruction

In today's schools education is directed towards mastery of knowledge, habits and skills (ZUNY) rather than towards the promotion of individual identity.

Such important components of education as experiencing a wide range of activities, working out an affective and purposive orientation toward the world, practice at interpersonal relations, are all given short shrift. As a result education is disbalanced and the very educative nature of the school is attenuated.

The emphasis upon mastery of knowledge, skills and habits is the consequence, on the one hand, of the "technocratic" direction taken by pedagogy and, on the other, of the traditional approach to education which focuses upon the transmission and explanation of information (*informatsionno-ob'iasnitel'nyi podkhod*) According to this approach, all energy is directed towards delivering ready-made knowledge, and progress in education is understood as adding to this knowledge through expansion of traditional courses or addition of new subjects or disciplines.

The results of such "progress" are well-known: an overload of course subjects; presentation of such subject as adaptations or watered-down versions of courses taught in the universities (which by no means made them science-based); the loss of the integrity and systematic unity of educational content, and the transformation of the curriculum into a catch-all of truncated, poorly organized, drily academic sets of information, the purpose and utility of which often remain a mystery to both teacher and pupil. The consequence is overloading of both teacher and pupil, an attenuation of interest, and a decline in the quality of education received by graduates of such schools.

The situation is exacerbated by the fact that the school, which is often regarded as the only purveyor of knowledge, in fact faces many powerful competitors. Above all, we have in mind the mass media. According to criteria of novelty, accessibility, and degree of influence upon the child, the "canonical" school-type education loses out in this competition.

Thus, the emphasis, characteristic of the school curriculum, upon accumulating information is, in substance, yet another manifestation of the school-centered philosophy whose day has passed. The overriding concern for passing on and accumulating information within the framework of the "frontal" approach represents the *extensive* approach to the content of methods of education. The transition to an *intensive* approach can be implemented through resort to the *activities method* in education.

The activities method is oriented not merely toward the mastery of knowledge but toward the way this knowledge is acquired, toward patterns and modes of thinking and acting, toward the development of the cognitive skills and creative potential of the child. This approach contrasts with the verbal forms and methods by which packaged information is mechanically transmitted, with the monological and impersonal style of verbal, or "talk-and-chalk" teaching (*slovesnyi podkhod*) and passive learning, with useless knowledge, skills and habits which are never activated in real life.

The principles of the activities method apply to all sides of schooling, to the cognitive process, to upbringing and to the labor principle. The child's activity is the basic factor in development and self-definition.

The content of school education is an inseparable, organic unity of two components: that which provides markers giving orientation in culture, and that which is activating and creative. It represents a "museum" of the history of human culture (the arts, science, technology, crafts, the professional world), the exhibits of which are designed to foster during youth an integrated theory-driven representation of the surrounding world. It is also a "workshop" in which the younger generation learns how to acquire that knowledge necessary for practical activities and how to apply this knowledge in a problem-solving way.

The basic sources of the content of education must be drawn from the fundamental spheres of human self-definition: the individual, society, nature and the noesphere.

Self-definition in the sphere of human values is provided by the humanistic underpinnings of the education and life-activities of the individual. In the societal sphere, self-definition takes place through the acquisition of such values and notions as homeland, humankind, socialism, internationalism, popular power, democracy, glasnost, the law-governed state, the family, labor, civic responsibility, etc. In the sphere of nature and the environment emphasis is given to recognition of one's place in the natural world, to heightening the level of ecological awareness and the notion of generational accountability in one's use of natural resources. The noesphere includes establishing moral accountability in the application of the fruits of scientific and technological progress, and mastery of approaches to culture as an instrument of change.

Reliance upon those spheres by which identity is given definition offers fundamentally new approaches to organizing the school, to the content and methods of education, to the cognitive side of instruction, and to *vospitanie* as a factor of self-definition in life-activities.

First and foremost in giving definition to content and approaches in school education are the following basic principles: realistically defined goals; a focus upon fostering personal identity, and democratization.

A Core Curriculum for the School

The curriculum of today's schools, which is unwieldy, remote from the child as well as from the real world, must be replaced by a content which is realistic, concise, near to the child's immediate needs in cognitive and practical terms, and which fosters individual development. Above all, educators must locate that which is fundamental to growth and enhances individual potentialities, which provides links between the individual and society, the present and the past. This makes up the core of general education and provides a guarantee that the new goals of education will be realistic and attainable.

Establishing the core curriculum (*bazovyi komponent*) involves defining an optimal core of ideas, values and representations reliance upon which ensures mutual understanding between individuals, and fosters cooperative interaction. Without this core curriculum the channels of socialization are destroyed, and it becomes difficult if not impossible to integrate people into the society or into the economy.

The core curriculum is not a static but an evolving type of education responsive to scientific and technological progress and to changes in society. Nevertheless it remains a relatively stable part of the general educational cycle. It serves as a base for supplementary and accelerated instruction in the general secondary school.

Establishing the core curriculum has great importance in societal as well as pedagogical terms. At the societal level it ensures the satisfaction of particular historical demands of a given system of education, and provides guarantees for a system of ongoing education accumulating and enriching the intellectual potential of society. Application of the core curriculum allows state and society to assess the actual conditions and dynamics of education in the country as a whole, in various regions and different schools. At the pedagogical level the core curriculum serves as a point of departure with which to realistically organize a developmental education. The gap between mandatory and accelerated levels of instruction provide a much needed space, *the zone of proximal development* of the child. From this precise criteria emerge allowing the teacher to guide and to accelerate rather than to follow behind the child's spontaneous development.

A Humane Education, an Education in the Humanities

Ordinarily, when we think of a humanities education we have in mind augmenting the relative weight of the humanities cycle in the school calendar. But the real meaning of enhancing the humanities in education (*gumanitarizatsiia*) lies in the special, distinctively human form of mankind's interrelations with the world.

Augmenting the humanities in education is provided by linking the school with world culture, global history and spiritual values. Increasing the status of the humanities is achieved by renovation of subject content, by liberating them from an uninspired, vapid-fleshless rationalism, by bringing out in these subjects spirituality and human essence. Making the humanities more meaningful means a fundamental restructuring of content to enhance oral and written speech, to promote understanding of peoples of other times and places, to enlarge historical understanding and foster better relations with the environment. The subjects included in the arts (aesthetic) cycle (literature, music, the fine arts) must be fundamentally recast into a cycle of courses centered upon artistic creativity. The natural sciences cycle will cease to be a "package" of ready-made knowledge: it will unfold as a living process of searching and discovering, invention, as a historical drama of ideas and people, showing the interlinking and mutual influence of science and technology, of economic science and economic management (or economic structure and economic practice), and as a process of becoming aware of the global problems of the human community.

Augmenting the humanities in education will serve to overcome over-reliance upon technocratic approaches and the alienation which follows. Aiding this will be the process of humanizing the content, methods and forms of education, redirecting education towards promoting individual identity. Specifically, humanization takes place through a consistent individualization of the entire educational process (taking into account the personal distinctiveness of the child) and through "personalization" of this process (taking into account the individual qualities of the teacher).

Individualization of the content, methods and forms of education requires reorganization to fit the actual experience and levels of the child, the pupil's personal inclinations and goals. Since the pace of learning and the individual capacities of the pupil differ, the school is obliged to provide material which is pitched at different levels of complexity and difficulty, in both objective and subjective terms.

The orientation of a renewed pedagogy around the notion of personal identity corresponds well with the obvious fact--unfortunately overlooked in today's school--that the teacher is also a culture bearer, who can make a major contribution to education. The issue is just how to incorporate and realistically fit this personalized aspect of schooling into the curriculum, how to learn to value the teacher as the primary carrier of that culture which is transmitted in the school, and how to nurture the teacher's individual potential.

Art plays a major role in humanizing education and the school. In essence, it is a universal mode of forming and developing creative potential, thinking in images, and individual aesthetic sensitivities in general. At all developmental stages it emerges as a distinctive form of spiritual and practical activity, through which the emotional self-definition and value-orientation of the individual takes shape. Therefore, all art subjects deserve full and complete recognition in the school curriculum from first year to last.

The harmonious edifice of aesthetic *vospitanie* which must be built in the school, must have its foundation in art. The school cannot advance along the path of humanization as long as the subjects of the arts cycle are not accorded their deserved place in the school calendar, and the sense of beauty, serenity, spirituality and empathy (stemming from the practice of art) is not allowed to permeate all other subjects and all other aspects of school life.

The humanization of the school must not be restricted to the sphere of spiritual development. It calls for doing away with the "residual principle" when it comes to the child's physical development. Physical education must be given back its rightful place in general education, and must be liberated from a one-sided emphasis upon sports in favor of a genuine *physical culture*, which is an inseparable component of the comprehensive and harmonious development of the individual personality.

Physical upbringing must be oriented first of all towards promoting the health of the child, which has today become a nation-wide problem. Daily physical exercises beneficial for the child's health must be added to regular classes in physical culture in our schools. A task of utmost significance facing our educators and society is to work out a comprehensive, well designed curriculum promoting the physical growth and health of our children.

Labor Education in the Schools

The labor principle in the schools is of profound and broad import, and is inseparably linked with the general activities orientation of the new education. Labor emerges as a leading factor in the promotion of individual identity, and as a means of creative assimilation (apprehension) of the world, of acquisition of age-appropriate experience in various spheres of labor and as an indispensable part of general education, significantly aiding in giving shape the general education component, and as just an indispensable part of physical and aesthetic education. Labor emerges, finally, as a real, socially productive contribution of a polytechnical rather than a narrowly craft-oriented nature--which by no means excludes the possibility of teaching handicrafts, particularly in the early classes.

In today's school the labor principle has been reduced to a narrowly utilitarian, production-oriented approach, treated either as a mere appendage to the formal curriculum or as an artificial means of vocationalizing general education. Such labor is too tenuously linked to the goals and content of general education, to promising trends in the economy, to the genuine needs of a given region, and to the interests and demands of the pupils themselves. The socializing impact of such labor, especially when no choice is available, is of a negative nature.

Labor in the school--and here we have in mind cognitive efforts as well-- must be goal-oriented, well thought-out, and diversified activity, having a significance both for the individual and for society, and taking account of the distinctive psychological and physiological aspects of each developmental stage. Fragmentary acquaintanceship with isolated tasks will not suffice. The schoolchild must participate in a complete work cycle producing palpably useful results/output.

The mission of the school is to equip children with all that is necessary for a constantly changing work environment, for lifelong self-education, for a resourceful, innovative approach (*ratsionalizatorskii podkhod*) to any work-related activity. Here it is necessary to define a core curriculum of labor culture: the very basic, foundation-laying elements of the productive work experience.   On the basis of the core curriculum of labor activity can be constructed the ABCs of work skills, organically entering into the core curriculum of general education, and forming part of the common cultural core (*bazovaia kul'tura*).

In order to implement the goal of a developmental labor education, diversity, choice, and variability of types of labor must be provided, in order that the pupil can find his or her place, his or her calling in the world of work.   Labor activity should incorporate the spheres of social services, of projects to protect the environment and to restore historically valuable edifices or monuments, and include age appropriate internships with various governmental or public organizations.   This will augment the links between school and the outside world, and will enhance the ability of labor to foster a better understanding of the nature of social relations.

The labor orientation of the school is meant to provide generalized work skills, modes of practical and cognitive activity, and to facilitate a contextual understanding of labor process and labor culture.   The labor, activities-oriented school creates a space for the diversified and harmonious development of individual identity, for the healthy psychological development of the child, all of which is inconceivable without both mental and physical labor.

Democratizatizing Education

The unity and integrity of the educational process in the renewed school can only be genuinely instituted through the democratic process.   The significance of democratization of content, forms and methods resides in providing access for each and every one of us to the higher levels of culture, in the maximal unfolding of the child's potential, and in the removal of all obstacles barring the path of personal development.

In order to provide children of diverse background equal access to culture, education must provide broad and flexible opportunities for children of the most diverse capabilities.   This calls for refined techniques of individualized instruction and upbringing, but also for an open-ended curriculum, for an enormous variety of text material and teachers' guides, for a diversity of approaches, and for adjustments to take into account cultural and regional distinctiveness.

Variety and openness of content and methods are provided, first of all, by student choice among diverse course offerings and types of activities, by progress evaluations based upon individual achievement in relation to previous stages of development.   Finally, openness and variety (diversity) follow from differentiation of the entire educational process in tandem with a corresponding spectrum of flexible instructional approaches.

The public should have the opportunity to review, correct, adjust and even offer alternatives to the curriculum and syllabi, with due consideration for the genuine needs, interests and capabilities of both children and teachers, for the level of intellectual readiness at any given rung of the educational ladder, and for the zones of promimal development of the child, and, finally for local and regional distinctions.

The competition offered by these home-grown, alternative curricula, the analysis and selection among such alternatives, comparison with other programs drawn both from nation-wide and from foreign experience, and resort to both public and official expertise should lead to selection of the optimal curriculum variants. At the same time, corresponding methodologies will have to be worked out to ensure that the curriculum can be enacted and that students be able to complete both basic and advanced general education cycles.

Such an open-ended approach to developing a new content of education facilitates, without undercutting the existing curriculum, the *gradual and unforced* "cultivation" of a new program for the schools. We have in mind that which simply cannot be put forth in finished form in any draft, but which can serve as the "launch" mechanism for an ever-evolving cultural and historical educational project.

Looked at as a whole, the new content will be structured as follows: the mandatory core curriculum will take up seventy to eighty percent of the school day; in addition, there will be "offshoots" encompassing national and regional cultures; further, there will be a portion devoted to topics fulfilling the school's own profile; and a part added by local teachers and finally, a portion entirely given over to the child's inclinations. Accompanying such a program must be original, lively and diversified single-author textbooks, teachers' handbooks and other aids and guides.

The pedagogy of cooperation provides the main guidelines for the democratization of education; the significance of this pedagogy extends far beyond narrowly methodological concerns. At the same time the pedagogy of cooperation is an integrated methodological approach. For the first time in decades it offers the teacher and the mass school a rich and diversified range of methodological tools designed to facilitate child development.

At the core of this methodological system is a set of fundamental ideas. Among them:

- the exclusion of compulsory methods from the classroom and the exclusive reliance upon motivation to draw the child into the common project of learning, stimulating the gratifying feelings of progress, success, development;
- the idea of "challenging goals," (*trudnye tseli*), that is, encouraging the assumption of personal responsibility, and a belief in the educational role of overcoming obstacles (associated with Vasily Davidov).

- the idea of "support signals" or "key words" (*tochki opory*) allowing even the weakest pupil to systematically advance (associated with V. F. Shatalov;
- the idea of "challenge" (*operezhenie*), which provides a special boost for pupils who are particularly strong and capable in a given subject area (linked with the work of Sofia Lysenkova);
- the idea of "large blocks" (*krupnye bloky*) allowing pupils to master what is most important, pivotal concepts, linkages, and significantly increasing the volume of learning while sharply reducing the burden on the pupil;
- the idea of maintaining a correspondence between the form and content of an activity;
- the idea of those forms of supervision and evaluation which are supportive of learning without compulsion (support signals, ungraded instruction, "learning parades," [*obshchestvennye smotry znanii*] etc.);
- the idea of self-analysis, or creative group self-organization, and cooperative learning with parents.

All the above, as well as other ideas and principles stemming from the pedagogy of cooperation are furnished with a full array of well-defined as well as diversified methodological tools.

The pedagogy of cooperation is not a finished, much less a closed pedagogical or methodological system. It is open to any and all ideas and approaches which do not violate the individual dignity of the child or the teacher. It is enriched through a process of collective striving, and as a part of the renewal of Soviet pedagogy.

In the light of the activities approach to education creative and active methods of instruction gain particular significance. Such methods include various types of problem-solving, the inquiries approach, the project and project-constructivist method and others. This does not entirely exclude resort to conventional approaches or use of methods of the program-algorithmic variety (the latter is a reference to the "step-by-step" approach embodied in *programmirovannoe obuchenie* which became popular in some circles in the late 1970s), but the priorities, nonetheless, in the new system of methodology, are elsewhere.

The new methodological system does away, as well, with the preponderance given to the frontal forms of instruction, to the monopoly of classroom lessons. Today, as a result of the dominance of the frontal approach, some students find learning too difficult, others find it uninteresting and unchallenging, and a large percentage of students become conformists. The activities approach gives new life to individual, club, and group forms of learning, in which the composition of given groups is not age-segregated and is often changing. The project method is in wide use, as are simulations and role playing (*rolevaia i delovaia igry*), issue-oriented consultations (*problemnoe konsul'turovanie*) and other modes of creative instructional organization.

The transition from the frontal type of instruction to the activities-oriented developmental approach, is also linked with the appearance in the classroom of a new technology of instruction, including personal computers with a variety of software, video-computer data bases/information sciences (*informatika*), which permit the pupil to freely pursue a range of interests with powerful information resources at hand.

The Results of Instruction

The restructured general education school should be able to provide qualitative and quantitative indicators of progress. The grading system (the so-called five-ball system) is not appropriate for providing benchmark (short-term) assessments of progress. Only at the end of the school year (or quarter or semester, according to the decision of local school boards) should evaluations of pupils, based upon qualitative assessments, and taking into account professional psychological evaluations, be given according to the five-ball system. All efforts must be made to eliminate the use of grades by poorly-qualified teachers as a means to *enforce* learning.

The measure of a pupil's achievement, and therefore of the success of the school, lies in the capability of the child to acquire new knowledge (and not merely to assess the amount or quality of knowledge already acquired), in the ability to apply knowledge (*poznanie*) already or recently acquired to conceptualize and solve a variety of problems and tasks, to identify and formulate one's own way of doing things and one's own goal-oriented worldview.

Restructuring Upbringing in the Schools

For long years the upbringing/socialization functions of the school were proclaimed to have priority over instruction. It reality such proclamations represented no more than demagogic sloganeering, a parade-type mentality, conspicuous display, and a concern with making the records look good. *vospitanie* boiled down to "requirements," to compulsion. In the school administrative, disciplinarian ways of influencing children prevailed. Such an approach to *vospitanie*, rather than facilitating, actually obstructed child development.

The ideology of renewal of *vospitanie* is based upon the following ideas:

The Setting of Goals. The all-round development of personal identity is a socialist ideal, a goal of the Soviet school. A realistic goal today is to foster comprehensive personal development, utilizing individual gifts and abilities.

The way to this goal is through individual mastery of the foundations of culture (*bazovye osnovy kul'tury*). From this stems the core of the content of upbringing as the "core culture" of the individual personality (*bazovaia kul'tura lichnosti*). This notion encompasses a culture of personal self-definition, (orientation in the spheres of) work and the economy, politics, democracy and law, morality and ecology, art and physical well-being, and family relations.

The core culture includes, on the one hand, eternal, universal values and, on the other, values accruing with the progressive development of a socialist society.

The Idea of Cooperative Interaction of Children and Adults. The school in the period of perestroika is giving new life to the genuine core of *vospitanie*. This essence can be found not in the influence exerted by adults upon children, but in the process of joint mutual interaction, based upon cooperation, and aimed at growth on the part of all involved.

The mutual search of children and adults for moral paradigms (*obraztsy*), for the best models of spiritual culture, of an activities-oriented culture, and the working out on the basis of this search of personal values, norms and codes are what make up the content of the work of *vospitanie*, guaranteeing that the pupil play an active role in the process. Without the idea of cooperation there can be no nurturing environment for bringing out the creative nature of upbringing. Here cooperation is directly juxtaposed to the authoritarian idea.

The success of the idea of cooperation depends upon expanding its zone (of application) from the school to the broader social milieu.

Only through creative cooperation with adults can children be provided with the necessary pedagogical guidance. Wherever cooperation is lacking, the formalistic guidance which exists will be ineffective. As he or she grows, the child, deprived of the genuine influence of adults, moves in the direction of amoralism and law-breaking. The contemporary wave of aggressiveness observable among youth stems from that "pedagogy of proclamation" which set all-encompassing directives, and functioned in a context of rampant societal hypocrisy. This led to the isolation of many adolescents from the older generation. When adults are unable to provide moral leadership, they replace it with authoritarianism, and the process of *vospitanie* is replaced by a process of relentless re-education (*perevospitanie*), which exhausts both child and adult. The choice is stark: either cooperation in upbringing or a war with children—there is no third way.

The Idea of Self-Definition. Developmental *vospitanie* calls for the formation of the integrated personality—a person with firm convictions, democratic views and a defined stance towards life. Self-definition includes the process of integrating distinct qualities into a (complete) personal orientation (*lichnostnaia napravlennost'*). The primary goal of efforts in the area of *vospitanie* is to develop a culture fostering personal self-definition.

Life orientation is a broader concept than professional, or even civic orientation. A culture of personal self-definition stamps the individual as subject of his or her own destiny. It is precisely in harmony with the self that civic, professional and moral self-definition must take place.

The Idea of Personal Orientation in Upbringing. Not curricula, measures or forms and methods, but the child, the adolescent, the youth, should be at the centerpiece of all efforts at upbringing, for the child is the highest goal, and what gives meaning to all pedagogical endeavor. It is precisely individual inclinations and interests, unique personal attributes and the sense of self-worth which merit sustained attention, which must in all instances be taken into account and nurtured. Progress from that which is closest to the interests of the child to an awareness of the higher spiritual needs should become the cardinal rule of *vospitanie*.

The Idea of Group/Collective Orientation (Napravlennost'). In the work of *vospitanie* we must overcome that attitude towards the collective that sees it exclusively as a tool of compulsion or a rigidly confining structure capable only of suppressing individual identity rather than fostering moral and spiritual capacities. If the cooperative milieu--the classroom group, the brigade, the circle--all serve to level personal identity, to promote blind conformism and submission to authority, rather than independence and a human, civic sense of personal dignity--then no matter how politically noble or socially significant the goals we set, such groupings (*obshchnosti*) are merely a surrogate for a community ethos (*kollektivnost'*), having little in common with a genuinely communist upbringing.

The school must make optimal use of the powers and traditions of the socializing collective, of group opinion and of self-government towards the end of moral suasion, and must promote an evolution from a spontaneous patriotism and internationalism characteristic of the milieu of the child towards a more genuine, consciously thought-out patriotism and internationalism.

School self-government merits particular concern. Its contemporary variant replicates the bureaucratic *apparat* in the child's milieu, remote from a democratic culture. Changing this situation presupposes directing all institutions of government and self-government to defend individual rights and interests; regular turnover of the *aktiv*; recognition of the right of each collective to work out its own rules and regulations; mandatory accountability of both the leadership of the school and of the institutions of self-government before the collective; directing energies towards transforming the surrounding world; and utilization of the methods of collective, creative upbringing.

Established practice suggests several possible approaches to changing the process of *vospitanie*. The first involves the creative development of humane and democratic principles and techniques within the framework of the traditional approaches utilizing the classroom collective, the pioneer detachment, the komsomol group, and by enhancing relations between teachers and taught on the basis of cooperation. The second is brought to fruition through a structure of inquiry. It provides pedagogical collectives the opportunity of devising and implementing their own, new, individually designed, or "authorial" projects for organizing the work of upbringing. For example, such work can be organized on the basis of productive labor, or in terms of student participation in the transformation of the school, or in the establishment of larger unities bringing together school and university-level or PTU collectives.

The organization of activities clubs must become one of the most promising directions of upbringing aimed at democratizing the school. It presupposes the bifurcation of the life of the school into academic (mandatory, course-related) and club-related (voluntary, personally gratifying). The school (or inter-school) club is a distinct and independent societal institution, serving as a partner of the school in the achievement of educational tasks. The relationship between the school and the club must be built upon a base of mutual interest and aid. Instead of relations of subordination and domination, there should be every effort at cooperation.

At the same time, school instruction and clubs are but part of a broader educational process, which is not fully played out within the walls of the school. This is not merely a matter of taking into account the influence of family, of mass media, of youth subculture, of various societal institutions, but of finding realistic modes and forms of co-organization. By this is meant finding new types of co-organization which organically evolve out of daily life: academic-*vospitanie* complexes; centers for aesthetic (expressive) and physical training; inter-school agricultural and industrial combinations; schools linked to universities or to research institutes and cultural institutions. . . .Certain of these types of organization are feasible in large cities, others in regional centers, and yet others in the villages. A task today is to build upon the existing base of new and vital schools to establish centers of innovation with laboratories, courses, workshops, in order to offer all who are interested the opportunity not merely to observe, but to actively participate when appropriate.

Linking the school and the outside world is a key condition of renewing the content and techniques of education, creating opportunities for moving away from levelling tendencies to promoting more diversified personal development; from rote, dogmatic learning to apprehending and transforming the world; from authoritarianism and alienation to humaneness and cooperation.

In the schools, perestroika of the education is inconceivable unless connected with the renewal of socialistic society in general. The idea of societal renewal is the foundation of the ideology of school perestroika.

The Elements Key to Renewal of Education

Changing How We Run the Schools

The chief obstacle to change in the schools is the obsolete system of governance of education. It is precisely in administration of the schools that we can see all of the key problems confronting renewal, and a fundamental restructuring of school management is the first, decisive step towards a general restructuring.

There are three essential shortcomings in the existing system of school governance: a lack of democracy, extreme centralization and a militantly, bureaucratic style. Such a system excludes any public participation in education, and takes no account of the social and educational, cultural and ethnic distinctiveness of diverse regions or of the needs of a given school. Instead it operates through paperwork, surveillance and control, working primarily for itself rather than for the public interest.

The perestroika of school governance has as its mission eliminating such shortcomings. Its basic approach is an emphasis upon profound democratization and a style of management which promotes school growth.

Democratization is the transition from a state to a joint *public-state* approach to running the schools. It implies inclusion of the public in school governance and simultaneously fostering school self-government and self-development. This represents replacement of the administrative-command methods of running the schools with methods grounded in socio-economic realities and educational needs.

The transition from a state to a public-state system of managing the schools involves not merely restoring equal rights, parity of state and society in school affairs, and not merely a rejection of the approach, embedded in the bureaucratic consciousness, of issuing commands "from above" and expecting compliance "from below," or even of the very notion of above and below as such. The essence of this transition is in joining the efforts of state and society in devising solutions, in an organic merger of official and non-official in the mechanisms of school governance.

The new public-state type of school management is to be implemented by education boards and school boards established in accordance with the intentions of the original Leninist decree on education (1918). These boards are to function to facilitate the joint efforts of state and society in carrying out a unified set of school policies designed to adequately supply the schools, to promote educational advance in general, and to heighten public awareness of educational issues.

At the first stage of school restructuring, education soviets will be created at the level of the city or district (*raion*). In order to combat the deep-rooted bureaucratic tendencies permeating not only official structures but even newly emerging societal formations (public organizations), such education soviets will be elected only for a short term. In pace with the establishment of democratic mechanisms of school governance, soviets of the next round (summons) can be established on the basis of self-government with a term of office identical to that of other organs of Soviet power. At the next stage, the principle of governing through soviets should be implemented at all levels of the educational system.

The impending reform of the Soviet political system will deepen and expand the tasks and functions of the education soviets. The path to democracy in education is through the transformation of education soviets into institutions of popular self-government.

At the level of the school, the principles of socialist self-government are already becoming predominant. Such principles are embodied in school collectives and school boards, whose membership includes teachers, parents, pupils and the public at large. Through these boards the school is emerging as a self-governing societal unit. From a socio-pedagogical perspective the boards enact the principle of co-governance of children and adults, of cooperative intergenerational endeavors.

The most urgent and significant aspect of democratizing the system of educational governance is decentralization. Decentralization represents a redistribution of functions and powers between the central, regional, and local authorities. It signifies the expansion of the rights of regional and local organs and of the schools themselves as well as an increase in accountability for affairs entrusted to each level or unit. It signifies an end to stereotypes of "uniformity," of the monolithic nature of the system of running the schools, and reliance instead on flexibility, heterogeneity and diversity in accordance with local conditions. The monolithic drive which still defines our strategies of school management is nothing less that the surviving core of the bureaucratic mentality of the period of stagnation.

In a decentralized environment, the main function of the central organs of governance will be to ensure the necessary conditions for successful completion of established minimal competencies (*dostizhenie urovnia obiazatel'nykh trebovanii*), and for dynamic advance in education as a whole. The center will focus its energies upon drawing up a philosophy (lit.: ideology) and strategy for the development of a system of lifelong education, upon establishing its priorities, upon large-scale experiments in education and upon fostering advances in applied psychology pertinent to the schools, upon analysis of public opinion, and upon informing the public about conditions in the schools, problems encountered, and future perspectives.

The basic thrust of activity at the regional and local level of administration is to develop the local system of education in accordance with nation-wide standards, with local socio-economic conditions, with local traditions and cultures, and to balance the various types of education and types of schools.

Local and regional institutions will deal with issues pertaining to finances, the supply of personnel as well as of equipment and other material needs, will coordinate the activities of all schools at the regional level, and will develop programs for teaching re-training and educational enhancement. It will be their mission to defend the rights of the citizen in educational matters, to take a non-bureaucratic approach to school concerns, to ensure public input, to support and stimulate creative directions taken by teachers, to nurture experimental programs, and to work actively to introduce innovations to the mass school.

As institutions of school governance, school collectives and school boards are delegated broad authority in the organization of the life of the school. They are accountable to society and to the state for providing the individual with access to schooling, for correlating the type of schooling provided with the age-specific psycho-physiological traits of children, with their individual interests and inclinations, and for achieving results on the level of the mandatory curriculum.

The establishment of a democratic, public-state system of school governance is one of the key factors in renewal of education, and represents a major step towards embodying in the sphere of education the Leninist notion of a transition from power for the people to power by the people.

Priority Financing and the Financial Autonomy of the School

Any state which pinches pennies on education is condemned to a perpetual game of catching up. In civilized societies education is an extremely important social and economic force (lit.: program). Ultimately, the level and quality of education achieved determines a country's level of well-being. Precisely for this reason, capital investments in education are generally considered to yield high returns.

Investments in education represent the most humane mission of any economy. They represent investments in the individual, in unleashing his or her creative potential, in forming an important strategic resource for the country.

We still don't fully recognize that human capital--the collective human intelligence--is, with every passing year, becoming the single most productive, not to mention creative, force of culture and civilization. It is time to recognize that we must treat the mind as the greatest resource, as the highest value and the goal of societal development, and not simply as a means of solving current problems.

It is absurd in economic terms to invest resources in industry, in agriculture, science, while withholding resources from the education of those very people who will be employed in these sectors. What this leads to is amply demonstrated by the "economics of frugality" of the past twenty years. We are not wealthy enough to skimp on education, especially since humankind has not yet come up with a cheap quality education.

Over the past thirty years the share of gross national product (national income) which has been spent on education has declined from 10 percent to 7.2 percent. The funding of education lags behind funding material production tenfold. In the sphere of the economics of education we have fallen hopelessly behind the developed countries. "Economizing" in this sphere has led to irreplaceable material and spiritual losses, on which it is impossible to place even an approximate price tag.

If we want to see our country genuinely revitalized, if we want to see it advance to the front ranks in the world community, we must give systematic priority to education, reject the "residual" principle by which it is financed, and increase the share of public input into education.

It is equally important to move towards decentralizing outlays on education and to financially emancipate the school itself. Setting the sum total of outlays on education should be the task of local as well as central institutions. The practice must be rejected of making deductions in the central budget of that proportion of an enterprise's budget which will then be allocated to education. Such resources can be directly handed over to local representative institutions. The local education soviets should also have the right to adjust wage and salary scales, as stipulated in the Law on State Enterprises (1987), and to allocate for educational ends a portion of the tax on cooperative enterprises, and on the self-employed.

A most important task of the soviets of people's deputies and the education soviets is to establish regional endowments (*fondy*) for educational development by attracting local and sectoral resources, contributions by enterprises, other organizations and private individuals, and to set up local industries producing directly for education.

The financial emancipation of the school must proceed along two rails. First, the school must be given the right to independently dispose of the resources budgeted it. Secondly, schools should be given the right to establish endowments, which could be disposed of according to the discretion of the school board.

Today, the school is bound hand and foot when it comes to the budget. The budget is meticulously divided into hundreds of specific items, and there is virtually no flexibility or discretion. Unfortunately, life doesn't arrange itself so neatly. It requires dynamic reactions to situations, business-like decisions, and socialist initiative.

The school must have the right to independently draw up its own budget within the limits of its allocations, and to distribute resources as it sees fit, as long as norms concerning salaries and benefits, school diet and debt service are met. Salaries can be derived from two sources: from state allocations, within limits set for given positions, and from the local school endowment.

Such a school endowment can be set up from the following basic sources: allocations from the local budget for the schools; specifically targeted allocations by the ministry, or by departments responsible for specific sectors of the economy; by local industries; by higher education institutions; by public organizations; cooperatives, etc; by voluntary contributions from parents or other citizens; by profits from pay services provided by the school, including renting out of the premises or equipment or from economic activities launched by the school itself (school businesses; workshops, student brigades, etc.).

The financial resources of the school must be fully at its disposal and not subject to exactions. The school board can funnel these resources towards key targets, can establish, on a contractual basis with other schools, extramural and scientific organizations, state and cooperative enterprises, a variety of inter-school combinations, programs, production units meeting the needs of the school, and school cooperatives.

Such activities will liberate the school from the spider web of countless financial instructions and norms now surrounding it, and will enable it to move freely, which in turn will provide a tremendous stimulus to growth.

Renewal of the school is the path:

- from arbitrary bureaucratic practices to popular empowerment;
- from residual to priority financing of education;
- from the financial enserfment of the school to its economic independence.

Teachers' Gazette
August 23, 1988

10

You Won't Get Anywhere
on the Sidelines

Among the many concerns of our time, the school must rank high. Such concern was expressed with extreme candor in a collective letter to *Pravda* (March 5, 1990) by deputies to the Supreme Soviet, entitled "The School is Still in a Tailspin." The facts as presented in that letter are undeniable. Nevertheless, the emerging situation in education is rather contradictory and many questions remain to be answered. This *Pravda* correspondent interviewed Mr. Edward Dneprov, director of *VNIK-shkola* of the APN, on the impediments to perestroika of the schools. VNIK is well-known for its innovative research into how to renew our school system.

Edward Dmitrievich, do you agree with the conclusions expressed by the deputies in the open letter?

Completely. The letter expresses the anguish we feel about education being marginalized in our society and state. You might say that this is the primary reason for the declining prestige of education and knowledge. Being pushed to the side creates a feeling of marginalization and deprives the teacher of hope for the future, of expectations of growth. But, in addition to the general opinions expressed by the deputies I'd like to add at least five more reasons of an internal nature for the lag in school reform.

The first is the legal confusion over who holds authority over the schools. On the one hand, the new Temporary School Statute, adopted by the State Committee of Education, is in force; at the same time the old 1970 Regulations (*Reglament*), passed by the Council of Ministers of the USSR, has not been abrogated. This serves as ample cause for sabotaging the new Statute, which in many areas is simply not in force.

In addition, for all practical purposes, the "amicable agreement" between the State Committee and the Ministry of Finance concerning the legal empowerment of the new State, and its economic stipulations in particular, is simply not working--local bureaucracies responsible for finances are paying no heed to it. So, here we are bouncing off a wall of financial ice. To make matters worse, those experienced functionaries over at the State Planning Committee got it into their heads to introduce the new economic mechanism of the school on a trial basis, for a year only. Now tell me, how many highly audacious school directors are you going to find who are going to introduce something like the new economic mechanism with the knowledge that they will suffer for such an act in short order?

Well, you won't find many. And, by the way, in no small way because of the failure to replenish the ranks of the educational bureaucracy. Here, just as in old times, the same old bureaucrats make all the decisions. Despite the waves of energy in support of renewal, moving from top down and from bottom up, bureaucratic channels continue to block the flow. This bureaucracy remains wedded to the principles of stagnation, and it is only thanks to the new faces at the level of the republics and lower that we might finally be able to end this bottleneck.

The chronic paralysis of official pedagogy shows no signs of mitigating. In the world of educational thought all kinds of new forces are emerging and working side-by-side with the old. But the hardliners are still in a strong position. The command-driven pedagogy is experiencing the same convulsions that are shaking the administrative-command system as a whole. A struggle for survival is underway. The last defenses are being fortified with the barbed wire and anti-tank defenses of antiquated dogmas. Myth-making tendencies, self-hypnosis, self-delusion are all rife. And we can understand this. After all, from time to time, Brezhnev's bushy brows seem to be ascending once again over the horizon.

Much more troubling are the occasional signs that here and there teachers are becoming alienated from perestroika, in education as in other spheres. We can detect a faltering in the teachers' movement. And after all, it is teachers, working hand in hand with the press who have been the driving force for renewal in education.

Moreover, among the "aristocracy of educational thought" we can detect a growing nostalgia for the tranquillity of the past. More and more we hear anguished cries for "clarity and definition." We hear that the "rank-and-file teacher" isn't prepared for such changes, and feels uncomfortable. Why? Because it's no longer so snug and cozy?

Evocations of such a mood are but one of the manifestations of pedagogical neo-conservatism, a defensive reaction against all innovation. To provide substance to such a defensive reaction all kinds of argumentation are trotted out, both practical and theoretical. There is too much democracy in the school! The time is out of joint! Nobody is ready to unfurl the banners! Well, are the banners really not yet unfurled? Maybe they are just being cleansed of all the

accumulated filth. Personally, I am much closer to another position, one stated
by one of the new leaders of the ideological section of the Central Committee,
V. Riabov: "The comprehensive democratization of the educational process, of
the entire life of the school, serves as an enormous, indeed the key reserve force
of perestroika in education." One could hardly overstate the importance of this
statement. After all, only recently right there, in the former section on science
and education under the Central Committee, was located the main brake on
education.

*We often hear that what is most important right now is finding more money
for the schools. What do you think?*

Money solves a lot of problems, but by no means all. I would even risk
saying that today money is not what is most important. In essence here, as in
agriculture, we can identify two fundamentally different approaches. The first
is the resource-consuming, *extensive*, command-driven way, which preserves the
old productive relations in the village (read: school). The second is the *intensive*
approach, aimed at transforming productive relations in society and the economy
and transforming the very model (paradigm) itself.

Of course the schools are in desperate need of money. But the extensive
approach, if seen as a panacea, can lead to conservative outcomes, for it takes
no account of the all-important internal mechanisms of perestroika. Even more,
it can serve as a justification for doing nothing: there's no money, so what can
we do? Enabling the internal mechanism, on the other hand, will bring to bear
the most important resource of perestroika--freedom.

What the school needs today is: economic freedom, the freedom of self-
government, the freedom for teachers' to unleash their own initiatives, freedom
in thought and action. "We have returned to the socialist slogan of 'freedom'
in the broadest, most comprehensive sense of this word," said Michael
Gorbachev in his concluding address to the Second Congress of People's
Deputies. So, let us return that word to the banners of our schools as well.
And not merely in thought, or in the Temporary School Statute--it's already
there. But in reality as well.

*I agree. But still, how can we lift the school out of its impoverished
condition? By improving its material status. Who would disagree that there is
a direct causal link between such improvements and the cultural, scientific and
technological advance of a society?*

In my mind the financial levers for enhancing the school are closely
connected with granting high priority to education as a whole. This by no
means can be reduced to direct investments in schooling alone. Changes in
financing must be wide-ranging. Above all, we have in mind taxation policies
which provide incentives to investment in education and culture, as is done
throughout the globe (such incentives are no less effective than direct investments); taxes specifically earmarked for education; tax-credits and write-offs for
educational initiatives and for construction in education based on local funding.

Finally, we should not forget about the resources already available within the educational sector. According to the estimates of our house economists, changing the terms of operation of the schools could lead to internal savings to the tune of four to five billion rubles each year, more than a third of the annual budget. Nobody has calculated what kind of savings *structural changes* in the schools could produce; changes such as eliminating supine higher education institutions or combining daytime and evening schools.

Another, often neglected, source of great importance is connected with the establishment of a new sector, one that might be called the *educational industry*. This sector not only requires no additional expenditures--it should actually contribute to restoring fiscal health in education. One of our problem spots right now is the shortage of goods and services available on the education market. For example, the population spends about two billion rubles annually on preparing for the entrance exams to higher education institutions primarily through private tutoring. Needless to say, most of this sum is not taxed. There is a shortage of books for children, for teachers, and for the educational community as a whole. The existing infrastructure does not provide children the opportunity to pursue their diverse interests or effectively develop their own talents.

The experience of the developed countries testifies that pay-as-you-go educational services would be very popular and could bring in substantial revenue, the bulk of which could be put back into education. Isn't it time that we learned from this global experience and set about creating our own educational industry--a network of public educational research and development centers, joint state and cooperative enterprises to produce instructional materials, small-scale publishing firms and other production-oriented workshops? Judging by what has happened elsewhere, all this could be done in a relatively short time. Such activity would of course directly benefit education, but it would bring into circulation some of the population's presently unused savings. Most important, it would directly involve broad segments of the population in addressing the country's educational needs.

I have outlined what could be a program of short-term economic measures for education. Such a program would help emancipate public initiative, and open up new vistas for societal activism.

Despite what you call the continued enserfment of the school, today we can discern the distinct outlines of an emancipated world in education: experimental sites, authorial schools, new types of schools such as gymnasia, lycées.

A graphic example of the changing pedagogical, or more accurately, moral, climate can be found in many of Moscow's schools. Over the last year we have worked closely with many administrators, directors and teachers in the Moscow schools. And it has been rewarding indeed. We have been impressed by the inventiveness, boldness, and originality of thought. Now as during the initial stages of school perestroika, it is been precisely these people, responsible for the day to day activities of the school, who have carried the burden of leadership. And tomorrow their energy will be decisive. The mission of educational scholarship and of school policy must be to give these people guidelines and provide them support in their efforts.

Pravda
March 20, 1990

11

Vseobuch: A General Secondary Education for All --from Illusion to Reality

The problem of universal secondary education turns out today to be a knot of contradictions in which the basic threads representing various aspects of school affairs have become entangled. Restructuring the schools depends above all upon disentangling these threads. Therefore, isn't it finally time to cut that Gordian knot, to tackle one of the most massive problems which has accumulated during the years of stagnation in our school policies, which are still affected by a spirit of illusion and pipe-dreams.

We know that reaching each new frontier in education, whether it be universal literacy, universal primary education, or universal secondary education to the eighth grade, leads to a reorganization of the school: its internal organization, content and methodologies. In a word, at each juncture the fundamental questions of what and how to teach rises anew. But the purveyors of our program of universal secondary education neglected to do their job, and there were no internal changes in the school corresponding with the achievement of universal secondary education. This goal was simply proclaimed, and the school was left to fend for itself. And it did adjust, through reaching an implicit "compact" between teachers and pupils. The teachers turned their gaze from their students' academic weaknesses. Otherwise, how could the mandatory quotas (*sredneobiazatel'nyi val*) have been achieved?

Towards the close of the 1960s our school curricula began to be enriched and elaborated. But not even one generation of schoolchildren was allowed to test these curricula, to study with the new textbooks before the law on mandatory secondary education forced the school to use them to teach all children, including those who did not want to be in school and those who found learning difficult. The teachers well understood that the academic content was simply too much for many in the new expanded contingent to master. So they kept two scores: two (failing) in their mental calculations; and three (passing) on the records. The negative social, moral, and pedagogical consequences of the impetuous introduction of universal secondary education are now obvious to all.

Objectively speaking, the 1984 school reform reflected problems in secondary education. Attempts were made to develop secondary education in three directions: the senior (tenth and eleventh) classes of the general secondary school; the SPTUs (specialized vocational schools) and the technicums. But once again changes were made arbitrarily, with little thought to consequences. First of all, universal vocational training was tacked on to the goal of universal general education. And to this day it is unclear what this vocational training means in terms of the school. Second, all vocational-professional schools (*proftekhshkoly*) were converted to SPTUs, with little heed given to doubts about the latter's ability to combine professional training and a general education. In the end we have general schools inadequately providing job training, and vocational schools providing a second-rate general education. Now we are engaged in a strenuous effort to overcome the deficiencies created during the period of stagnation and exacerbated by the 1984 reform, all connected with the implementation of universal secondary education. Our efforts are in vain, because we are looking for a way out of a dead end. The problem is that we have artificially combined universal secondary education with preparation for the university, with so-called "readiness for college" and have tried to bring all students, at whatever cost, to a level at which they could function at any VUZ. But no matter how hard we try to turn slogans about "equality of opportunity" into reality, both research and experience show that university-level competency is achieved by only a fraction of school graduates (in the other socialist countries between twenty and fifty percent). Even the ubiquitous grade inflation of our schools cannot conceal this truth. No wonder our teachers call universal education (*vseobuch*) "universal mandatory secondary (or average) punishment." To be sure, recently we have been reluctant to mention on paper the notion of mandatory secondary education, but it continues to exert its influence. Incidentally, almost nowhere in the world is a complete secondary education mandatory for all.

We can overcome our "universal mandatory secondary self-deception" only by rejecting, at long last, the illusory linkage of all schools to high education. A bridge between the school and the VUZ has long existed in the form of private tutoring and preparatory courses. So, are not contemporary needs best met by a different model of schooling--mandatory, general, *basic* secondary education consisting of two rungs (four plus five years)? Mandatory basic secondary education corresponds best with global practice.

Let us try to describe this model in greater detail. On the basic school we superimpose a third rung of secondary education: universal professional instruction. Here, there are three paths to follow, two of which are directly college preparatory and the third of which, as we shall see, is not terminal either.

The first path--the tenth and eleventh grades of the school, is differentiated in orientation. For example, in the Estonian variant, there are four directions: humanities, physics and mathematics, chemistry and biology, and economy and technology. These grades will provide professional and vocational training as well to fit the profile (*uklon*) chosen (for example, computer programmers, pre-school educators, laboratory technicians). Classroom activities in these grades can be organized according to the principle of funneling (*voronki*). For example, during the first semester of the tenth grade in a group pursuing the bio-chemistry cycle, the student might not yet have decided what branch of the natural sciences best fits his or her inclinations. Here, optional courses can help in making the choice. But during the second semester, optional courses are replaced (or supplemented) by mandatory subjects in the chosen area. During the course of the eleventh year, core courses can be supplemented by a specialized cycle of lessons designed for the future chemist, medical profession-al, livestock specialist, or agronomist, in line with the resources of the school. Regardless of the profile of the individual school, the curriculum must include a range of social science, literature, art and physical culture courses as well as thorough training in a foreign language. Depending upon local conditions, the tenth and eleventh grades can be combined with the general school or set up separately (as is the case in most countries). We believe that entrance examinations in the designated specialty should accompany the transition from the second to the third tier of pre-university schooling. After completion of the eleventh class, the graduate will be eligible to enroll in a VUZ institution or technicum or to take up work in his or her specialty.

Graduates of the basic secondary school may also choose the second path: enrollment in a technicum, an SPTU, a pedagogical or medical college (*uchilishche*); in short, in an institution providing thorough professional instruction, which also can serve as a basis for enrolling in a VUZ.

Finally, the third path--the variety of vocational schools and colleges with a varying term of instruction. Here the way to the university can also be found through extension, evening, or correspondence courses. Evening and correspon-dence course schools must be made equivalent to the senior classes of the general school and the SPTU.

In adopting this model, society can provide every young person with a mandatory basic secondary education, guarantee a broad-based professional training, and enable everyone who so wishes to acquire the courses necessary for entrance into the university. Offering everyone the opportunity to prepare for higher education is the duty of society; (competitive) access is the right of every person.

In our view, perestroika of the schools must begin with the emancipation of pedagogy, with a rejection worn-out dogma. But to this date, the upper ranks of the educational world find it hard to part with these dogma. One group denies outright that the schools are impersonal and monolithic. Another, more flexible group, recognizes the degrading aspects of this type of uniform education and agrees on the need for change, but only at the top level of the school system. As for the lower levels, they remain, in this view, tightly integrated, "wrapped up" in one package--that of the "state requirements" (*gosstandart*).

In the original legislation on which, subsequent to the 1917 Revolution, the foundations of the Soviet school were laid, the notion of "state requirements" did not exist. Instead there was the term "curriculum minimum" (*programnyi minimum*) (or minimum competency). The minimum, however, always has a built-in predisposition toward the maximum. And standards are standards; they impose strict boundaries on the curriculum, inhibit variety, limit its capacities for enrichment, and restrict the possibilities for adaptation in the diverse republics, regions, or individual schools according to the level, abilities, interests, and enthusiasm of the teacher or pupil.

How can we create a unified yet diverse mandatory basic secondary education? How can we introduce diversification in this context?

Up to the sixth or seventh grade differentiation makes sense only as elective courses within the framework of the general core curriculum. Further along, there should be mandatory courses according to the profile or path chosen. As the student moves up the educational ladder, the proportion of required courses in the selected discipline should increase. The possibility of changing one's profile (midway) should be offered through a cluster of electives or through supplementary courses taken outside classroom time.

With this organizational approach, we can create conditions in the basic school favorable to bringing out children's individual inclinations and abilities, to unleashing the creativity of teachers, and to attracting creative societal input. The basic school need not be impersonal, standardized and mass in the pejorative sense of this word. The school must develop the capacity for self-emancipation and internal growth. The establishment of an extensive web of specialized courses within the basic school would help students make a more informed choice about their future educational direction and about their future in general. Particularly gifted adolescents could pursue an accelerated education through extension courses.

Let us recall that the basic principles of the Soviet school have always emphasized the promotion of the student's individual identity. In losing sight of this goal, we distorted the content of education in the manner of the worst types of schooling of old.

A basic general education must give students a unified (common) level of academic and labor preparation--not for higher education but to make informed decisions about life. And precisely for this reason it must not be entirely undifferentiated or homogenous. The richer the school's palette, the richer society will be. Enforced "dumbing down" or levelling processes (*usrednenie*) ultimately destroy a people's intellectual roots.

A new *Concept* of a general secondary education and a corresponding new strategy for educational growth must include at their core the idea of a multiplicity of school models, the right of the individual school to define its own creative path, the right to a choice of textbooks, of technologies, of ways of organizing the entire learning process. Without such choices there simply cannot be perestroika or democratization of the schools.

Moreover, this new *Concept* must be drawn up along with a program for its implementation, in a truly democratic way, with glasnost and public input, in the spirit of our times. In the final result, the fate of the younger generation is in the hands of the school. The educational leadership, and the entire educational community for that matter, cannot simply assume the role of arbitrators of the destinies of the young. Educators are but the delegated authorities of the people in the affairs of education. The art of educational governance is nothing more or less than the adept conduct of education in the context of society's constantly evolving needs.

Izvestiia
January 9, 1988

12

Dneprov's Principles

In the halls of the Academy of Pedagogical Sciences, the new Minister of Education of Russia, Edward Dneprov, has the reputation of one who likes to make waves, of an incorrigible reformer. Today, this is no longer something to conceal--quite the opposite. And in reality Dneprov was the force behind the founding of VNIK-shkola (Temporary Research Collective--School, recently renamed the Center for Pedagogical Innovation), that vociferous organization known for its revolutionary endeavors. He is the author of many unorthodox works on the history of education, and of numerous articles (on contemporary education issues) in the central press. Today Dneprov has what is most important: a fulcrum with which to reform the existing system from top to bottom. Admittedly, it is not yet clear whether the levers exist to carry this out, but the new minister is of a most decisive cast of mind. The ground under him is, for the time being, stable. His ten principles are holding firm.

These principles (Dneprov relates), were developed by *VNIK-shkola* while we were working up concept papers for reforming the schools two years ago. When I presented these principles at several international meetings, Western scholars noted how far away we had moved in education from authoritarian pedagogical traditions.

Edward Dmitrievich, let's look at each of these principles in turn, beginning with the first.

. . . Which is democratizing education. For us, first of all this means taking the government out of the school. In April, 1987, when I first talked about this at the Academy of Pedagogical Sciences, and shared my thoughts with readers of *Teachers' Gazette* I was picked apart. This historian of the pre-revolutionary school, Dneprov, they said, had forgotten what century he lived in, and was off by a century or so. Only later did it begin to hit home (especially after speeches by Gorbachev) that our entire world, including that of the school, had been paralyzed by pervasive state control.

Destatization simultaneously implies demonopolization, but at the time I refrained, held back from using that word. . . In the Constitution it is written that everyone has the right to an education. But nowhere is it written down that this education must be obtained through the state alone. Therefore, we want society to have the right to create its own educational structures.

This is all kind of unfamiliar terrain for us. . . .

Another, directly related principle is that of creating a multi-tiered or variative (*mnogoukladnoe*) system. We plan to encourage alternative forms of education, which in the future will become parallel educational structures. Why shouldn't "privatizers" have the right to their own schools?

If I am correct, UNESCO defines as private any non-government school.

Because our society has such an allergic reaction to the word private, I prefer not to use it officially. Here it is important to understand what is central: the state should be obliged to provide a minimal sum, regardless of the school in which the child is enrolled. And there must be a choice here. An open-ended education--that is the fourth principle. Our education, like the society as a whole, is a closed one. And this is the cause of many ills. Self-enclosed economies, self-enclosed school systems, just like walled-off societies, are incapable of sustained growth. We want to tear down the walls, but here everything depends upon de-ideologization and de-politicization. We have to turn the communist party organizations out of the school. As for the Komsomol and Pioneers, this is a more complicated question. Children still want to join the Pioneers, and so we should not force matters here.

The fifth principle is that of challenge, or acceleration (*operezhenie*). Education can retard, or lag behind developments in general, or it can move slightly in advance of society. At those decisive turning points in history such as we are today experiencing, schools can be made an accelerator of change. For us this is particularly important if we hope to restore the country's exhausted gene pool (*genofond*: the notion that Russia's gene pool was "exhausted" by Stalin's depredations is widespread among the intelligentsia).

As far as the remaining five principles are concerned--augmenting the role of the humanities, making the schools more humane, differentiation, lifelong education, and developmental education--they are already in operation in our education.

This is all so unfamiliar. We graduated from the regular old Soviet school, and nobody ever thought it was possible to study elsewhere, in a private school for example. Reality was accepted as a given, and no questions were asked. "Dear Leonid Ilyich (Brezhnev)," and that was that! "The Party: the mind, conscience and honor. . . " these were axioms, and these were the slogans adorning the schools. You know. . . .

And this is precisely the tragedy of recent generations. The state didn't have any need for thinking people, it needed "cogs", and the school fulfilled this "state requisition." Today, as we move toward the market, he who is incapable of finding his own way, of self-actualization, is doomed, especially if he only sits and waits until someone walks him on a short leash.

You've taken on some difficult tasks. Do you think that in the present circumstances you can pull it off?

Of course, but not in the old way of orders from above: simply issue a decree and in one fell swoop everyone starts to follow the new principles. One of the worst evils of our politics, including school politics, was that of issuing imperial, global proclamations. The new team we have brought to the Ministry of Education follows a different approach: that of providing models, of "kindling a flame."

Today everywhere you turn--Tuva, Mordvinia, Moscow--we have the same education. But we want diversity, vitality, a throbbing pulse. I told our regional school administrators that whoever can come up with a good program--social, economic--will be given full freedom. A municipality knows its own needs best. This is true throughout the world. And most funds for education come from the municipality. Our (prerevolutionary) zemstvos, for example, spent up to forty percent of their budget on education. Schools should turn to their local soviets when it comes to economic concerns.

Certain people argue that what our schools really need is money, better material conditions. Is this so, or do we need something more?

This approach--the pragmatic one--is just as unpromising as it is, say, in the agricultural sector, where we have literally buried in the ground millions upon millions of rubles, and still demand yet more investments, investments, investments. Of course the schools are hurting for money, in fact they are impoverished, but money alone, particularly in the form of direct investments, will accomplish nothing. We simply cannot make a claim on a big piece of the pie, it doesn't exist, the flour has been all used up. We've got to turn to more conventional economic policies, by using tax relief and other inducements to interest cooperatives and enterprises to invest their money in education.

But I have always believed, and continue to do so, that the main resource for promoting educational development is freedom.

How do you plan to go about breaking the existing practices of governing through decrees and inspection?

I wouldn't employ the word "breaking," for it has highly unpleasant connotations. Instead the basic principle should be "don't even think of issuing commands." Our neologisms are often very revealing. For example, *terorgany*, which means "territorial (administrative) organs," but which are indeed "organs (instruments) of terror," which paved over the field of education with asphalt, just to be sure that--God forbid--there were no unexpected growths! And how much we have lost! In the early thirties instruction took place in 104 languages;

today we have slightly more than forty languages of instruction but fifty three autonomous national education systems enjoying constitutional status. We have no intention of forcing indigenous languages and cultures down anybody's throat, but we want to create conditions guaranteeing each people full access.

On September 1 this year did our children and teachers have any tangible way of knowing that during the summer a new minister of education had been appointed?

I'm afraid not, we simply haven't had time to do anything concrete yet. But we did prepare and discuss at the committee level of the Supreme Soviet of the Russian Federation a set of emergency measures for the rural school.

Who are "we?"

I had a fine team at *VNIK-shkola*, and brought much of this team with me to the ministry. My closest associate, Vladimir Borisovich Novichkov, became the first deputy minister, and Evgeny Fedorovich Saburov, who drew up the new economic mechanism, became deputy ministry for economic affairs. I tried to keep this team together, so we could work jointly to implement our plan for renewing education.

Some people say that Dneprov is a theoretician who will be broken by reality and crushed by the bureaucratic apparatus.

I have always been interested in both theory and practice. It's hard to imagine being broken by work in the trenches. In any case, I won't give up easily. As far as the bureaucracy is concerned, there is definitely some palpable resistance. This is natural. The Ministry of Education has never been in the forefront of change: instead it has embodied a rather rigid conservatism. However, when I sat down and talked over our plans with individuals, it became clear that there were people here as well who were frustrated by the lack of change. I think we can find a common language. But this is not to deny the reality of resistance. There were blatant attempts to undercut the traditional August meetings (with teachers), and complaints have already been filed against me. This is familiar stuff. We don't plan to back down; in pursuing our program we will be firm, but not, I must add, punitive.

One more from the rumor mill. They say you don't have a degree in education. They say further that you are a specialist in the lower schools and predict the collapse of higher education institutions.

The principles we have discussed apply to the entire system of education, and not just to the secondary or primary school. But if you follow that logic, then you might predict the collapse of vocational education as well. I am an historian of education. So what is history? It is the present projected upon the past. And if some worked in a narrow specialty--didactics, methodology, the secondary school or university, I looked at the whole picture. My own specialty was in three areas: the politics of the schools, the public educational movement, and the development of the system of education as such. I emphasize the word "system" which encompasses everything from pre-school to the university. I cannot claim to know everything--that would be absurd. But I consider myself open to learning, and hope to apply myself with real energy to those areas where I know little.

Do you have school-age children? Do they talk to you about the schools? Don't your, well, "ministerial-level" impressions clash with that other level of reality, i.e., daily life?

I have two grown-up children: a son twenty eight and a daughter thirty one. So they are already through with their schooling. But I have a new family, and an eight-year old stepdaughter, who points me to many problems (with the schools). For example, when I perused her textbooks I was horrified. We must put them into a museum of horrors on how to scorch the soul of a child. Blatant, raging socialist realist dogma. There is no mention of (the great Russian educator, Konstantin) Ushinsky. Lev Tolstoy is mentioned once. Yes, contact with my stepdaughter puts many problems into focus. Well, this is true of all kinds of personal contact--this is my work, from morning till night. There is no other way of going about it, for the situation I have inherited is an unenviable one.

Sobesednik
August, 1990 (No. 35)

13

The Russian School: A New Era?

Who will become the minister of education in the new Russian government? It comes as no surprise that this question has attracted a lot of public attention in recent days.

A year ago, the venerable old building located on Chistoprudnyi Boulevard underwent a name change: the Ministry of Enlightenment became the Ministry of Education of the RSFSR. In our times, so inclined to name changes, few would have taken note of this change were it not for the simultaneous arrival here of a new group, well-known in educational circles for the struggle they have waged against stagnation in the schools. This was, as was noted at the time, a case of the opposition coming to power, an opposition which had criticized the system for its uniformity, standardization (*odnomernost'*), myopia and dogmatism. But along with the wave of criticism they set in motion, they also put forth a set of constructive proposals. Edward Dneprov, who became the minister, is the director of the Center for Pedagogical Innovation, and before that of the renowned Temporary Scientific Research Collective on Schooling, which drew up a new set of guidelines for education, the *Concept*, aimed at democratizing and humanizing education. This *Concept* won approval from the All-Union Congress of Educators some two and a half years ago.

Dneprov brought with him to the ministry a group of individuals who had played an active role in drawing up the new strategy for education. Among them were teachers who had moved up various rungs of the administrative ladder, as well as scholars: educational specialists, sociologists and historians. Many of them had already become prominent through their scholarly work as well as through their articles in the press aimed at a wider audience: among them are deputy ministers V. Novichkov, E. Saburov, E. Kurkin and advisors of the minister V. Slobodchikov, V. Sobkin and V. Abramov. Saburov is one

119

of our few specialists in the economics of education. Kurkin is a pioneer in education, the founder of an innovative school. Gazman is a gifted organizer of children's extramural activities. Remarkable individuals, they brought with them to the ministry a group of like-minded thinkers. They described their own approach succinctly: don't order people around, but try to govern *processes* in education. But in order to govern processes, one naturally must study, analyze and monitor them. Therefore, in moving to the ministry the new group has been determined not to break its ties with scholarship.

Moving to a contractual hiring relationship with its employees, the ministry underwent a significant change in personnel. This period of transition was difficult, even painful, as this, to put it bluntly, atypical group came together. Nevertheless, at the same time the ministry also began a radical shift of policies. A Federal Council (*Sovet*) was established to represent at the national level the interests of the former autonomous republics, which have not acquired sovereignty. The practice of running things from top down has outlived its time; the time has come for a dialogue among equals between the center and the various territories, among the diverse groupings of nationalities. The previously dispersed productive capacities of the ministry have been joined in a single grouping. The idea has been broached/posed of reorganizing the entire administrative structure of education, drawing upon the instructive example of pre-revolutionary Russia.

I attended a simulation or brain-storming session (*delovaia igra*) which brought together administrators from the regional and district levels, deputy ministers at the level of the republic and school directors, and saw for myself how difficult it is to get across new ways of governing the schools. What was encouraging was that at this session nobody imposed the new approaches, nobody trumpeted them; instead people were brought to them in stages. And soon after this, the need for a new structure of governance for education became evident through the press of events. In Moscow, when prefects and municipalities were created to replace the old soviet institutions, the Moscow Education Committee, headed by RSFSR Deputy Minister of Education L. Kezina, was ready to link up with this reform process. The vertical lines of school administration now join the school through the school district (*shkol'nyi okrug*) at the level of one of 124 municipalities with the educational district (*uchebnyi okrug*) at the level of the prefect and, finally, with the Moscow department of education. This vertical line, it is hoped, will allow a more professional and flexible system of governing the schools insulated from the political process. In this structure the school itself has far greater independence and discretion.

The March 1991 All-Russian Education Conference approved the program worked up by the Ministry of Education for stabilization and growth in education during the transition period, a program calculated for a two-year period. The first decree of the Russian President, which brought the schools within his purview, bodes well for change in education. Dneprov himself announced that once his program is implemented, he will consider his job done. This puzzled many people, although in point of fact there was nothing surprising here. These scholars who have come to the ministry do not see the job they have undertaken as a career to be clung to, but rather as a means of bringing into focus in real life the ideas and experiences that have accumulated over a lifetime. But events have suddenly made the departure of the minister a real possibility, not in two years, but right now, as (Premier) Silaev's cabinet is going through the confirmation process.

Meanwhile, the Ministry of Education is an archetypally unfinished construction site (*sploshnaia nezavershenka*).   After all, the legislative underpinnings for the new school are only now being put in place. A draft Law on Education in the RSFSR was circulated for discussion just recently. This draft originated in the ministry, then was discussed jointly with the Committee on Science and Education under the Supreme Soviet of the RSFSR. The bill is scheduled to go before the parliament at the upcoming session.

When Dneprov was appointed a year ago, conservative educational circles reacted with hostility. And now the opportunity has arrived to get rid of this figure, who has been entirely too independent and decisive at his ministerial post. Is he vulnerable? Too little time has elapsed (to accomplish much); here and there matters have been decided in too great haste. It's not hard to point to errors and shortcomings among those who joined him at the ministry. But the progressive segment of the teaching profession are pinning their hopes upon this group. Work is underway on new textbooks and new curricula. Educational institutions of a new type are just now beginning to appear. While only last year there were but a handful of gymnasia and lycées in Moscow, Kezina now can list literally dozens of such unorthodox institutions. Kezina is in close touch with the needs of the time. But not everybody in charge of education today has such a finely developed awareness. The school has only begun to emancipate itself. And let's be frank: reforms are always linked up with specific individuals who are in a position either to advance or to retard them. And so it will be a bitter pill to swallow if it turns out we have underestimated (the importance of) the appearance of these energetic individuals, ready to provide support for Russian reform where the soil is most fertile to raise a future generation of activists and supporters--in the schools.

Izvestiia
August 14, 1991

14

One Hundred Days,
and a Lifetime

The following article discusses eleven "sensitive areas" or "pain points" identified by the Minister of Education. These are "zones" where the minister hopes to achieve a major "breakthrough."

The Rural School

Virtually all (90 percent) rural schools are housed in adapted facilities. But if only this were the sole problem! Administrative centralism, which is in essence a modern version of bonded labor, is the main tragedy of the rural school. A new program of renewal presupposes above all:

- targeted financial investments;
- collaboration with the (local) soviets in mobilizing local resources (incidently, in 1906 the local governments, or zemstvos, invested 20.4 percent, and some up to 40 percent of their budgets in education);
- giving high priority to ensuring that schools have teaching materials and equipment;
- supporting smaller schools (those villages where the school closes down subsequently die).
- protecting the living standard of the rural teacher.

What will the future village school look like?

School Legislation

The school is still locked in the grip of the bureaucracy. This bureaucracy is willing to surrender economic and other *concerns* to the school, but as a rule, retains the privilege to boost its own salaries.

Whether in theory or in practice, there is no sign of the needed legislation on education. We are in urgent need of a Law on Education for the RSFSR. We just as urgently need statutes for higher education, for general secondary education, for vocational and professional training, and for pre-school institutions, etc. Such new legislation must dispense with the traditional proclamatory nature of laws on education and create real mechanisms for renewal and development. It must be of an enabling rather than a restrictive nature. School legislation is also needed in order to keep in check the bureaucratic mania for norms and regulations.

Schools for National Minorities

We have "lost" more than seventy five nations and peoples during the period of Soviet power. In 1934, in our country instruction took place in 104 languages, while in 1988 the number was thirty nine. This, despite the fact that there were fifty three independent administrative units (i.e. regions) for national minorities. Our educational system, like the administrative-command system as a whole, takes no account of national minorities.

Nations without a culture perish. And without schools, both nations and cultures disappear. Depriving education of an ethnic or national component detached it from popular culture and led to the destruction of cultural traditions, to a rupture of the linguistic ties between generations, to the birth of *mankurts* (a reference to robot-like, brainwashed and docile characters in the popular novel by Chingis Aitmatov, *One Day Lasts a Hundred Years*), and to nihilistic attitudes in ethnic affairs.

Every people (and each belongs to the "family of man") must have the right to create and restore a national system of education. But as a start we must decentralize governance in education, restore the first stage of schooling where instruction is provided in the native language, and work systematically on curriculum development in this area for the first two rungs of the educational ladder. We must also establish a republican-level fund to promote the education of the smaller peoples and nationality groupings. . . .

Scholarship

At present there are in Russia twenty one research institutes working on educational topics. The quality of their work is reflected in the current conditions of the school.

Without fundamental organizational changes there is no way to dig Russian pedagogical science out of the pit into which it has fallen. The new program for education renders superfluous the Academy of Pedagogical Sciences (it has been observed that a multi-branched academy is always more a bureaucratic system than a scientific research system). But what is needed is a muscular branch of pedagogy and psychology within the "Big Academy" (the Academy of Sciences of the USSR) which would rely heavily upon regional and nationality research centers. The new branch would concentrate its efforts upon curricula development.

Governance

We need a new system of governance, not "from above", but hand-in-hand with the school, the local soviet, one which builds from within. This, so to speak, is the administrative plane of the pedagogy of cooperation.

The goal of the "new management" is to develop an open, pluralistic, self-developing system of education which does away with "school-centrism." Such a system will rest upon the principles of decentralization, the delegation of authority from below rather than from above, a strict delimitation of relations among the various administrative layers, and contractual relationships. The new system of management will aim to ensure both the smooth functioning and the development of education.

The New Economic Mechanism

Normative (state minimums) rather than "levelling" (*srednepotolochnoe*, or, roughly, state ceilings on) financing of education, together with the financial emancipation of the school are the core elements of the new economic mechanism. Their introduction, by the most conservative estimates, can increase the school budget by four to five billion rubles, that is by more than one third.

What is most important is unleashing economic initiative and protecting such initiative from prosecution. But this is not enough. Favorable conditions must be ensured for those who take upon themselves the effort and risk involved in implementing the new economic principles and norms.

The new economic mechanism envisages the growth of a market for fee-paying educational services. Also long overdue is the establishment of an educational industry--service centers, educational development centers, joint stock companies, joint government and cooperative enterprises, to produce educational materials, commercial banks and workshops to promote innovation in education.

Parallel Education

Alternative public educational structures could serve as a catalyst for a qualitative renewal of the schools, for genuine democratization and demonopolization of education, and for removing the state from education (*razgosudarstvleniia*).

Such new structures represent the first step in forming a multi-tiered educational system and in recognizing the equal property rights of state and society in the domain of schooling. Needless to say, for the initial period we need a set of measures to protect the new educational institutions from social deformation (i.e., from the baneful consequences of economic decline and social dislocation), to enhance the quality of programs, and to ensure societal as well as state supervision over the content and moral aspects of the pedagogical process.

Professional and Vocational Education

Before our very eyes our system of vocational and technical education is disintegrating. The transfer of schools to individual ministries or enterprises did not help; on the contrary, it only emphasized the narrowly utilitarian and short-sighted aspects of training, and led to a decline in the quality of general education offered. The unification of the Ministry of Education and the Committee on Professional and Vocational Training was a purely "architectural" decision. Today the vocational school and specialized secondary education systems are in a state of war. Yet the sooner we change our perspective on the PTOs, the better the chance of achieving success with the economic reforms.

One other consideration must be brought up. According to the calculations of VNIK, with the transition to a market economy some thirty million people will be looking for work. The system of vocational and professional education, which has assumed for itself the role of retraining, will undoubtedly be important in this context.

The Teacher

Society reaps what it sows. Applying the "residual" principle to the teacher (i.e., education, and the teacher, gets what is left over once other, priority needs have been met) ultimately leads to a decline in a country's intellectual capacities.

The new educational program calls above all for salary increases for teachers. This necessitates a revision of wage scales, with a reduction of the uncompensated share; the introduction of differentiated salaries; increases in entry-level salaries for young teachers; a reexamination of the system of salary supplements (*doplaty*), and introduction of bonuses (*nadbavki*) as the new economic mechanism is implemented It calls for changing to a contractual system, reviewing the pension law, and so forth.

The Briansk Program

On April 26, 1986 few could have guessed what the Chernobyl explosion would lead to. It took more than one year for us to understand that this was not a run of the mill accident, one of the hundreds, even thousands that take place throughout the world. This was a global catastrophe, perhaps mankind's last warning that we stand on the brink of extinction.

The present official definition of safe levels of radioactivity (thirty five *bery*) is both dangerous and criminal. It was introduced in order to calm the public's fears and to reduce social tensions, at least temporarily. But today we suddenly discover places where radioactivity has reached 45 curies per square kilometer-- this is an emergency situation by all international standards requiring immediate evacuation, especially of children. But our people still live there, and it is four years later. And who knows, perhaps irremediable damage has already been done to their health.

The ministry's Briansk program will be implemented jointly with the Ministry of Health. Among the most urgent measures are: a complete evacuation of the contaminated areas; provision of uncontaminated produce for all the schools and rehabilitative institutions; changing the structure of classroom lessons/activities; organization of a special rehabilitative-psychological service in the affected areas; introduction of "fresh-air" summer programs in uncontaminated areas.

Textbooks

What must the textbook be like, in order not to deprive the child of all interest in learning? In order to teach the child how to think and how to learn?

In order that it be a companion rather than a dictator to the child? By the way, who are textbooks designed for anyway, for the teacher or the student? And how many textbooks do we need for each subject? But maybe it's not worth spending a lot of time fretting over these questions: maybe we should just reprint the old textbooks used in the pre-revolutionary gymnasia, and that's that! You see, we have a bunch of questions to deal with here. No wonder the ministry has come up with a separate program to deal with the textbook issue.

Teachers' Gazette
August, 1990 (No. 34)

15

"Power Was Dumped in Our Laps": What Happens to the Former Opposition When It Ends up in the Corridors of Power

When I came to the new RSFSR Ministry of Education I was handed a lot of intelligent documents (new laws, decrees, programs). I saw a lot of fine people with the same intelligent, but also slightly melancholic expressions. If I had to be brief, in the terse style of the "new journalism," that would be all I'd have to say about this new ministry and its people, about the recruits of the so-called "Yeltsin muster." There are no sensations, no scandals to report about, and the reader is tired of hearing about new ideas—good as well as bad. And about new laws—good and bad. People are also sick of encountering "talking heads" on television or in the newspapers, because they, or their ideas, don't seem to have any real impact in changing our stultifying reality.

"The third choice"--that's how the new minister of education, Edward D. Dneprov, describes the situation confronting his generation, people of the sixties (*shestidesiatniki*), today. The first choice was in 1956, the year of the Twentieth Party Congress. The second was at the inception of perestroika. And now, as perestroika falters, when, seemingly, there is no light at the end of the tunnel, is the third time of choice. And this is the most difficult one, for earlier there was inspiration. This time there is none.

. . . Dark corridors, high ceilings, huge, faded portraits of Ushinsky, Krupskaia, Lunacharsky, a lonely bust of Makarenko, covered with dust and shoved into a corner, as if guilty of some serious infraction. . . .

"I'd like to burn the whole batch," is the despairing response of deputy minister Novichkov to the new pile of daily paperwork on his desk. "This is not

128

a program--it's a bunch of illiterate nonsense," is the furious public comment of another deputy minister, Kurkin, to the work of yet another deputy minister. They blow up, then relax, embrace and laugh at themselves.   Is this a kindergarten or a ministry?

And in the house cafeteria I saw Dneprov guiltily jump to his feet when the cashier approached him (rather than waiting for him to come to the counter) with his bill.

Well, and here are the people--sociologists, psychologists, philosophers, not the kind you (and especially I) would expect to have shown up here, in this utterly moribund setting, a year or so ago. Here, this very place which had done so much to suppress their creative energies throughout their professional lives.

Dneprov was a navigator on a warship, an officer in the navy. To be sure, he barely managed to get out of the navy, and then only after a scandal. A humanist to the core, he became an historian with a quite unusual specialty-- pedagogy.   He surfaced in our pedagogical circles sometime early in the eighties. At that time we, educators, journalists, and scholars in this field, were a forlorn, beaten-down lot. The battle between Stalinists and "humanists" had not abated during the period of stagnation, had raged on long before the battalions of perestroika had taken up the struggle in a larger arena, and as early as 1970 had cost the life of (the reformer) Sukhomlinsky. After his demise, others such as Shatalov, Shchetinin and other innovators had suffered. The contest was not an equal one: against the Central Committee of the Party, the Academy of Pedagogical Sciences, the Ministry of Enlightenment, all they had was the pen, the idea, the fragile world of children acted out in the schools and clubs under their protection. Therefore, I recall the startled enthusiasm with which our small minority registered the arrival at the auditorium of the APN of this outstanding, fearless and sardonic orator. Calm and self-possessed, this striking man made his way to the podium, dispelling the somnolence of the auditorium, like a destroyer knifing its way through hostile water. He aimed at his opponent his refined, passionate logic in defense of the new pedagogy of freedom, humanism and democracy. And he was followed on the tribune by a number of like-minded bold, solitary individuals.   And this marked the appearance, at the dawn of perestroika, of the "Dneprov team," which then, in 1988, brought together scholars and educational practitioners, at the initiative of (Chairman of the State Committee on Education of the USSR), Gennady Iagodin, in *VNIK-shkola* (Temporary Scientific Research Collective) to work up a new ideology, a new conception of education for the country. It was an exciting time!

And here we are now, the Spring of 1991. We are at the All-Russian Conference of Educators. As for them, they are up front, at the presidium. Out of habit I look around, and I catch myself feeling that it is lonely and boring without them next to me in the auditorium. There is nobody to disturb the tranquillity by uttering harsh commentaries, nobody to rush to the front of the hall ready to pounce upon the speakers' presentations.

The former opposition is now in power. So where can we find new, equally talented forces? Nowhere. The thought occurs to me while listening that Dneprov the minister is not as sharp-edged, and not as distinctive as Dneprov the rebel. Those intelligent, precise thoughts, now carefully dressed up in restrained, scholarly garb, lose some of their brilliance, bite, and significance. In the auditorium one can discern a subdued, alienated murmur, which clearly distresses the minister, for it is not like old times. . . .

Intellectuals in power. . . what a catastrophe! They pushed and pushed, and now see where they have gotten! After all, by its very nature, the creative intelligentsia must be an opposition force, otherwise it disappears as a "species." But, as matters have turned out, across the globe in a number of countries today it is precisely intellectuals who have come to power, and above all those in the humanities: publicists, writers, lawyers, economists, actors, directors. It seems as if all at once they have assumed charge of governments, of states, of ministries, all with an unprecedented, unique societal mission: to dismantle totalitarianism, this cancerous tumor of the twentieth century. They have an unenviable fate.

"Power was dumped in our laps," says Oleg Gazman, advisor to the minister on childhood socialization (*vospitanie*). This minister was certainly not standard issue (i.e., he didn't rise through channels). He didn't even have his own apartment; instead he drifted from rented apartment to rented apartment, dragging with him his huge library. And all year long, almost to the present day, he remained a "homeless minister." And the team he put together in the ministry, well they are not the kind who usually go in for this type of work, either. Dneprov had to practically beg each of them: "Hey, fellows, I can't do it all myself."

"Earlier I was a sought-after, respected guest before any audience," recalls Vladimir Novichkov, deputy minister. "I had the reputation of a scholar with progressive ideas, linked to something important and exalted. But now, I feel like I'm being led to a jail cell, and I read in the audience's eyes: "Ah-ha, a damned bureaucrat! And then it begins: What about salaries? What about living quarters? Where can we find light bulbs, window glass?"

As I write these words, (Leningrad mayor) Sobchak is telling them the same thing on television--how he dreams of leaving politics. But, he corrects himself, he'll do this only when he can say to himself, "We've gotten the job done, and aren't needed anymore."

Intellectuals, scholars in power--this is a new phenomenon, in psychological and moral as well as political terms. In contrast to the ruling party nomenkla-tura, which held on to power for decades, such intellectuals see a departure from power not as civil death, or oblivion, but rather as a liberation. They see such a departure as an opportunity to return to a more normal, natural, full-blooded existence, more conductive to creative endeavor. And so, in power, they retain an inner freedom and independence.

. . . No, this is not a clique which has seized power. On the contrary, *this is a team which hands back power.* They have rejected the ministerial tradition of retaining the right to confirm local education officials, instead turning over this "lever" to the regions and localities themselves. They have rejected the notion of imposing a uniform program of school development, or uniform curriculum upon the schools throughout Russia, retaining only the power to formulate a general strategy and to develop guidelines for a common "core" (*komponent*) of global and federal components (leaving a significant portion to be locally and individually defined). "No self-respecting people will ever willingly relinquish to the central authorities control over local culture and education. And we support this."

Of course only "abnormal" people, profoundly indifferent to the privileges of power, could avoid succumbing to one of the most powerful human passions--revelling in power--could dismantle such a remarkably well-oiled machine like the former Minister of Enlightenment!

This was the situation: there were, let us say, seventy territories with, for example, two thousand problems. We take one of these two thousand problems (say, school catering), apply it to one of these territories (say, Perm region), put together a large ministerial commission, tour the area and "investigate the problem" of school catering in Perm region (or suicides in the Komi Autonomous Republic). The outcome is the removal by the commission of the local educational leadership (*rono*) a decision communicated in an order along with a document entitled roughly "On the Situation in. . . ." The director of a given school reads such a document, takes fright, and knows exactly where he has to get his paperwork in order before the next inspection. And although there is no change in the quality of catering, and no reduction of suicides, and although no issue is resolved, but only "investigated," the well-oiled machine continues to function smoothly. Ah, those were good times!

But now, tell me, who is going to pay attention to, not to mention go along with, the progressive steps taken by the new ministry if it doesn't have the power to dismiss (since it doesn't have the power to confirm appointments)? They relinquished power, and what did they get in exchange? And these madmen argue that one cannot govern people but only processes. In a word, this is an odd bunch. It should come as no surprise that among the "normal" functionaires of the Ministry of Education one can find a truculent, antagonistic attitude toward these "smart asses."

Anyone who has been the inalienable property of his state will have difficulty exercising his rights over his own life. Exercising such rights is difficult, risky, burdensome and fraught with responsibility. This is yet another reason why the democrats place so much hope upon instituting private property: private property in land, in stocks; ownership of one's own enterprise, one's own business, will stimulate a demand for education, they feel.   Indeed, only a truly free, independent person will be able to fully appreciate what is implied in the *Concept* for a new school: nurturing the vital, truly emancipated, individual personality. The most that the majority of our citizens today hope for from the school is that it will lead into the university, and hopefully, that their children won't be beaten or verbally abused there. In a word, in the Dneprov camp the democrats are all "free market advocates" as well, if only because they are (genuine) educators.

While our opposition, unlike that in Eastern Europe, did not move directly from prison, or rise from the position of janitor (the kind of position that dissidents were often forced to hold), to their present position of power, each one of them could no doubt write a book about the art of survival.

Viktor Slobodchikov, a psychologist who was himself brought up in an orphanage under the tutelage of the legendary Semen Kalabalin (one of the heroes of Makarenko's *Pedagogic Poem*) believed that the "sixties mentality" resides not in an ideology nor in a shared fate, but instead in the capacity to retain a firm sense of individual identity. Both during the period of stagnation and now, during the present "intoxication": "The way I see it is that society is still functioning primarily through the activities of this stratum of individuals, those who are today from forty to sixty years old."

Isn't this how the popular bard Gorodnitsky put it in his song about the statues of Atlas at the entrance to the Hermitage Museum: "They were placed here (to hold up the heavens), but nobody ever came to spell them."?

In recent years we encounter with growing frequency requiems to the spirit of the sixties. Just a few days ago, in connection with ceremonies marking a year since Andrei Sakharov's death, the newspaper Moscow News summed up matters thus: "The death of Andrei Dmitrievich was but a symbolic marker of the passing of the classical era of the "generation of the sixties," of those men and women who had emerged during the decline of the Khrushchev era of half-reforms and who had tried to realize their potential twenty years later."

It had also often occurred to me that their time was limited, that their historical era had passed, that they were ill-fated hostages of their own lofty illusions, of their thirst to "save the world," incapable of simply living like "normal" people. But each time that I mixed with them I was once again swept away by their ingenuousness, their directness and youthful innocence, by the humane gifts of this generation, inspired not only by reform but, at least as important, by the powerful wave of poetry publicly performed before huge audiences and of homespun songs sung around campfires.

As for their infamous "romanticism, idealism, sentimentalism," which the younger generation treats with such condescension, as if it were wiser and more profound, aren't these traits but a manifestation of their inextinguishable spirituality? Spirituality, by the way, is a trait very hard to come by, even among our present-day intelligentsia, which does obeisance to it on every possible occasion. This is a rare gift, the capacity to spiritualize one's life and work, especially in the corridors of power.

"I believe that we now find ourselves in an unprecedented, a unique situation with all kinds of creative possibilities," asserts Slobodchikov. "Even the ideology of fascism was not as destructive (as communism), for it did not exert its sway nearly as long. Moreover, it was protective of the German people, while we built prison camps for our own people. We are confronted with the task not merely of restoration or even of rebirth, but of resurrection of the dead. We cannot become people of the late nineteenth century, so we must create something new, a new life. And education is a pathway by which this new existence can be created in a normal, natural, humane way."

As I listen to him I think that even in Hell the generation of the sixties will find "an unprecedented, unique situation with all kinds of creative possibilities." Incidentally, this is a quality independent of any particular generation or age group. Where a "normal" person encounters a dead end, a hopeless situation, pitch darkness, even torment, such people find genuine opportunity. Take, for example, the new, completely unexpected vision of Grigory Iavlinsky (a prominent economist and advocate of marketization) put forth in his program for rescuing our country from its plight.

Well, after all, when everyone is exhausted, drained of hope, all that remains is to place one's faith in talent—one's own talent, and that of others. In Russia, for the first time in memory, talent and power are not confronting each other across the barricades. Maybe this is no small matter?

Komsomol'skaia Pravda
May 25, 1991

PART THREE

The Opposition in Power

16

The Attack on the Minister

A few years ago an obscure scholar, Edward Dneprov, known only to a narrow circle of educators, was labelled an enemy of the Soviet school and education, the wrecker of glorious traditions, an opponent of party and government decisions. Why? The answer is that he dared to utter the truth about the crisis of our schools. Even more, he became the leader of a movement to implement immediate remedial measures to save the schools. In the Fall (1990), the Supreme Soviet of the RSFSR appointed Dneprov Minister of Education of Russia. But the campaign to undercut him, far from receding, has only grown in intensity.

Our school history is exceptionally laden with reforms. Each such reform was labelled epoch-making, radical and progressive, but for some reason, after each reform the Soviet school only sank deeper in the mire of routine and formalism.

The old gymnasium, with its high standards of learning, was eliminated. Methodological forecasting *(Metodologicheskoe prozhekterstvo)* was eliminated, along with the search for new instructional approaches. Innovation in the school was labelled "pedagogical distortion" and wiped out, along with the study of the living child (pedology). And children were dressed up once again in the uniforms of the gymnasium and segregated by sex, only to be reunited once again when the next round of progressive reform was instituted. And school and life were "reunited" (apparently the implicit understanding was that they are somehow separable). Vocational and general education were combined, and then separated, and so on.

This is how we arrived at the last in sequence, the "historic" school reform of 1984. It was proposed during a break between two sessions at the party congress, in the room set aside for the presidium, and in a classic manner: "We talked it over and came to a decision. . . ." I recall asking the then Minister of

Enlightenment of the USSR, M. A. Prokov'ev, if he had been involved in the preparatory work laying out the foundations for such a reform. Michael Alekseevich shrugged his shoulders and replied that the first he had heard of the reform was at the congress. Soon after this the apparatchiki within the party began to prepare the reform (i.e., the educational bureaucracy within the ministry was not involved) and the so-called "Chernenko reform" underwent the ritualistic public discussion, received gushing accolades, and was proclaimed the panacea for the ills of our long-suffering school.

By 1987 the situation had radically deteriorated. It was admitted that the reform had "stalled" and that there had been no sign of improvements in the school. It was at this time that I first talked with Edward Dmitrievich Dneprov, then Laboratory Head at the Scientific Research Institute on General Pedagogy at the APN USSR. This conversation was a formative one, both for my interlocutor and for me, as it drew us into the swirl of events which have since enveloped both the school and public life as a whole.

"We are dealing with a pseudo-reform," he said. "This fiction, constructed on the nostrums of the pre-perestroika era, will only further imbalance the school, lead to the multiplication of errors, the exacerbation of school problems, and the decline of education in general."

Soon after this, a central newspaper published his article, in which his basic thesis was tersely expressed in the phrase: "reform of the school reform." What happened next can be easily imagined. He was labelled the chief enemy of the Soviet school, violator of its traditions, the opponent of party and government decisions, a hare-brained schemer, an ignoramus, and a mud-slinger. Oh, how it would be nice to let the curtain descend on that not so glorious page (sic) in the history of our educational thought, but even today, as the reader will soon see, such a hope is premature.

Incidentally, this "mud-slinger and violator" provided a very precise explanation of the causes of our crisis in education: the total statization of our school; its isolation from the world about and transformation into a strict-regime institution; the emphasis upon uniformity and elimination of national cultures (*denatsionalizatsiia*); the suppression of creative impulses among the teaching profession; the lethargy of official pedagogy; the conversion of general secondary education into what teachers call "universal compulsory secondary punishment"; the large-scale pseudo-vocationalization of the teaching profession. But how in the world did our theoreticians of education, who treat the history of our school and pedagogy exclusively as a triumphal march from one victory to the next, forgive all these accusations?

Even more surprising: the State Committee of Education of the USSR then established *VNIK-shkola*, with E. D. Dneprov as its head! This group of like-minded thinkers, working feverishly for a year and a half and under constant fire from the guardians of purity in educational doctrine, managed to prepare dozens of research papers and documents laying the groundwork for genuine educational reform--the first in our history not generated by the bureaucracy, not driven by fantasy, and not destined to be restricted to the paper on which it was written.

Perhaps the storm of accusations and insinuations against this troublemaker Dneprov would have subsided had not the unexpected then occurred: the Supreme Soviet of the RSFSR named him Minister of Education. The attacks against him picked up, even before he first opened the door to his office. The role of finger-pointer was adopted by the so-called "Soviet Association of Educators and Researchers" in the person of its chairman, L. I. Ruvinsky and his mouthpiece, *Pedagogical Herald*, which he also edited. Issue after issue was dedicated exclusively to Dneprov and ran screaming headlines; judging by them, Dneprov belonged in the electric chair, not at his ministerial post! These educators and researchers seemed to see their basic mission as unearthing every possible detail in the life of their beloved hero. In this they achieved some success, perhaps partially compensating for the total lack of other research in education that might be attributed to the association.

Dneprov's colleagues urged him to respond to the onslaught, but he shrugged it off: "We haven't got time for this, we've only been at our posts for three months and there's so much to do, and isn't it already clear that this is merely opportunistic garbage?"

Indeed, the character and the style of the denunciations levelled by Ruvinsky and company are not of the sort meriting a serious response. What can one say, for example, when in the lead article in the first issue of *Pedagogical Herald*, editor Ruvinsky commits the newspaper to "helping enhance the spiritual and moral level of culture and intellectual life, as a condition of its renewal," and then, in the sixteenth issue snickers at the concocted "military service related and other sins" committed by Edward Dmitrievich" and then produces the following refined utterance: "Well, come to think of it, didn't our brave fellows in naval uniform sound the alarm for the October Revolution way back then? So why not let our little sailor carry out his own revolution in education!" (This is a sarcastic reference to the role the sailors of the Aurora gunship played in the October Revolution of 1917.) What do you think: doesn't this type of phraseology and style of discourse significantly enhance the level of our culture and intellectual life?!

I fear that the reader might nevertheless conclude that I am somehow trying to whitewash specific "sins" committed by Dneprov and so stridently trumpeted by *Pedagogical Herald*. After all, a criminal is a criminal, and I'm not about to deny that. "In the corridors of the old estate on Chistoprudnyi Boulevard (where the ministry is located) groups of disheveled "boys in blue jeans"--as the professionals at the ministry call them--are gathering. "Hey, Ed, when you're finished eating we'll wait for you at the exit. . . " that's the democratic way they address the minister!" Well, this certainly is a fine kettle of fish! After all, he is a minister! In his position, he should make his exit down the carpeted grand stairway, and should maintain a regal bearing as he passes by his former friends and colleagues, extending only two fingers in acknowledgement to the present-day department heads within the ministry. No, no, he's not maintaining the dignity of the post! It's true, it's difficult to tell how these "kids in blue jeans" found their way into the corridors of the ministry. The old *VNIK-shkola* crew! The fact that these "kids" are in their forties, or even fifties, doesn't count here, nor does it matter that I've never noticed any particular liberties in their behavior or bearing. I don't know a single one of the colleagues at the ministry who tutoyers Dneprov. Well, perhaps only his first deputy. And for that matter, who cares?

Perhaps we ought to drop this matter of Dneprov's biographical sins? Yet the truth requires that we respond to some of these "awful" accusations, repeated endlessly in this newspaper. You see, the minister has "never worked in a school!" What can you say to that. . . ? Maybe it's not too late to require that the minister pick up the teacher's pointer? Remember the time when a certain enterprising general suggested that our President, as Chief of the Armed Forces, go through basic military training? I can only comment that Dneprov's historical research as well as his efforts concerning the contemporary school, his innovative initiatives, all point to his eminence as a specialist in the area of education.

And what about the bizarre criticism of Dneprov's statement that "our basic principle is to rely upon like-thinking people." This, it turns out, is "elementary monopolism and cronyism: only our ideas, only our people, only our team." And how is it supposed to be? As if the ministry, taking charge of reform, will rely upon alien ideas and recruit from among proponents of the old command style pedagogy. What a strange way to conceptualize how ministers and presidents are to put together a team!

I don't even know how to respond to the fantastic claim that teachers as a whole do not support the VNIK program. In fact this is what is keeping today's progressive teachers going. At the section on general secondary education at the Congress of Educators, VNIK's Statute on the General Secondary School, as well as the *Concept* were resoundingly approved by an overwhelming majority. Newspapers such as *Trud*, *Literaturnaia gazeta*, *Komsomol'skaia pravda*, *Izvestiia*, and *Teachers' Gazette* were inundated by letters from educators, who saw in VNIK's activities the prototype of a revolution in education. Comparing the two programs advanced respectively by VNIK and the APN USSR, the newspaper *Komsomol'skaia pravda* commented: "The notions of democratization, humanization, and diversification are fundamental to the VNIK *Concept* while they are but tacked on to the APN system, which remains wedded to the old." Virtually all of the changes now beginning to be implemented in our schools have one source: VNIK, Dneprov and his colleagues.

What is the purpose of the unprecedented smear campaign now underway at *Pedagogical Herald*? Well, perhaps I was too hasty in employing the word "unprecedented." In reality, he is not the first leader of the Russian government who had the hounds unleashed on him as soon as he was chosen for his post. I feel that the attack on Dneprov is but part of a campaign, whose strategic goal is not as much his removal as it is targeting the entire program to reform the Russian school. This program threatens to undercut antiquated pedagogical dogmas and the authoritarian model of education. The proponents of the old pedagogical nostrums have too much to lose if the reform succeeds.

And what about Ruvinsky? Why has he adopted the pose of an implacable warrior? It doesn't take a genius to figure out the answer. It is sufficient to recall the scandalous events--which drew the attention of the state prosecutor--connected with the illegal registration, at one stroke of the pen, of one hundred thousand teachers in the mythical "Association of Educators and Researchers" at a time when Ruvinsky was promoting his own candidacy as a people's deputy (apparently he used this association to claim an automatic seat in the Congress of Deputies as leader of a public organization). *Mirabile dictu*--our country witnessed the appearance, as if by order, of yet another public organization with a given right to a quota of delegates at the nationwide Congress. The true story was fully recounted on the pages of the authoritative *Literaturnaia gazeta*. As for Edward Dneprov, he was unfortunate enough to have to provide a detailed account of this distasteful episode on television on "Searchlight on Perestroika" (a popular program).

It's hard to say if we're going to see yet more denunciatory articles. Although it seems that the tactics pursued by our "truth-seekers" are changing; after all *Pedagogical Herald* is not exactly a widely read newspaper nor does it enjoy particular renown. Apparently, someone has decided that it is more effective to "circulate a rumor" as the wise empress Catherine II suggested in such cases, on the off chance that it will stick in people's minds and serve as a convenient prompt. A number of curious colleagues have already inquired if it is true that Dneprov is going to be sent packing somewhere far away. And I've heard tell, in complete confidentiality, that he is already employed as a manager of the pharmaceutical network--in Tiumen! (In Siberia, a major stopping point in the old route by which political prisoners were sent into exile.) Maybe they really believe it, a type of wishful thinking that all of these reformers and reforms would just go away, finally--would be scattered to the winds. And then the school would get back on the old, well-worn and secure rails, and proceed on its unhurried way, even if this way leads inexorably to derailment.

Rossiiskaia gazeta
April 21, 1991

17

Decree No. 1 of the President of the Russian Federation: On Priority Measures to Promote Education

Acknowledging the exceptional significance of education for promoting Russia's intellectual, cultural and economic potential, of ensuring that priority be given to education, I decree that:

I. The government of the RSFSR:

1. develop and submit for approval of the Supreme Soviet of the RSFSR by the end of 1991 a State Program for the Development of Education in the RSFSR, including in this program measures to establish an educational fund and support for non-state educational institutions;

2. in elaborating the structure of executive power in the RSFSR and formation of administrative structures, provide for direct subordination of the official structure of educational governance to the office of the President of the RSFSR;

3. in formulating the extraordinary budget of the RSFSR for the second half of 1991, allocate the resources for education necessary to provide for pay increases for employees in educational institutions, as well as supplementary outlays for catering and other aid to pupils, students and teachers in line with price increases;

4. propose to the Supreme Soviet of the RSFSR that all institutions, enterprises and organizations connected with the education system be

exempt from all forms of taxation, duties or exactions, that these sums be allocated to promote scientific and academic activities as well as to enhance material conditions and the social benefits provided by educational institutions;

5. establish, in accordance with the laws of the RSFSR, tax relief for all enterprises, institutions and organizations, regardless of affiliation or form of ownership, commensurate with the proportion of their resources devoted to promoting education;

6. provide for the state social protection of the sphere of education by:
   - developing and providing for an integrated set of measures under the rubric of "Russia's Children";
   - developing and implementing a set of guaranteed state instructional and financial norms for wards, pupils, and students at the various types of educational institutions; and introducing indexation of these norms to the rate of inflation;
   - providing for priority allocation by the state of material and technical resources to educational institutions, in first order to institutions for orphans, wards of the state, handicapped children, and special-needs children;

7. provide for inclusion within the *goszakaz* (system of state requisitions) all construction projects, including dormitories and other living quarters designed for educational purposes;

8. grant, on a priority basis, material and technical resources for construction, repair and utilization of educational facilities;

9. provide for publication in adequate print runs of textbooks, instructional and other classroom materials; allocate to this end sufficient resources and printing facilities;

10. establish the newspaper "Russian Teachers' Herald," and the journal "Russian Education."

11. develop a system of state support for pupils and students; namely, direct establishment of unified social protection endowments for students at educational institutions.

II. Beginning January 1, 1992, institute a salary increase for employees in education.

Increase the average wage or salary in education to:
   - for instructors at institutions of higher education--twice the level obtaining for industrial workers;
   - for teachers and others employed in pedagogy--no lower than the average salary in industry in the RSFSR;
   - for instructional support and other personnel in education--the average salary obtaining for comparable work in the industrial sector;

Maintain the above wage and salary equivalencies until January 1, 1995;

III. Establish, from January 1, 1992, a scholarship fund providing for:

- fellowships for graduate students equivalent to the average wage in industry;
- scholarships for students in institutions of higher education no lower than the minimum wage; for students at specialized secondary schools and at vocational-professional *uchilishche*, no lower than eighty percent the minimal wage established by RSFSR legislation.

IV. In order to expand the opportunities for citizens of the RSFSR to receive an education, to carry out scholarly research, to exchange scholarly and pedagogical experience and results, and to develop international cooperation (the President further instructs the government of the Russian Federation to) send abroad on an annual basis no fewer than ten thousand students, graduate students, teachers and educational researchers.

V. Establish, from September 1, 1991, an annual vacation of no fewer than 36 work days for shop instructors in educational institutions.

VI. Leave at the discretion of educational institutions all hard currency earned from international activities of these institutions.

VII. Grant perpetual usage without payment of all plots of land now utilized by educational institutions, enterprises and organizations. Provide that plots of land be granted on a priority basis to all educational institutions under construction.

Teachers' Gazette
June, 1991 (No. 29)

18

Al'ternativa

"I will not allow school to interfere with my education."
Huckleberry Finn

Being by profession an historian, I'll begin with a little excursion into recent history--that of the past two years--before turning to substantive issues.

Since the very moment when Gennady Alekseevich Iagodin decided to establish *VNIK-shkola*, we have specifically worked to promote non-state schools. But inasmuch as we also sought to be politically realistic, we took a gradualistic approach and were delighted when we were joined by *Teachers' Gazette*, which came out in active support of private schooling.

I believe that the contribution made by *Teachers' Gazette* has been a very important one. In an article by, I believe, Vladimir Zhukov, we encounter the argument that we should have introduced the public to the notion of unofficial (non-state) structures and private schools. But this is already the second stage. First we had to plant the idea that the school is not only, indeed not first of all, an institution of the state, but rather a societal institution, working for the individual, for society and for the state. We spent three years on this, and only then began to refer to non-state educational institutions.

When *Teachers' Gazette* published the proceedings of the First Gathering of Promoters of Private Schools, it included a speech by my former first deputy minister, Evgeny Saburov, in which he argued that I, Dneprov, had concocted first the idea of combined state-societal schools, and then of societal-state, and finally, of societal schools. No such "inventions" ever took place. Instead, there was a deliberate--though, to be sure, partly concealed--strategy for normalizing the situation in the school system by moving from unadulterated state structures (and here you can already notice the theme of destatization) toward the four possible types: state-run, state-societal, societal-state, and societal. Such types can be encountered in school systems across the globe. We--I repeat--had to undergo a certain evolution of public awareness in order that the importance of (such a transformation) be recognized.

From the start the Ministry of Education in Russia set about promoting the non-state sector in education. I say *non-state* rather than private, because we had to take account of our social psychology, our level of public consciousness. . . We have always had a severe allergic reaction to the word "private," and for that reason you will not find it mentioned in any of my speeches or articles. This, despite the fact that according to UNESCO terminology, *"private" is everything which is not of the state.* For that reason, we should alter the title of our "Statute on Private Schools," and refer to non-state educational institutions, *a non-state educational system.*

Our first draft (of this Statute) was rejected by the collegium (of the Ministry of Education). The second, now before you, is more or less acceptable, but it also needs some serious modification. The Russian draft Law on Education has already significantly outstripped the Statute. In the latest version of the draft Law, state and non-state schools are given equal legal rights. Even more, the draft provides for the most indispensable benefits and advantages for the non-state school system. We are planning to move this Law through the Supreme Soviet in the very near future, at the upcoming session.

We have heard a proposal here that an official program of educational growth should be developed by November 1. Such a program already exists, and will soon be presented to the Council of Ministers. I promise and guarantee you this.

How can the policies of the ministry be explained? The people now running the ministry did not come from the *nomenklatura* (ruling elite) but from this very auditorium. For that reason we have common viewpoints. There is no conflict here.

Personally I am convinced that *a far-seeing state must create its own competition if it wants to survive and develop.* And from the draft Law you can readily see that we are creating not one, but two alternative systems. I have in mind, first of all, the *non-state (or private) sector,* and second, *home instruction,* which, for all practical purposes, was previously non-existent.

For us, all of these non-state or private schools serve as a very powerful experimental launching site. If we are to speak of moving in the direction of the market, then it is only natural (indeed necessary, given the inflexibility of the state system) to establish a market of educational services. Consider, for example, the publisher *Prosveshchenie.* We have a persistent problem with textbooks. Our way of producing them simply doesn't meet the needs of the market. Instead, we must create an alternative network of publishers.

In all of Germany, only one region, Rhine-Westphalia, and only one institute in Zoost has undertaken, using its own paper and at its own expense, as a form of humanitarian aid, to publish forty textbooks for us, with print runs of from ten to forty thousand. Other areas are willing to do the same. And in Norway twelve textbooks are being published; in Holland another eight. There could be others, but, unfortunately, we haven't yet managed to prepare such textbooks for publication.

Here you don't need to pose the issue of generating new textbooks. Instead, write them and make them available to us. We'll work together to get them published.

Consider now the *issue of differentiation.* We are able to confirm that in our (i.e., ministerial) schools we have introduced 177 new programs (curricula). But do you know how this was brought about? I am convinced that many new types of schools, new approaches to education (Freinet, Montessori, Waldorf) can only take root here, in the non-state sector. But I hasten to add that we are ready to involve any part of the official state system in this process.

I agree with the argument that alternative education as such can thrive both within and without the state system of education. Initially, of course, we were all proponents of alternative education. But I feel, nevertheless, that the non-state system should be a *parallel, legally empowered education system.* . . .

I want to call your attention to the so-called "war of laws." If we compare the two "Statutes" (by the State Committee of Education and the Ministry of Education) on private schools we can readily see the underlying sources and reasons for this "war." I will name the four principal differences between the two "Statutes."

We apply the principle of *registration,* not of requiring permission nor of preserving the right to forbid (opening such schools). And recently, when I was handed a committee report drawn up by our bureaucracy, according to which permission of the local executive committee (of the soviet) needed to be obtained and a petition submitted from the regional or municipal school authorities in order to open a school, I was indignant. Such proposals are against the law, and we are adamantly against them. I repeat: the only principle here is that of registration.

The second, and most important, is the *issue of finances.* The State Committee of Education is not about to finance private schools. As for us, ever since the beginning--1988 that is--we have argued that no matter what school the pupil is enrolled in, his or her schooling must be financed through state monies allocated according to a per capita norm (the *gosminimum*). The state *must* finance the child's education. This comes under the category of social measures to protect children and it underpins our own draft "Law on Education" as well as our "Statute on Non-State Educational Institutions." We will hold our ground here, and our position is shared by the Russian government and the Supreme Soviet.

What do I think needs major clarification, more thorough and precise enumeration in the "Statute" (even if it can be found in the "Law")? Why, if an educator moves into the private sector does he, like those working in cooperatives, fall out of the system and lose his pension and other benefits? Is this what you call social justice? Here too, the positions of the State Committee and the Ministry of Education are at odds.

In general, the returns on education are delayed. For this reason we must eliminate rigid controls over the school. In our "Statute" we call for verification through exit examinations at the several transition points in the system, and nowhere else. As for all exercises in local ingenuity, such as yearly or quarterly verifications, they have been cooked up in order to bind the teacher hand and foot. We should insert in the "Statute" a provision for expert review once every two years. This, like the registration principle, will serve to protect the private school. Accreditation, we insist, will serve not as a means of control or supervision, but rather as a means of protecting these non-state structures.

Now, concerning the future activities of the ministry in this direction. We are establishing a new Main Board on Alternative Education which will include a special sector concerned with private schools. We are setting up this board not to exert control, but to facilitate mutual endeavors. We have prepared a research project "The Non-State Institutions of Russia," and (if approved) will immediately grant funding.

If you prepare such a document we will also finance that (project). I ask you that it be done by the end of the year. If your ask for four hundred thousand rubles, we'll give you four hundred thousand. We must consider what from such a project could be inserted into the "Statute" (once again, the issue of protecting the social status of the teacher); what needs to be deleted (professional qualification exams, which might well turn into yet another type of leash.) Let's agree that you won't spend your time addressing inquiries to the ministry. Instead, why don't you work up proposals, find the right people, and we'll work together.

What is most important is legal provisioning and financial support. We have already established an Innovation Fund for educational growth. Unfortunately, the Ministry of Finance allocated nothing to this fund, but we managed, through our own efforts, to extract seven million rubles, and these monies are now available. We will give you one million rubles as start-up capital. With these millions you can work through the Innovation Fund or, if you prefer, establish your own federal fund for promoting private education.

About norm-based financing of the schools. We are now beginning to lean heavily in this direction, and have put together a group of specialists to work on it. We'd like you to take part in the effort. By the end of the year the first version of these norms will be ready, but there are monumental complexities here, particularly when it comes to rural schools. We won't be ready in this area by the end of the year.

About personnel. We're hardly in a position to send one hundred specialists abroad on an annual basis (as has been proposed). Nevertheless, we will work to include a quota for private schools as well. It is essential for creative educators to be able to share experiences, to participate in international seminars.

As far as preparing teachers is concerned. . . I believe that we cannot rely exclusively on pedagogical universities. There are, in any case, an inadequate number of such universities, and certain of them are elitist and do little for the schools. . . . I propose to you a Russian institute for teaching retraining. We will establish a department working specifically for the private schools and which can set up permanent programs.

Concerning the *information base for your system,* here it has been proposed that an information bulletin be created with the name of "New Educational Institutions in Russia", and with a print run of one hundred thousand copies. But we spend too much time trying to create new items instead of working to exploit better what is already available. We already have *Teachers' Gazette,* which is doing a fine job. The journal *Public Education* is finally, after long hesitation (which was in large resolved by the events of August) lining up on the side of Russia. This journal will include a special section dedicated to your concerns, and it has huge press runs, putting it in every school. We also have the *Education Herald,* which comes out once a month. We are ready to put it out twice a month and dedicate space to your problems. Here too, the print runs add up to 450,000 and *Educational Herald* is in every school. I beg you, take advantage of these opportunities!

We are also going to be putting out handbooks on education, the first will come out in 1992. This is very important, as one example will illustrate. You are right now following the same path as we did in organizing student cooperatives. First there was a laboratory under VNIK, and then we established the Association of Student Cooperatives. . . Later, amendments were inserted in the Law on Cooperatives and guidelines as well as a statute were worked up. And then a Code was drawn up, a series of methodological handbooks put together, etc. Still later, a Russian Federation Internal/External (*ochno-zaochno*) School of Young Entrepreneurs was established. There you have a summary of two years of endeavor. A major factor here was accurate information, including knowledge of the overall Soviet experience with student cooperatives, study of foreign endeavors in this area, careful record-keeping for each school involved. I propose that we work together to create such a handbook, as soon as you are ready.

On taxation. Let's not beat around the bush here. Neither state schools nor non-state schools should be subject to any form of taxation.

On organizing an information bank for long-range research. I propose we establish this not in 1996, but now. And we don't plan to establish our own bank, but will provide you the technology on the basis of our Russian Federation Russian Information Center. And later, when you have formed your own association, you can strike out on your own.

The establishment of an association is a most welcome idea. If we are to establish a Russian Federation Teachers' Union, it will be organized, unlike the USSR Creative Teachers' Union, on an associational principle. Associations and methodological groupings will make up its foundation, its skeletal structure.

. . . We wholeheartedly welcome the establishment of a Russian Association of Non-State Education. We are ready to become a member and make a contribution. We don't expect any dividends. We hope only for your help and for the growth of the non-state system of education. This is our deliberate personal, political, and civic stance.

Teachers' Gazette
December, 1991 (No. 49)

19

The State of Education
in Russia Today

Foreword

Our society has entered a period of fundamental change in its socio-economic and political relations. Nobody any longer challenges the need for such change and for the transition to qualitatively different types of relationships, but it is much less clear where we are going and how to get there. The search for answers is made more complicated in the sphere of education by the profound internal crisis it is now undergoing. Finding a way out of the educational crisis, given the significant uncertainties surrounding the socio-economic changes taking place in the country, is possible only if we have a detailed, well-worked out strategy which takes into account not only the present situation in education, the tendencies and relations now prevailing therein, but also various scenarios for the future direction society might take. Such a strategy must be the basis for elaborating a flexible tactical program capable of constant adaptation to changing circumstances.

The text before you is a draft report to the Council of Ministers of the RSFSR, presenting a detailed strategy of action in the transition period, and based upon an analysis of contemporary conditions in the republic and upon a prognosis of changes in the economy and society. . . . This strategy aims to resolve three basic tasks: to protect the educational system during the transition to a market economy, to stimulate the development of this system during the transition period, and to promote growth in the long run.

In drawing up its plans, the ministry assumes the need for fundamental organizational changes in the legal, economic and socio-psychological relations

148

which have evolved to date in the sphere of education. The primary deficiency at present is that the system does little to stimulate initiative from all involved in education at whatever level, does little to encourage effectiveness, and does not provide the enabling circumstances for those who strive to improve education. But without qualitative changes, without innovation, there can be no development. On the other hand, the mechanism of implementing educational reforms from the "top down," when decisions about who, what and where are made only at the very top of the administrative apparatus, are demonstrably ineffective. Thus, if in the near future we are not only to protect the system of education from the threat posed by the transition to a market, but to take advantage of the opportunities created by the new socio-economic conditions, the prevailing relations in the sphere of education must be changed such that enhanced effectiveness becomes a vital necessity at all stages of the process and for all involved in education. Decentralization of the system of administering education is a must, excessive regulation must be eliminated, and all those involved in the schools must be empowered. . . .

The Structure and Administration
of the System of Education

Education in the Russian Federation can be described as jointly state and public (*gosudarstvenno-obshchestvennoe*) and is structured as a continuous chain, each rung of which presents a stage of instruction and socialization serviced by a wide variety of educational institutions. The state system of education in the Russian Federation includes pre-school education, a general secondary education, secondary vocational and professional education, higher education, post-graduate education and advanced professional training as well as inservice training and skills upgrading (see Figure 19.1).

Structure

The basic functions of **pre-school institutions** established for children up to age six or seven. . . are to protect and nurture the physical and psychological health of children in the system; to ensure their personal and intellectual development; to promote the emotional well-being of every child; and to work with the family to foster enhanced child development. Pre-school institutions are divided into general, special-education, extended day care, and combined.

General secondary education is the central rung in the system of education in the Russian Federation. Under this rubric are: general education secondary schools of a variety of types, evening schools, boarding schools (*internaty*), special schools for learning-disabled children with physical or mental handicaps,

FIGURE 19.1 The State System of Education in the Russian Federation

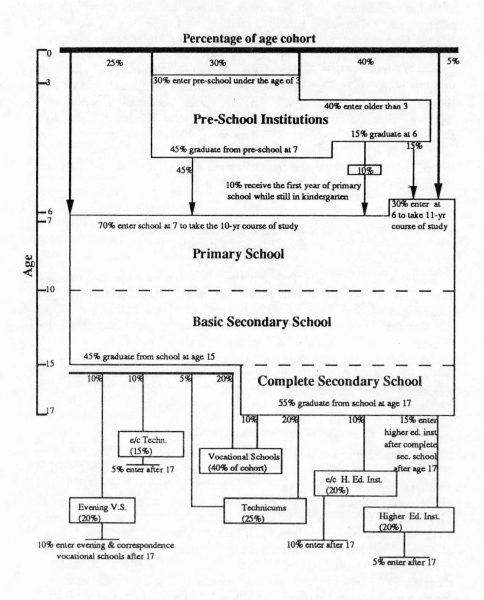

Percentage of age cohort

special schools (for the gifted) and a network of extramural educational institutions.

The general education schools, while diverse in content, form, approaches and organization, share common tasks: to establish favorable conditions for the intellectual, moral, emotional and physical development of the child; to foster a science-based world view; to ensure that children master a core of unified knowledge about nature, society, humankind and the world of work, and likewise master habits and skills of independent activity.

The system of general education includes: the primary school (the first level of a general secondary education, lasting three to four years); the basic school (the second level, *bazovoe srednee obrazovanie*, lasting five years); and the senior school (the third level of a general secondary education, lasting two to three years).

A secondary vocational education is the first level of a professional education and is oriented toward producing trained personnel for all sectors of the economy. The population is serviced by a network of technical institutes (*tekhnikumy*) and vocational schools (*uchilishcha*) with a technical, humanitarian or arts profile, as well as by schools offering comprehensive training.

Higher education is oriented toward preparing highly trained specialists and is implemented through the universities, institutes, academies, factory-technical universities (*zavody-vtuzy*), academic centers (*uchebnye tsentry*) and other scientific, scholarly, and pedagogical complexes.

Post-higher education is the top rung in a system of lifelong (continuing) education. Post-higher education can take place through forms of professional self-enhancement, provided for by a network of departments, institutes and courses for this purpose, and also through graduate training.

Provision for the pursuit of diverse educational interests by children and youth as well as adults is through **supplementary structures of lifelong (continuing) education.** Among these structures are: musical, arts, dance, and sports schools, arts centers, children's clubs, stations (clubs with a narrowly defined focus) for young technicians, naturalists, outdoor-lovers, institutions, cultural homes, ensembles and diverse types of institutions for vocational-professional education; institutions of the VDSO "labor reserves," people's universities, lecture series, parent counseling and education programs, sports clubs and bureaus at factories and other enterprises as well as at trade unions, and other organizations dedicated to spreading knowledge about science, technology, society and politics, art, etc.

In 1990 the Russian Federation state budget allocated to education of all types 15.3 billion rubles (excluding capital investments), or 3.9 percent of the republics national income. The sum total of expenditure on education in the Russian Federation from all sources was 33.4 billion rubles (the state budget and other state resources, cooperative organizations, collective farms, trade unions and other public organizations). Resources were allocated as follows: to pre-school institutions--14.7 percent; to general education institutions--51.7 percent; to *internaty*--8.2 percent; to extramural institutions--4.4 percent; to vocational-technical institutions--15.8 percent; to specialized secondary schools--2.3 percent; to higher specialized institutions--2.9 percent.

Administration of the Schools
in the Russian Federation

There are several tiers in the hierarchy of the administrative structure of the schools: the Ministry of Education of the RSFSR; the ministries of education of the autonomous republics, the *okrug*, regional, *oblast'* branches as well as district, municipal administrations and the structures of individual schools. Educational institutions and organizations operating in the territory of the RSFSR can also be subordinate to the central state organs and distinct departments both of the central and the republican-level bureaucracy.

The structure of administration is not strictly hierarchical: that is, administrative structures created by the supreme soviets of the autonomous republics and local soviets of people's deputies are not subordinate to the Ministry of Education of the RSFSR. There is a long list of administrative functions falling exclusively within the competence of local institutions at various levels.

Nevertheless, in reality the structure of educational governance remains highly centralized. Until recently not only local educational structures, but even the Ministry of Education of the RSFSR could not pursue independent budget policies. Norms of expenditure by budget line were set by central organs and the role of the Ministry of Education of the RSFSR was limited to compilation of the budget. All questions pertaining to changes in the existing system of financing had to be decided at the central level. Such a system made it impossible for the various levels to effectively utilize the funds allocated them. This deficiency became particularly evident in recent years in connection with the mounting shortages of goods on the market. Because it was impossible to redistribute funds to different lines in the budget, large sums of money remained unspent (in areas where no goods were available). Thus, in 1989, some 254.7 million rubles remained unused. The situation today is virtually the same. To this date the budgets of educational institutions are strictly allocated to various items of expenditure, and adjustments can be made only with permission from the top. Restrictions on the disposition of funds were accompanied by strict regulation from the center of all educational institutions, of teachers and of pupils. As a rule, local administrative units fulfilled the role of surveillance, making sure that all norms and rules were observed. Every type of educational institution was deprived of independence (autonomy) in the selection of syllabi, curricula, classroom organization, salary and reward structures, and in management of economic affairs.

According to a sampling of teachers from general education schools conducted in 1988, 86 percent of all teachers would be happy to work in a school freed from the supervision of the district educational bureaucracy. Roughly 48 percent of all teachers noted that bureaucracy was the main factor impeding change in the schools. Today, the teachers are even more convinced of the need for more autonomy.

The transformation now underway in legal relations between schools and the local administration has created significant problems for the latter, since bureaucracy is now being shorn of its mission, and has nothing to control. Thus, the old paradigms of governance no longer apply, but new ones have not yet been worked out.

The situation is exacerbated by the lower quality of existing managerial methods and the lack of innovative approaches in this area. The natural desire of any supervisory system to have precise performance indicators by which to evaluate the units under supervision has led to an emphasis upon measurements such as average grades, the proportion of repeaters and conversely, of prize-winning students, the number of underachievers (*neuspevaiushchie*). This has perverted the goals of the schools, which have been forced to work for the "numbers" rather than for the "consumer." Today we still have no reliable way of assessing the quality of education, of evaluating teaching performance, or of measuring ways of organizing the educational process, in order to gain a realistic picture of the state of education at the regional or the national level.

In its approach to teachers, the administrative-command system displayed a high degree of arbitrariness and unchecked behavior (*voliuntarizm*). As a result, today there are no reliable personnel policies in place. In their endeavor to achieve the required results, administrators relied primarily upon compulsion rather than stimulation. But such an approach no longer meets the needs of the system. At the same time the existing structure of wages and bonuses does little to encourage the efforts of teachers and must be fundamentally changed.

The old system emphasized proper functioning over growth, and growth was thereby neglected. In substance, questions of change (lit.: development) were left entirely to the top levels of the bureaucracy, and only they had any real opportunity to say what kind of schools should be in existence or to alter their content, forms, methods of schooling, reward structures or teacher training. A central task to be resolved is how to bring all levels--regional, local, and school-based--into the decision-making process.

One of the key deficiencies of the old administrative system was its "functional disunity (segmentation)." As a result the innovative process remained scattered, unintegrated. New curriculum and methodological approaches were not brought into the system, since teacher training, publishing schedules and supply schedules took little heed of schedules to implement new course content. The unchanging proportion of budget line allocations year after year testifies to the fact that financing was generally insensitive to the real priorities of educational development.

The way in which relationships came to be structured in the educational system discouraged innovation and the efforts of teacher-innovators. As sociological surveys have demonstrated, among teachers as a whole only 8 percent experience a degree of conflict with school administrators and only 7 percent with the RONO (district level school bureaucracy) bureaucrats, among innovative teachers the proportion is 30 percent and 21 percent respectively. Roughly 25 percent of innovative teachers noted that they had been harassed by administrators for one reason or another, while among teachers as a whole only 4 percent experienced such harassment. Few would dispute the need for renewal in the schools today. But in the system of education, we have yet to develop an organizational mechanism to facilitate development, we have no models for such a mechanism, and administrative personnel are not trained to work in such a way as to encourage innovation--here too, as a rule we don't know just what such training should look like.

The State of Pre-School Education

The existing system of pre-school institutions in the Russian Federation still lags far behind the needs of society and state, and is failing to fulfill its basic functions: to provide a stimulating, healthy and emotionally stable environment for the child. While proclaiming support for individualizing approaches to the child, this system did not put such approaches into practice. For all practical purposes, the system of **upbringing** was charged with instilling in children an ideological orientation provided by the state and a specific level of factual knowledge (ZUNY). The hyper-organized and hyper-regulated life of the child, and of the adults (responsible for this child) was highly detrimental to the child's emotional well-being, his curiosity, his imagination and his value orientation. In its present state the pre-school system does not have the capacity to meet the basic needs of education.

A Description of the Network
of Pre-School Institutions

At present there are in operation 87,100 pre-school institutions in the RSFSR with 9,634,700 children enrolled, of whom 7,376,700 are from urban areas, and 2,258,000 are from rural areas (see Table 19.1).

The expansion of the network of pre-school institutions has consistently lagged behind demand. Over the past five years, the proportion of children serviced by the system has remained at approximately seventy percent. At the same time the number of applications rejected for lack of space rose from

TABLE 19.1

The Network of Pre-School
Institutions (in thousands)

Number of Institutions	1980	1985	1989
Urban	43.2	45.9	47.1
Rural	31.3	35.9	40.0
Total	74.5	81.8	87.1
Number of Places for Children	1980	1985	1989
Urban	5,843	6,427	6,873
Rural	1,645	2,246	2,518
Total	7,488	8,645	9,391

871,000 thousand in 1985 to 991,000 in 1990. Moreover, enrollment in urban pre-school institutions exceeds capacity by more than 500,000 children. The increase in the number of unsatisfied applications can be explained by the decline in construction of pre-school institutions in the last three years. In the first eleven months of 1990 only 108,300 new places were created--37 percent of the annual plan.

In recent times a serious problem has arisen in connection with pre-school institutions under the control of a given branch of the bureaucracy (74.5 percent of the total, with 7, 010,800 children). Here two negative developments have been observed. First, children of parents who are not employed in enterprises connected with this sector have been dropped from these institutions, which has only exacerbated the shortage of places. In some places such parents have been required to pay for the full cost of providing child-care, an amount of 50 to 120 rubles a month. By the close of 1990 some local soviets had succeeded in halting these practices. . . but elsewhere local government has been unable to successfully intervene. With the onset of market relations the situation will be ungovernable: with the increase in prices the costs of providing for a child will skyrocket, affecting ministerial (*vedomstvennye*) institutions far more than municipal ones. At the same time the autonomy of enterprises will increase as they gain full freedom to dispose of their resources.

The second observed tendency is for branches of the bureaucracy/industry to hand over their pre-school institutions to local soviets (Belgorod, Novosibirsk, Tiumen oblasts, the Komi ASSR, etc). But the state budget has made no provision for such institutions.

The existing network of pre-school institutions is poorly differentiated. In urban settings there exist only institutions for healthy children and those for children with health or developmental disabilities. In addition, in rural locations there are also some 275 combined kindergartens and schools, making up .3 percent of all pre-school institutions. For decades we have seen no new types of pre-school institutions; such institutions might provide flexible entry and departure times and diverse educational services. And the conditions do not exist for the efficient utilization of existing pre-school institutions: opening small-group daytime, evening, or even overnight, vacation and holiday facilities on a short-term basis; facilities offering a flexible schedule; and small groups with a specific educational orientation. The conditions do not exist for creating a network of new, alternative-type pre-school institutions.

Providing for Pre-School Institutions

The pre-school system is financed according to the "residual principle." The state budget for 1990 allocated 558.9 rubles per child. Over the past decade this figure has risen by 163.9 rubles, which by no means compensates for the increase in prices for construction, furniture, equipment, food and other goods and services. Today, a significant proportion of pre-school institutions (33 percent in rural locations and 18 percent in the RSFSR as a whole) do not satisfy minimum standards. These are buildings not originally designed as pre-school institutions, often heated with a Russian stove, lacking running water or indoor plumbing. Almost one fourth (23.3 percent) of all state-run pre-school institutions (excluding those under industry) are in need of major repairs. And the proportion of such adapted facilities has actually increased since 1980 (from 16.4 percent to 18 percent). To this date, despite the dangerous environmental conditions in a number of regions, which clearly threaten the health of children, no money has been allocated, and no provision made, to provide land for children's facilities outside the cities as dacha communities are built. At present only 2 percent of children are being taken outside the cities to such healthful sites.

The provision of food for children in pre-school institutions is constantly worsening. Between 1949 and 1984 the official norms governing school catering remained virtually unchanged. In 1984 by decision of the Council of Ministers, food norms were increased by 33 percent to 100 percent for a number of basic items (meat, milk, vegetables, cottage cheese). However, the monetary sums attached to these norms cannot today meet the needs of a growing child. Over the past twenty years these norms have increased only by 17 to 27 kopecks (i.e., from a range of 67 to 80 kopecks per day to 84.1 and 107 kopecks a day--the minimum applying for children remaining up to 9 hours a day, and the maximum for children remaining 24 hours).

Kindergartens are inadequately furnished. . . .

Curriculum and Methods in Pre-School Institutions

In terms of programs, our pre-school institutions are also out of step with the times. Between 1962 and 1985 a mandatory, uniform *Program for Upbringing in Kindergartens* was in force, being reissued nine times without substantive change in that interval. In 1985 a new *Program of Instruction and Upbringing in Kindergartens* was adopted, and remains in force today. With a uniform curriculum in place, it was inevitable that the content, methods and forms of education in pre-school institutions displayed little variety. Educators were forced to work with uniform standards, to rely exclusively upon the calendar age rather than developmental stage of the child, and to ignore individual distinctions. A tightly regulated curriculum drove all creativity out of the educational process.

Methodological and classroom aids were made, as a rule, in accordance with the uniform curriculum, and reflected all of its shortcomings. The assortment of such aids available is extremely limited, and remains unchanged year after year; the volume of output of children's games and other school classroom materials is very low.

Correspondingly, with so limited a range of selection and choice, educators are forced to stick to one and the same curriculum. A major effort must be launched to ensure that in the near future educators are given a choice of curricula and approaches to their work.

Teachers in Pre-School Institutions:
The Situation Today

Pre-school institutions of the RSFSR employ 968,300 directors, upbringers, senior upbringers, music teachers, speech therapists, and special educators (*defektologi*). Of this number only 78.5 percent have a degree in education (in the village 68 percent)--and only 16.7 percent have a higher education degree (see Table 19.2).

The limited professional and educational training of the majority of teachers in pre-school education is detrimental to children's development and their emotional well-being. In training teachers a uniform, inertial system has evolved, in which there is little observable difference in the training provided

TABLE 19.2

Educational Qualifications of
Pre-School Personnel (in thousands)

	1970	1980	1985	1990
Higher	33.8	70.1	119.0	161.3
Inc. Higher	11.6	15.9	19.8	23.5
Specialized Sec-ondary	-----	-----	556.4	704.2
Other	-----	-----	105.0	79.3
Total	359.8	547.5	800.2	968.3

specialists of different profiles working in quite different environments. Future *vospitateli*, methods specialists, and administrators all receive the same training. Instruction provides the future teacher with little opportunity to master the practical skills of learning how to play and interact with children and how to work together with parents.

Our pre-school system provides little stimulus to quality education. The position of *vospitatel'* at a pre-school institution pays poorly and lacks prestige. The average salary of an employee at a state pre-school institution in the RSFSR in 1989 was only 45.8 percent the wage of employees in the economy as a whole. Salary increases have lagged behind inflation (see Table 19.3).

A base salary increase for pre-school *vospitateli* mandated in 1990, along with a 30-ruble supplement for (out of class) work with parents was to have come from local budgets where available. As a result in many areas no increases were implemented. Other categories of pre-school employees were also denied promised salary increases.

Employees in the sphere of pre-school education are not extended the benefits provided teachers in the schools: preferential access to housing; the right to retain a full pension while continuing to work in urban pre-school institutions; free housing for specialists in urban areas who continue to work after pension age; reductions in the work load for *vospitateli* from 36 to 30 hours weekly, and for special education professionals from 24 to 20 hours weekly; and extended vacations. Qualified specialists in pre-school institutions are not eligible to be awarded honorary titles such as "Merited education employee of the RSFSR," or "Merited teacher of the RSFSR."

TABLE 19.3

Monthly Salaries of Pre-School Personnel
(By education level) (In rubles: range)

	1965	1985	1990
Directors			
Higher Education	75-136	160-195	190-250
Secondary Specialized	65-126	140-175	190-250
Secondary	60-126	-----	-----
Methods Specialists and Senior *Vospitateli*			
Higher Education	70-91	140-160	170-210
Secondary Specialized	60-82	120-135	170-210
Vospitateli			
Higher Education	70-91	130-150	110-160
Secondary Specialized	60-82	110-130	110-160
Secondary	55-82	-----	-----
Assistant *Vospitateli*			
Lacking a Specialized Secondary Education	70	75	90-100

The existing situation has led to an ubiquitous shortage of personnel--roughly 37,700 vacancies exist in the pre-school system of the RSFSR, and the need for support personnel is only 50 percent-70 percent satisfied.

Legislation and Regulation of Pre-School Institutions

From a legal point of view, pre-school institutions are in unsatisfactory shape. . . . Teachers, parents and children, those most involved, have little real opportunity to exert influence over pre-school institutions. Three basic legislative documents have regulated pre-school affairs for decades. Until 1960 pre-school institutions were governed by the 1944 Statute (*Ustav*). In that year a Temporary Statute was promulgated, and in 1985 a Statute on the Preschool Institution followed. In addition, a thicket of instructions and rules has been created, more than 200 since 1960 alone, tightly regulating the life of both child and adult in pre-school institutions, and imposing a uniform standard, limiting the opportunities for creative applications.

A major shortcoming of existing legislation is that it provides no economic stimulus for educators to try new approaches, or to organize new types of pre-school institutions, including alternatives to government-run schools.

The existing health and sanitary regulations in pre-school institutions are unduly restrictive, and significant efforts to increase diversity as well as to create an emotionally nurturing environment. For example, the health codes governing the construction and maintenance of pre-school institutions call for strict observation of the practice of age or group segregation, for windows to be located only on specific sides of the building and for rigidly defined usages of pre-school buildings.

Research and Academic Support, Information and the Media

The number of scholarly institutions (or sub-institutions) working in the sphere of early childhood education is extremely limited: there is one Institute for Pre-School Upbringing within the Academy of Pedagogical Sciences of the USSR (in comparison, there are roughly 20 scientific research institutions--NII--concerned with the school working under the APN); there is one laboratory in the Institute of General and Pedagogical Psychology of the APN SSSR, a number of specialist in the department of psychology of Moscow State University. At the level of the Russian Federation there is a small laboratory under the Scientific Research Institute for the School. There are a number of departments at pedagogical institutes concerned with early childhood education, but the quality of their work leaves much to be desired.

Scholarly research in this area is dispersed, there is no general plan of action and research proceeds in a haphazard manner. Over many years a significant volume of theoretical and experimental research has accumulated, but existing designs and guidelines for pre-school institutions take little account of this research, and for this reason do not meet contemporary expectations.

The unsatisfactory level of research is also reflected in data on scholarly publications on early childhood education, the volume of which is steadily shrinking. Thus, the *Questions in Psychology* contained 34 articles in the past three years, with the annual number declining from 14 in 1987 to 9 in 1989. These articles were little read by employees in pre-school institutions. The only journal linking research in the areas of pre-school pedagogy and psychology is

Pre-School Vospitanie. Founded in 1928, it has changed little since. Over the past twenty-five years its circulation has risen only by 220,000,[1] and its size has shrunk by 23 percent, despite the fact that the journal is aimed at a broad readership, including *vospitateli*, administrators, methodologists, music teachers, activities specialists, as well as teachers and students at pedagogical schools, and even parents.

The content of scholarly articles on early childhood education is unsatisfactory, and the number limited: over the past 15 years we counted only 69 publications; in 1987 there were 8 articles and in 1988 only 9 articles.

The need for a family-oriented journal in this area remains unsatisfied. In the sole journal in this area, *Family and School*, over the past 10 years there were in all 57 articles on early childhood.

The periodical press and mass media in general show little interest in meeting the demand by parents and educators for both scholarly and practical information about bringing up children at home and in school.

The State of General (Secondary) Education

The mission of the school, seen as a societal institution, is to fulfill the educational demands made of it by the individual, society as a whole, and the state. However, in its present condition, the school is incapable of fulfilling its mission. For all practical purposes it has one master--the state. Having evolved into a bureaucratic state institution, the school until quite recently functioned according to a strict regime of uniformity in thinking, direction and control. Carrying out the basic design of the administrative-command system in producing "cogs" for the machine, the school aimed not at growth but at a general levelling and elimination of individuality. The school trumpeted the goal of comprehensive and harmonious development of individual identity, but the content, methods and forms of instruction and *vospitanie* did nothing to further this goal. The artificial *shkolotsentrizm* of Soviet childhood (the striving to encompass the entire life of the child within the walls of the school) essentially turned the school into a "warehouse" for children.

To put it bluntly, education in our schools is in a state of profound crisis and in need of fundamental perestroika. According to sociological surveys, some 73 percent of all teachers believe this to be the case. The crisis is also reflected in the opinions of parents and children. Roughly 22 percent of schoolchildren would like to transfer to another school, and roughly the same proportion of parents have a negative view of the school in which their children are enrolled. They and many others are very critical of many basic aspects of schooling. For example, in various regions of the RSFSR only 26-35 percent of students and 36-42 percent of parents believe that teachers are adequately trained. Only 2 to 20 percent of pupils and parents believe the school offers sufficient opportunity for accelerated study of individual subjects. Specialized instruction in production-related skills satisfies only 10-12 percent of students and 47 percent of parents. There is a significant amount of tension/conflict between parents and children, on the one hand, and educators on the other. Thirty seven percent of teachers complained of perennial problems with certain of their students. Roughly the same proportion (33 percent) of pupils complained of conflictual relations with their teachers. One in five parents and 42 percent of senior students believe that teachers manipulate grades. Thirty percent of pupils and 15 percent of teachers complained of rudeness and cruelty in teachers' interactions with students. Thirty six percent of parents and 29 percent of pupils complained that their teachers were apathetic and indifferent about their work, and 37 percent of teachers noted the same about their own colleagues. In addition, 60 percent of teachers believe that the family plays little role (*samoustranilas'*) in child upbringing, and 47 percent remarked upon their pupils' indifference toward learning.

As a consequence of the misplaced goals of the schools, and of relationships prevailing in the schools, they are incapable of fulfilling their basic mission in society: to provide for individual growth and self-realization, to socialize and provide culture and to help choose a career. As a result, the overwhelming majority--over 90 percent--of seniors do not believe that school instruction facilitates growth or self-realization; around 85 percent feel that the school does nothing to help them find their way in life; 83 percent feel that the school does not assimilate them to culture and, finally, more than 90 percent deny that the school provides them with a professional orientation. . . .

The School Network

At present there are 20,000,000 students in general education school, of whom 14,300,000 are in urban, and 5,700,000 are in rural locations (see Table 19.4).

TABLE 19.4

Enrollments in General Education
Schools (in millions)

	1960	1970	1880	1985	1990
All Students	18.6	23.0	17.4	18.3	20.0
Percentage in village schools	47.3	43.9	34.5	29.5	28.5

Source: Narodnoe obrazovanie i kul'tura v RSFSR (Moscow, 1989), p. 18.

Thus, in the past five years, enrollments have increased by 1,700,000. The increase in enrollments has outstripped the capacity of the system. In the 1989/1990 school year there were 64,293 schools in the RSFSR, of which 17,346 were primary schools (832 in cities and 16,514 in villages); 16,031 provided an incomplete secondary education (2,239 in cities and 13,792 in villages); and 30,916 were full secondary schools (13,839 in cities and 17,077 in villages--the reader is reminded that the term secondary school here includes all grades, including primary). Thus, the number of schools in the countryside is twice the number in urban locations, but the number of urban pupils is almost two and a half times (2.4) the number of rural pupils. This is testimony to the tendency of the urban school network to create huge schools (*shkoly-giganti*). Between 1986 and 1989 the proportion of schools with 30 or more classrooms (i.e., homerooms) rose from 20.6 percent to 26.3 percent.[2] Given current conditions, in the overwhelming majority of such oversized schools it is impossible to provide a decent education. Moreover, the tendency to merge schools reduces the opportunity for parents and children to select the school of their choice.

(Overcrowding has systematically increased in the last decade.) In the 1988/1989 school year 22 percent of all pupils were enrolled in second or third shifts, compared to 17 percent in 1980 and 19 percent in 1985. Between 1970 and 1980 the number of pupils for each place in the schools declined in the RSFSR from 1.56 to 1.18, but in the following decade it rose again to 1.35.[3] Here, the RSFSR is in eighth place among the republics, far behind the Baltic republics, Ukraine and Moldavia. At present, each pupil in the schools has 2.8 square meters of floor space, which is 1.5 times less than regulations require.

Over the last decade, the sum of money allotted to renovation of school buildings more than doubled, from 387.9 million rubles to 828.3 million rubles, but as a proportion of the school budget, increased only slightly, from 4.6 percent to 5.4 percent. Moreover, the sum allotted the Ministry of Education by the Ministry of Finance for repairs (.6 rubles per cubic meter) is less than the minimum requirement calculated by the former (2.5 rubles per square meter). Existing practice does not provide for adequate maintenance, for modernization, for enhancement in line with contemporary minimum standards.

Educational policies over the last decade have also had a significant impact upon the structure of the school system. In 1960 elementary schools made up 62.3 percent of the total, incomplete secondary schools 26 percent and complete secondary schools 11.7 percent. Today, the proportions are 26.4 percent, 23.5 percent and 50.1 percent respectively (see Table 19.5).

The basic change took place in the 1970s and 1980s, during the transition to a universal full secondary education. In this interval a sharp reduction took place in the number of primary and incomplete secondary schools, while the number of complete secondary schools rose. But a number of considerations suggest that further continuation of this trend would be harmful. First, a

TABLE 19.5

The General Education Network
of Schools (in thousands)

Type of school	1960	1970	1980	1985	1990
All					
Elementary	72.5	47.4	20.8	18.7	17.3
Incomplete secondary	30.2	27.0	19.8	18.2	15.4
Secondary	13.6	21.2	26.4	28.5	32.8
Total	116.3	95.6	67.2	65.4	65.5
Village Schools					
Elementary	67.1	44.7	19.8	17.8	16.4
Incomplete Secondary	25.0	22.1	16.7	15.3	13.3
Secondary	6.3	10.6	14.0	15.3	17.9
Total	98.4	77.4	50.5	48.4	47.6

continued decline in the number of primary and incomplete secondary schools would damage the infrastructure of smaller, especially rural settlements. Second, such schools have their own strengths; it is vital that the various stages of education (i.e., primary, basic secondary) be provided distinct schools. From the point of view of education provided, such separate schools can be more easily organized to fit the needs of children at distinctive developmental stages (early childhood, adolescence, etc.). Moreover, the transfer itself from one school to the next can serve as a powerful stimulant in the social maturation of the child. . . .

The existing school network can be described as displaying a low level of **differentiation**. It is only in recent years that new types of schools have arisen, such as lycées, colleges, gymnasia, and Sunday schools, and that commercial enterprises have been launched specializing in providing educational services to the population. Before 1988, only a handful of higher educational institutions sponsored schools, but today there are 198 such schools in operation. In the same period, the number of gymnasia and lycées has grown from zero to over 100. The tendency toward differentiation is a welcome development, in that it opens up new opportunities for satisfying personal needs in education and serves as a stimulant to growth for the system as a whole.

A major shortcoming of the existing school network is the virtual absence of alternatives to the state system. Today, the conditions do not exist to permit the establishment or development of a parallel, competitive network of such schools. The legal and economic environment is also not conducive to (developing such a parallel network). In turn, this absence (of competition) has a detrimental impact on the official state system.

Curriculum, Methods and the School

. . .(Contemporary conditions in our country require that educational content, implemented through curriculum and methods) provide differentiation and multi-level instruction of diverse subjects; that content include a nation-wide, a regional, and site-based component; and that education be **continuing** at all rungs of the school ladder.

Selective sociological surveys indicate that in terms of curriculum and methods our contemporary education is not up to par. For example, 89.7 percent of seniors, 47.4 percent of parents and 81.7 percent of teachers support differentiation in education, particularly the right of upper-class students to independently select their courses. In addition, 31. percent of upper-class students, 17.6 percent of parents, and 25.3 percent of parents support special classes providing accelerated instruction in given subjects. Moreover, 17.8 percent of upper-class students and 5.8 percent of teachers pointed out the need to create entirely new courses in line with student interests.

The urgent need for change in the direction of differentiation and sorting by levels (*raznourovnost'*) is indicated by parents' willingness to pay fees for supplementary programs (18.4 percent), for electives (11.1 percent) and other educational services provided by the school. The average sum paid by parents for such services, according to scattered data, is 10-12 rubles per month. However this figure naturally fluctuates according to region, number of children in the family, family income and level of education.

A study of curricula, syllabi, and other materials pertaining to methods and content indicates that certain changes have been taking place over the past three years. Right up to the 1988/1989 school year general education schools in the RSFSR operated according to a single course of studies mandatory for all schools. The first step taken toward differentiation was the establishment of four different curricula for the primary school, representing an attempt to apply an integrated approach. By the following year, the number of programs available to the schools had risen to 15. Different variants offered a measure of concentration upon the humanities, physics and math, or other disciplines. Other variants took account of differences between urban and rural settings. However, the changes introduced by these variants were primarily alterations of form, (notably, partial reallocations of time spent on each subject) rather than of **approach** to the presentation (lit.: organization) of educational content.

Moreover, the changes introduced encompassed only one to three classroom hours a week. Only the Twelfth variant of the school program proposed offered students a measure of choice among subjects. *At present the overwhelming majority of schools continue to use the basic variant of the curriculum.*

For the 1990-1991 school year, schools were offered fourteen different experimental programs, all based on the core curriculum devised by the USSR State Committee of Education. Each of these curriculum plans was drawn up on the basis of a three-tiered structure including nation-wide, republican, and school (site) components. The plans also incorporated the ideas of integration, differentiation and sorting by levels of instruction. A number of courses and sections were introduced reflecting the new emphasis upon the humanities in education. Analysis of the organizational approaches to content adopted by these curriculum plans shows, however, that like the variants of the basic plan (discussed above), these experimental curricula reinforce the prescriptive subject organization of instruction--to be sure, now within the framework of subject *cycles*. Roughly two to four hours weekly are given over to electives and supplementary courses, which, according to sociological research, are the least popular way of organizing classes. (Only 5.6 percent of upper-level students called for introducing electives.)

In short, the notions of differentiation and sorting, as well as the modular (*pokomponentnyi*) organization of content are only nominally realized by these experimental curricula, since change is limited essentially to a minimal redistribution of course hours and to reshuffling of the curricula. It is apparent that internal stability, this immutable underlying logic to the organization of curricula, exerts a powerful--if hidden from the view of the amateur "consumer" of education--pressure on all endeavors to alter educational content; pressure to keep curricula in line with established practices and set expectations.

Much more obvious is the understandable resistance put up by teachers to changes in the school day, resistance provoked above all by threatened salary reductions which would follow from reduction of the number of class hours in the new curricula, especially in the primary schools. This suggests yet another problem, which takes us beyond the issue at hand of content and methods, namely, the absence of adequate structures of compensation (i.e., wage scales), and of ways of measuring the quality of teaching (assessing performance).

Turning now to an analysis of course syllabi, by which is decided precisely which subjects are given how many hours, we note first of all the ripe age of existing syllabi. The basic schedules were drawn up in the 1960s and have governed the way textbooks and classroom aids have been drawn up since then. The frequent changes introduced, or reissuing of existing programs up to 1989 were the result of recurrent ideological zigzags, of the ongoing need to add supplementary materials to the curricula in line with recent developments in science and scholarship. But, just as with the structuring of curricula, as a whole, changes did not affect the fundamental logic of the program, which continued to reflect the underlying premises by which content was organized in the 1960s. Changes reflected, notably, a trend towards more practical applications, elimination of more theoretical material, simplification of the way material was presented, and freeing the teacher to allocate hours to themes as he or she felt most appropriate.

The elaboration and introduction of new syllabi and accelerated programs for core courses basically began in the mid-1980's. The number of such programs, like the number of programs for the basic courses, was limited to one for each subject. However, the manifest inadequacy of the print runs for such programs (ranging in the low thousands); at the same time sociological surveys show that no fewer than 25 percent of teachers, that is 150,000 at the middle and upper levels, experience the need for accelerated programs; the shortage of ready-made course materials prevented teachers from implementing these programs.

The virtual monopoly exerted by the centralized distribution of single variant course packages (*uchebno-metodicheskie kompleksy*) over each basic subject, by a single course outline and, correspondingly, a single, mandatory syllabus for each subject, resulted in the paradoxical situation whereby the schools were administered by the ministry not, in substance, through direct control (such prerogatives to district branches belonged to district branches, but rather through the uniformity of unvarying curricula governing the content of education, through uniform programs, and through publication of uniform textbooks and handbooks.

The bulk of such course packages were developed within the framework of the model curricula of the mid-1960s. With only insignificant modifications they have been published and republished in up to twenty editions (the record is the medieval history textbook, which "survived" 27 editions); on the average, new editions appeared every two years. So, in 1990 the situation in the schools is such that schools have on hand one set of course packages (the average supply, in terms of sets per pupils, is 100-120 percent), written by teams of authors in the late fifties and early sixties. From this perspective, even the appearance of new textbooks on new subjects (information sciences, computer technology) has little impact on the twenty to thirty-year old educational core residing in this complex of textbooks. We might add that research shows that the volume of scientific information available in the world is doubling every ten years.

Teacher training and retraining. . . is a particularly important issue in the context of attempts to introduce fundamentally new courses, subjects, and textbooks. The existing system (by which teachers are trained and their skills upgraded) emphasizes *replication* (i.e., adhering to old ways) and limits the ability of the teacher to assimilate new approaches. . . and to apply them, whether as supplements or as alternatives to the prevailing system. Moreover, as thorough study of a number of innovative approaches to teacher training demonstrates, serious difficulties arise from the lack of opportunity to publish experimental texts and teachers' guides in small print runs, the obstacles presented by the official curricula to testing new approaches in experimental settings; and the extreme difficulty of getting rid of the old bureaucratic authoritarian paradigm of classroom interaction, which students in pedagogical *uchilishcha* and institutes continue to absorb. . . .

The past five years has seen the proliferation of specialized classes and schools, the establishment of gymnasia and lycées, which have as their mission increasing the degree of *differentiation* of education and providing accelerated instruction in various subjects. At present there are 3,116 schools in the RSFSR providing accelerated instruction; this represents 6.6 percent of all schools. Most such schools (2,257) are located in cities, where they make up 15.7 percent of all schools; in the villages the corresponding figures are 559 and 1.8 percent. In terms of number of pupils, there are 1,190,000 (9.9 percent of all pupils) in accelerated courses, of whom 1,110,000 (12.8 percent) are in cities and 80,000 (2.5 percent) in villages. Enrollments in the fifth to eleventh grades of gymnasia and lycées total 138,072, of whom only 2,300 study in the rural areas.

While enrollments in schools with accelerated programs comprise 9.9 percent of all students, sociological research shows that more than 30 percent of all school-age youth would prefer to be in such schools. Thus, the network of specialized schools could be expanded at least three-fold.

It is particularly noteworthy that neither the specialized schools nor the new types of educational institutions such as gymnasia and lycées are decently provided with course packages or integrated programs. The absence of science-based and culturally appropriate syllabi, classroom materials and systematic approaches, are among the most important reasons for the formalistic, frontal approaches almost universally employed by such institutions, which in principle should serve as a "breakthrough zone" in the school system.

Teachers and the Schools

Throughout the 1980s the number of teachers in the general secondary schools steadily rose, from 944,100 in 1981 to 1,023,000 in 1985 and to 1,244,300 in 1989. In the same interval, the increase in the number of urban teachers was by 44 percent, of rural teachers, by 17 percent (in 1989 there were 716,300 teachers in urban schools, and 528,000 in village schools). In the village, the number of pupils for each teacher declined from 14 to 11, and in the cities from 23 to 20. But this process proceeded unevenly. In the elementary classes in the village, the ratio of pupils to teachers declined from 18.7:1 to 15.8, and in the city from 35.1:1 to 27:1. At the secondary level (grades 5-11) the ratio (in the humanities, math, and natural sciences) declined slightly in the villages, from 14:1 to 13.5:1, but in the cities it actually rose, from 23.6:1 to 25:1. Thus, the general strategy of improving education by reducing classroom size is being realized mainly at the level of the primary school, and the situation in urban schools remains quite difficult. At the intermediary and upper levels classroom size continues to grow for the basic subject. In addition, between 1986 and 1989 the number of *vospitateli* (here: activities-organizers) fell from 122,400 to 90,000 (see Table 19.6).

TABLE 19.6
Supply and Demand:
Teachers (in thousands)

	1982	1983	1984	1985	1986
Plan figures for admissions to peda-gogical institutes	53.0	53.2	55.7	58.3	58.4
Graduates	41.8	42.5	42.8	41.9	39.8
Demand	126.3	131.3	133.8	140.9	147.4

	1987	1988	1989	1990
Plan figures for admis-sions to pedagogical institutes	59.8	67.3	67.3	67.6
Graduates	36.1	37.2	38.2	--
Demand	154.6	155.4	133.5	147.6

In 1982, there were 53,000 spaces in pedagogical institutes for freshmen, 41,800 graduated, but there were 126,300 vacancies in the schools. By 1989, the respective figures were 67,300, 38,200 and 133,500, and in 1990 the number of vacancies rose to 147,600. Thus, the demand for new teachers has risen over the decade, the official target figures have stayed relatively constant as a proportion of actual demand (from 40 to 45 percent), but the actual output from pedagogical institutes has declined.

Moreover, while between 1980 and 1989 the attrition from general education schools declined (from 62,500 to 35,900 respectively), in 1989 the number of teachers retiring or transferring to other sectors of the economy rose sharply to

59,200. Migration has also been a powerful factor, and in the early eighties the flood of teachers out of the republic exceeded the number coming in. But in the second half of the eighties the flow reversed, and in 1989 the number migrating into the RSFSR exceeded the number leaving by a factor of 1.17 (in absolute numbers, there was a net gain of 2,800 teachers). Thus, at present inmigration took care of 2 percent of the need for new teachers.

We must also take note of the significant *feminization* of the teaching profession, a process which is accelerating in recent years: between 1975 and 1989 the percentage of males among all teachers declined from 21 percent to 17.3 percent. In the world's most advanced countries this distribution is reversed.

The age profile of teachers is germane here. The length of professional service of teachers is presented in the following table (see Table 19.7):

TABLE 19.7

Length of Service of Teachers
(in percent)

Length of Service	1980	1985	1987
Less than 3 years	13.2	16.4	16.8
From 3 to 8 years	18.5	17.2	18.9
From 8 to 13 years	16.3	14.4	14.8
From 13 to 18 years	14.4	15.4	14.0
More than 18 years	37.6	36.6	35.5

From the table it is evident that over the past two decades the situation has not drastically changed. A slight increase has occurred in proportion of young teachers with fewer than three years' experience. But the proportion of teachers with more than 18 years' experience in the schools substantially exceeds all other groups, and comprises more than a third of the total. Thus, the sphere of education is being profoundly affected by the "graying" of its personnel, for those with lengthy experience in general tend to be less active, more conservative about new approaches, and less dedicated. If we juxtapose information on the salary scales of teachers with averages for the economy as a whole, we immediately see that teachers are paid far less than others in the RSFSR (see Table 19.8).

TABLE 19.8

Average Monthly Wages of School Personnel
(In Rubles)

	1970	1980	1985	1986
In the Russian Republic	126.1	177.7	201.4	207.8
In Education	109.0	139.9	154.8	161.5

	1987	1988	1989	1990
In the Russian Republic	216.1	233.0	258.3	277.0
In Education	170.2	178.1	183.6	204.1

A sociological sampling of 1,700 teachers from different regions in Russia showed a direct relationship between length of service and salary. Thus, the average monthly salary for teachers with under three years' service was 173.8 rubles; for teachers with three to eight years' service, 215.1 rubles; with nine to thirteen years' service, 228.8 rubles; with 14 to 18 years' service, 232.7 rubles, and with over eighteen years' service, 254.8 rubles. Moreover, among teachers with fewer than three years' service, 60.6 percent were making fewer than 130 rubles monthly, and only 7.7 percent were making over 250 rubles. The relationship was reversed for teachers with over eighteen years' service: more than half (51.1 percent) had incomes of over 280 rubles and only 9 percent received less than 130 rubles. Thus, the data unequivocally demonstrates that length of service (rather than merit) is the determining variable in teachers' salaries.

During the eighties the proportion of teachers in the 5-11 classes (with a tertiary education) rose from 92 percent to 97 percent (this figure was achieved about 1985 and has remained the same since). In the primary schools the proportion of teachers with a higher education rose from 23.2 percent in 1980 to 38.3 percent in 1989; correspondingly the proportion with a specialized secondary education (i.e., a degree from a pedagogical *uchilishche*) declined from 71.5 percent to 56.7 percent. But in rural areas, only 24.8 percent have a higher education, and in general, despite the gains, the need for primary school teachers with a higher education is pressing.

The quality of teacher training today is a question of great importance. Sociological research demonstrates that 83.6 percent of teachers are unhappy with the quality of pedagogical education. Only 2 percent feel that the education they received "met contemporary standards"; 7.5 percent believe that it "provided them with a firm knowledge of child psychology"; 25.7 percent agree that it "gave them the professional tools necessary for interacting with children"; 28.8 percent believe that they were given "firm mastery of their subject"; and, finally, only 5.8 percent feel that their education gave them a solid grounding in culture and politics.

In the RSFSR there are more than 16,000 "dwarf" (*malokomplektnye*, or, roughly, "one-room") primary schools with 42,000 teachers, but only 11 pedagogical institutions have programs specifically set up to train teachers for such schools. Moreover, such programs are experimental, rather than core elements of the institution.

The conservative, rote, non-innovative approaches employed in today's pedagogical schools and institutes have a detrimental effect upon the future teacher's capacities for self-education. Sociological surveys show that fewer than 15 percent of teachers regularly read specialized journals; this indicates the very limited orientation of teachers toward ongoing professional improvement.

What about the existing system of teacher refresher courses? Every year roughly 20 percent of teachers undergo refresher courses through the IUU (Inservice Institutes) system. This corresponds to existing stipulations that one fifth of all teachers annually should upgrade their skills. However, the data show that during the eighties the proportion of primary school teachers taking such courses declined from 27.4 percent to 18.1 percent each year (in 1987). But, the real issue is not the numbers, but the quality of the training provided. Again, sociological research shows that 93.6 percent of teachers are unsatisfied with such courses. The existing system of educational enhancement through the IUU system does little to genuinely improve the professional performance, social status, or standard of living of teachers.

Technology and Equipment

Schools are inadequately equipped today. . . . Globally, we can observe a tendency to reduce the relative weight of equipment designed for *demonstration* purposes in favor of *laboratory*-type technology, facilitating independent research and experimentation. Technology should be of the kind that contributes to the reorientation of traditional instructional processes in the direction of "lifelong, creative and independent self-development." It should be appropriate for individual, small-group, or classroom instruction and for a variety of approaches. . . .

The system of laboratories in existence today was designed for one type of school, the general education school, while other types of schools such as the one-room rural school and the primary school in general, need fundamentally different types of laboratories.

Laboratories for the natural sciences often fail to meet hygienic or safety standards. The majority of physics labs are equipped with only 65-70 percent of the needed instrumentation for classroom demonstration, and only 55-60 percent for conducting experiments. A large number of chemistry laboratories are poorly ventilated, do not have electrical supplies, and have inadequate water piping to students' desks. Schools lack special facilities for storing and disposing of chemical reagents.

In recent years we can observe a decline in both the availability and the quality of school equipment. Inexpensive instruments are being replaced by expensive equipment destined primarily for specialized secondary and higher education institutions. Much of the instrumentation is incompatible, is used once or twice a year, and in design and measurement fits poorly with other lab equipment. Much of the instrumentation is defective. And there is no unity to the equipment produced, no system by which it can be utilized to present integrated laboratory work in physics, chemistry or biology, not to mention accelerated instruction in these areas. Instruments do not have the adaptors or details necessary for multi-purpose utilization in the classroom.

To sum up, inadequacies in technology and equipment include: backward technology; an antiquated selection; inadequate attention to the diverse uses and types of schools employing equipment; the absence of equipment facilitating the organization of instruction in ways promoting differentiation and individualization, or encouraging more effective utilization of classroom time; a supply system with dire insufficiencies.

The State of Evening Schools

The basic mission of evening school is to offer a general secondary education to adults lacking a degree and to adolescents who have already begun work. The bulk of the students enrolled in such programs are young people with limited knowledge and limited learning skills as well as inadequate motivation. Correspondingly, such institutions are stigmatized as second-rate.

Evening schools today do not satisfy the diverse educational needs of adults. The orientation of evening classes solely toward providing a general secondary education deprives it of organizational flexibility and limits the possibilities of developing new forms and approaches for educating adults. Changes in content and method have been fragmentary and take no account of the distinctive features and demands of the adult clientele of such schools.

In the past thirty years, the number of evening schools has sharply declined, as (after a sharp increase) has the number of students enrolled: from 12,100 schools with 1,700,000 students in 1960, to 6,900 schools with 2,100,000 students in 1970, to 6,000 schools and 2,600,000 students in 1980, 4,600 schools and 1,600,000 students in 1985, and to 2,100 schools and 500,000 students in 1990. Thus, the number of schools has declined sixfold, and the number of pupils threefold. *The decline has been most precipitous in the last five years, which testifies that the number of youth not receiving a complete secondary education has sharply increased* (italics added).

The significant shrinkage of the network of evening schools and of enrollments in them has resulted from a general decline in the number of working youth without a complete general secondary education and from improvements in planning the flow of enrollments to such schools. The educational bureaucracy did little planning in the areas of demographics, rational distribution of schools, or coordinating school activities with local industry or public organizations. Instead it strove at all costs to make sure plan targets for enrollments were met. Interactions between evening schools and industries were structured in terms of demands imposed on industry in order to maintain enrollments.

In addition to independent evening schools, working youth can receive instruction through regular daytime schools and at Instructional Consultation Stations (UKP) (see Table 19.9).

TABLE 19.9

Number of Independent Evening Schools,
Instructional Consultation Stations (UKP)
and Day Schools Offering Adult Education

	1987	1988	1989	1990
Evening Schools	2,394	2,203	2,084	2,049
(In rural locations)	534	443	418	408
Day Schools	7,211	5,646	4,865	3,839
(In rural locations)	6,089	4,703	4,004	3,149
UKP	2,384	2,688	2,920	2,922

As is evident from the table, between 1987 and 1990 the network of independent schools, classes and day-school groups continued to shrink. The organization of instruction through regular schools was most widespread in rural locations and the number of Instructional Consultation Stations has remained stable in the last two years.

The present situation can be explained by the fact that the educational bureaucracy does not regularly concern itself with the issue of educating working youth and correspondingly the appropriate statistics are not collected on the number of working youth lacking a complete secondary education. Neither is there any effort to coordinate efforts with the industrial bureaucracy, with collective or state farms in order to clarify the situation and real needs.

In recent years the basic contingent of students enrolled in evening courses has grown younger. Thus, between 1986 and 1989 the proportion enrolled who were fifteen years old or younger rose from 5.9 percent to 16.4 percent of the total, who were seventeen years or younger from 22.9 percent to 58.6 percent. This demographic change stems from the flow of students from the regular day schools and from the PTUs which do not provide a complete secondary education. It is common today for certain categories of youth to begin work after completing the ninth grade, and then to complete their education through evening schools. We can presume that this process will be accelerated as new economic relations take hold with the country's transition to the market.

As for teachers in evening schools, only one-fourth are full-time employees. The high proportion of troubled youth enrolled, and the low prestige of such schools turn away young educators with specialized training, and teachers from the day schools--who are moonlighting--bring with them, to instruct adults, the methods and approaches they employ during the day with children. Here we need a concentrated effort to retrain such teachers in appropriate methods by developing special courses and seminars.

Substantive improvement of the education provided by evening schools is inconceivable without a restructuring of content and instructional methods. The principles of diversity, flexibility and differentiation must prevail. Courses must be offered and choices made available to students with different levels of preparation and ability, electives must be offered providing accelerated instruction, and a variety of teaching aids, textbooks and study guides must be made available to facilitate independent learning.

Today, circumstances dictate not only a qualitative improvement, but also a fundamental reorientation of the evening school. The evening school must provide a general educational, but also professional training and retooling, educational enhancement in one's profession, links between education and recreation for the workforce, and open access to students and the population at large to learning.

These new roles for the evening school much be achieved not only through conventionally structured processes, but also through fundamentally new types of institutions, capable of integrating such functions. One possibility would be a Center for Adult Education--a multi-profile institution engaged in enhancing the general educational, professional and cultural background of working youth and adults. . . .

Minority/Nationality Education in the RSFSR

General Description

According to conventional definitions, a "nationality" school is one in which the native, non-Russian language is used at some (undefined) point for instructional purposes. At the outset of the 1989/1990 school year 1.7 million pupils, or 9 percent of all enrolled pupils in the RSFSR, were enrolled in such schools. At the same time, the non-Russian students made up 19 percent of the student body in the RSFSR. The gap between the potential and actual contingent of students enrolled in minority schools reflects not only the free choice made by pupils or their parents, but also the policy pursued until recently on a mass scale of changing the medium of instruction to Russian.

The situation which has evolved today has deep historical roots connected with the establishment of minority schools in the Russian Federation. As a result of successful school policies carried out in the 1920s instruction was carried out in seventy languages by 1931, in 92 languages by 1932, and in 104 languages by 1934. Accordingly, the number of textbooks published specifically for minority schools rose sharply, and a major effort was launched to train teachers for such schools.

However, beginning in the second half of the 1930s the situation began to change drastically. Administrative units representing the nationalities within the educational bureaucracy were abolished, as were minority districts (*raiony*) and minority village soviets. As a result the numerous minority enclaves (in the RSFSR there were 200 nationality *raiony* and 2,000 minority village soviets) were deprived of that foothold in the bureaucratic apparatus which would have allowed them to organize their schools on their own. Moreover, minority schools were persecuted as a "nationalist deviation" (from socialist ideology and socialist goals). "At the request" of the minorities, the written script was changed from latin or arabic to cyrillic and, finally, in 1938, by decree of the Central Committee of the Communist Party and of the Sovnarkom of the USSR a new law was promulgated: *On Mandatory Study of the Russian Language in the National Republics and Regions*--ushering in a half century of restrictions upon the use of indigenous languages in the schools. A number of languages previously taught were now eliminated: we no longer have not only textbooks, but even alphabets for the Tsakhurian, Karelian, Gypsy, Shorian, Udegean and Izhorian languages. Even today we have not yet resurrected these languages.

In the RSFSR, the stimulation of ethnic awareness, which is a profoundly natural process, is only at an embryonic stage, and is somewhat primitive and uncontrolled at this time. This stems from the decades-long rupture or degradation of nationality traditions, from the loss of local self-awareness (*microponimanie*), from the forcible destruction of traditional relationships between local cultures, nature and society, of traditional moral, cultural, work, demographic and cultural ties. Such was the outcome of implementing the idea, spurious from the beginning, of the perpetuation of cultures which are national only in "form," but unified and charged with ideology in "content." The cultural existence of the many peoples of Russia, the right to retain centuries-old legacies, was in reality reduced to the right to replication (lit.: reproduction) of a standardized, stereotyped set of norms in behavior and thinking, of equally standardized patterns of material and spiritual production. The decline of minority cultures is causally linked to the destruction of interactive milieux, to the attenuation and marginalization of established ways of life, and to a moral and spiritual impoverishment in human interactions with nature, society, and even self.

While retaining an isolated component of national identity--teaching of (but not in) the native language, the school in reality was transformed into an instrument of destruction of minority cultures. In some cases it became a direct cause of the profound degradation of ethnicity, for example among the numerous peoples of the North and the Far East.

Thus, we have reason to assert that the educational system, and above all the school itself--through which the entire population of the country must pass--must be decisively restructured to promote the rebirth of ethnic cultures and to serve the cultural needs of minority groups. We need a school which will provide children not merely with a certain sum of knowledge in the natural sciences, math and the humanities, but which deals with the whole person. Here the school can and must function to stabilize and to promote civilization(s) (lit.: to civilize); it must emerge as a genuine force in the sphere of culture.

Today, increasing enrollments in schools providing instruction (in and of) non-Russian languages suggest that we are entering a new era in the evolution of the schools of the Russian Federation. At the present time, of the more than 120 languages in the RSFSR there are only 66 in use in the schools. In terms of instruction at different levels of schooling the picture is an extremely diverse one, in terms both of medium of instruction and teaching of a given language. Thus, only three languages (Bashkir, Russian and Tatar) are used as a medium of instruction from grades one through eleven (most of the other minority languages are used as a medium of instruction in grades 1-2 or 1-4; a few are offered in grades 1-7). This underscores the existing imbalance between the potential ethno-cultural needs of the population and the services provided by the schools. At the same time, teaching of the native language is spreading at all levels of the school system. (Most of the minority languages are taught throughout the school cycle, but some are only offered in the early grades.)

Investigation of the various minority educational systems confirms the existence of substantial disparities in the highly important criterion of capacity for self-development. In terms of potential we can divide the various systems into several groups.

The first group comprises those autonomous areas disposing of adequate resources, provided with a self-sufficient scientific, economic, material and technical (including publishing) base. Included in this group are the schools of 34 minority peoples residing in 22 autonomous territories of the RSFSR and having their own publishing houses. With the proclamation of state sovereignty and the growth of national consciousness, the market relations now emerging should serve to stimulate governmental interest in promoting "their own" minority systems of education.

In the second group we include those minority school systems of peoples without autonomous status and scattered throughout several administrative territories of the RSFSR (the Nogai, Vepsa, Greeks, Gypsies, etc.). Meeting the educational needs of these peoples will be possible only through joint efforts of the ministry (of education of the RSFSR) and local departments of education. Here, however, the situation is aided by the fortuitous location of these people in highly-developed regions with advanced educational infrastructures (teacher training institutions, refresher courses for teachers, etc.).

Two peoples, the Germans and Koreans, fall into a third category. Their cultures have developed relatively independently of the prevailing socio-cultural environment in Russia, and they can more or less count on different types of support from their historic homelands.

The fourth group is made up of (migrant) peoples from other full-fledged republics of the USSR (such as Georgians, Kazaks and Estonians). Schools for these peoples have traditionally been provided for by the educational bureaucracies of the corresponding republics, and their further development is a matter of bilateral cooperation between the ministries of education of the RSFSR and the other interested republics.

The fifth group lumps together the numerous small ethnic groups of the North who, because of the socio-cultural conditions which have evolved over time are not capable of independent development of their own educational systems at this time. The situation is further complicated by the fact that the traditional European-type school is not suited to the way of life of these peoples. Moreover, the psycho-physiological specificities of the indigenous peoples of the North call for fundamentally different approaches to their education.

Yet, if we understand by nationalities school the entire complex of levels and types of institutions transmitting a given culture and shaping the child according to the dictates of that culture, it must be admitted that for all the groups and individual peoples considered above (including, incidentally, the Russians), there is no such school in existence at the present time. Accordingly, there are no systems (federal, republican, regional, etc) of education representing given nationalities. We can speak only of evolving fragments of a system of nationality education, visible in the appearance of various courses (required or elective) centered around ethnic cultures, or in the inclusion, with varying success, of a ethnic component in the traditional curriculum. Specifically, at present a large-scale pilot program is underway to include in the curriculum as an independent *blok* (component) instruction in ethno-pedagogy, translation, study of the applied arts and local industries of various ethnic groups (in the Chuvash, Mari, and Northern Ossetian autonomous republics, and the Evenk and Chukchi autonomous regions).

Nationality Education: The Instructional Side

At present, the nationality school has around twenty choices of syllabi. Among these syllabi, the basic ones are: 1) the unified syllabus, used by the majority of nationality schools; 2) a syllabus offering study of the local language as an elective; 3) a syllabus for the schools of the peoples of the North; 4) a syllabus offering accelerated study of both local and Russian languages; 5) syllabi stressing a humanities or other profile. Such syllabi provide more time in the classroom for instruction in the native language, in local geography, culture and history instead of striving for a fully integrated cycle of disciplines; this enhances the didactic side of things, but also creates the necessary space in the curriculum for language study.

The syllabi now offered to the schools are presented at prototypes, and local educational authorities have the right to alter them in accordance with local conditions and needs. It is important to stress, however, that variations in the syllabus are allowed (and they are most often allowed!) strictly within the framework of the given paradigm: the nationality school is that institution in which the local, non-Russian, language is in use, either as the medium of instruction or as a subject of instruction. Thus, analysis of conditions in the nationality schools must be based upon consideration of the "language component," except in isolated cases.

During the past two years we have seen an augmentation of the local and nationality components in syllabi in use. In the majority of territories having schools with a diverse ethnic student body a new course has been introduced (in russian) called "Local Culture, Literature, and History." In the 1990-1991 school year an experimental core curriculum was introduced which provides space in the syllabus for a local, ethnic (national) component. But this very limited variability does not present enough opportunity to teach the full diversity of local cultures within the curriculum. A more integrated approach must be designed for the schools.

In terms of classroom materials and methods the provisioning of nationality schools is extremely spotty: only three minority territories have produced, for the resident nationality, textbooks for the study of Russian from grades one through nine (Bashkiria, Tataria and Iakutia); seven territories from the first through forth grades (Buriatiia, Daghestan, Kalmykia, North Ossetia, Tuva, Checheno-Ingushetiia, Chuvashiia). Such textbooks take reasonably full account of the distinctive features of the local language relevant to study of Russian. Provision of the minority primary schools of the other territories of the RSFSR with appropriate textbooks for the study of russian is much less satisfactory; a key variable is the language family (Finno-Ugric, Abhazian-Adygei, etc.).

Beginning in the fifth grade, moreover, with the exception of Bashkiria, Tataria and Iakutia, all nationality schools go over to the unified syllabus, within the confines of which it is virtually impossible to take account of distinctive ethno-psychological features in the study of Russian. This substantially reduces the effectiveness of instruction and the degree of mastery of Russian. Thus, it is urgent to create a new generation of textbooks and teachers' aids for teaching Russian in each distinct territory.

The development of classroom materials for study of native languages and literatures, beginning with primers, as well as for history and geography, is being undertaken by the autonomous republics, regions and districts. Such materials include, in addition to conventional textbooks, works of literature, anthologies of readings on record and other audio-visual aids. However, the antiquated approaches, ideology-saturated content, and the failure to take into account ethnic and psychological aspect of the nationality at hand indicate that a new generation of classroom materials is needed. This, in turn, is impossible without establishing new working groups to put together such materials, and without breaking the monopoly of some existing groups.

At the same time the productive capacity of those publishing houses serving minority nationalities is already overstrained. A cluster of pressing demands make urgent a restructuring of the educational publishing industry: the marked tendency to continually expand the list of classroom aids included in packages for each subject; the appearance of new subjects related to local cultures (ethnography, local history, etc.); the need to put together new textbooks for study of the local language by those who do not know it, or have a weak command of it, by children of a given nationality living outside that autonomous region, and equally by Russians living within a given region and studying that region's indigenous language. During the interval between 1986 and 1990 2,243 titles were published for the nationality schools in the RSFSR; it is projected that 3,354 titles will be published between 1991 and 1995 (this, according to 1990 projections, which take no account of actual demand).

To make matters worse, publications for nationality schools are released in small print runs; given the rising cost of paper and of other printing costs, this has already resulted in an unacceptable increase in the costs of instructional materials, and has cut deeply into the government budget for such outlays. For example, in the republic of Tatarstan, the deficit incurred in publishing textbooks (i.e., costs over price) rose from about 394 rubles in 1989 and 1990 to 672 rubles in 1991.

Teaching Personnel

At present teaching personnel for the nationality schools are trained in the following specialties: teachers of Russian language and literature (taught in Russian); teachers of the native language and literature, in that language; early childhood psychology and instruction (in Russian); elementary education (in Russian); subject instruction (all in Russian).

The educational background of teachers of language and literature (*slovesniki*) is uneven; in recent years a gap has persisted between teachers of Russian language and literature, of whom 97 percent have a higher education and teachers of the native language and literature, of whom 92.3 percent have a higher education. Moreover, a gap of 6.5 percent exists between urban and village teachers of the same subjects. In a number of minority schools situated outside the given autonomous territory, the proportion of teachers (language and literature and other categories) with a tertiary education is only 52.2 percent. A chronic shortage of properly educated teachers is substantially vitiating the quality of education in such schools.

In 1988 and 1989 the tendency developed to train general subjects specialists in the native language: by 1995 the number of such specialists able to serve as subject instructors in the native language should rise to 34,785 from 7,440 in 1990. A similar trend can be observed in training for pre-school education. In addition, training has begun for multi-subject teachers to work in small nationality schools. In a number of teacher training schools instruction in indigenous applied arts are now part of the course offerings. In Dagestan and in Kazan, in the 1989-1990 school year, entrance examinations for pedagogical institutes were held in the native language for the first time.

Some negative aspects of teacher training for the nationality school also merit note:

- In Kabardino-Balkariia, Kalmykia, North Ossetia, Udmurtia, Chuvashia and Iakutia, teachers of the native language and literature are prepared solely at universities, which provide inadequate training in methods;
- There is no specialized training for teachers to work with pupils who are weak or entirely unprepared in their own native language, as well as with Russians wishing to learn that language;
- As a rule, teacher training institutions lack a cycle of courses centering upon ethnic cultures;
- The graduates of teacher training institutes generally have a very low level of general education and training in methods; this makes them unreceptive to new approaches in education;
- Inadequate use is made of teacher training classes for graduates with a general (secondary) education.

- The same deficiencies exist in the system of refresher courses and skills enhancement for teachers.

As we see, a qualitative change is called for in the personnel recruitment and training policies for the nationality school.

Research and Communications

To this date, the scholarly paradigm governing studies of the instructional process in the minority school depicts such a school as an educational institution offering instruction in the native language, both as the medium and the subject of study.   Therefore, virtually all research was reduced to the issue of bilingualism, understood as the foundation stone of the nationality school, and the central research organization of the Ministry of Education concerned with this topic--the Scientific Research Institute on the Nationality School, with its filials and local laboratories--fell in line with this agenda.

Over the years the Institute has done much to promote teaching of Russian and other indigenous languages in the various regions of the Federation. However, it has been obvious that in the current situation the further development of ethnic education calls for research in hitherto unexplored areas such as ethno-demography, ethno-psychology, ethno-sociology, ethno-geography, etc. But advances in these areas are unfeasible without a general theoretical foundation: a comprehensive conceptualization of ethnic development in the context of actual socio-economic conditions prevailing in the RSFSR during the period of transition to the market.   Here we observe a convergence of practical and scholarly needs on the part both of the nationality school and of society as a whole, which calls for cooperation between basic science and its applications in more specific areas.   In this connection what is needed is the timely transformation of the Scientific Research Institute on the Nationality School into a research institute on *problems* of ethnicity.[4]

In order to enhance the role of research local laboratories of this institute must also be turned into filials.   They should be called upon to serve as distinctive centers which, working hand in hand with local teacher training and retraining institutions as well as other methods centers, will provide articulated structures with unified goals and a practical agenda.   The potential of such centers will be significantly augmented by drawing up the talents of scholars from local pedagogical institutes and universities, from research institutes in the area of language, literature and history under the councils of ministers of the autonomous republics and the local branches of the Academy of Science of the USSR.   Another potential source of input is the membership of the various creative unions at the level both of the autonomous republic and of the country as a whole.   Joint international efforts in the area of multi-cultural education could also be highly productive.

There is no single centralized source of information on the nationality school in the RSFSR or the USSR as a whole. Fragmentary data can be found dispersed throughout a variety of educational journals. *Russian Language in the Nationality School* and its equivalents at the level of the autonomous republics are the only journals functioning in this field, and (as the title indicates) for only one category of teacher. Certain republic-level Inservice Training Institutes (IUUs) intermittently publish collections of articles or booklets devoted to innovative teaching practices. But such publications receive only limited circulation, even within the boundary of the autonomous territory.

State Aid and Support for Children

Present Conditions

The state of programs promoting the education and development of children in need of government help and support (this includes orphans, children separated from their parents, children with learning disabilities, children with affective or volitional disturbances, children from disadvantaged families, and children needing special learning environments) is directly linked to the level of socio-economic development of the country as a whole. It is in these programs that a society's "pain-sensitive areas" are reflected--areas such as the frequency of abandoned (orphaned) children, of developmentally disturbed children and adolescents, of juvenile delinquency, etc.

According to UNESCO data for 1988 on the condition of children throughout the globe, the USSR as a whole ranks 39 of 131 countries in terms of child mortality (based on a coefficient of child mortality of children up to age 5). In the Russian Federation every year 200,000 children under age fourteen die; another 30,000 are born with hereditary or congenital diseases. At present the number of invalid children in the republic under age fifteen surpasses 38,000. The overall number of children with mental or physical deficiencies is 1,000,000; of this number 702,000 are enrolled in incomplete secondary schools for the developmentally handicapped.

In 1989 adolescents under 17 committed 15 percent more crimes (or an increase of 20,000 infractions) than in the previous year. Every year, some 130,000 to 150,000 minors take part in violations of the law.

There can be little doubt that such a state of affairs reflects both the condition of the family in our society and the deficiencies of official programs for the younger generation. Data testifies that right up to recent years women were considered a vital part of the nation's productive capacity and that 27,000,000 women are working in conditions not meeting official health or safety standards, while women make up 44 percent of the labor force in industries deemed injurious to health. This, the intensive urbanization of the country, and a number of other factors, have attenuated family ties, reduced the potential moral and educational role of the family, and exacerbated tendencies such as "social orphaning," (*sotsial'noe sirotstvo*) that is, "orphaned" (i.e., abandoned) children of living parents. In 1990 alone 50,000 children were registered as orphaned or abandoned (left without parental support). In the past three years 40,000 parents have been deprived of custody of their children. In orphanages (lit. "children's homes" or *detskie doma*) and boarding homes some 68 percent of children have been removed from the custody of their parents (it is unclear whether the statistics in this paragraph apply to the RSFSR or the USSR as a whole).

The official system of child support and aid includes:

- orphanages and boarding schools for orphaned children and state wards.
- boarding homes, both general and specialized;
- special educational institutions for children with physical or mental handicaps;
- special schools and vocational schools for children needing distinctive learning environments.

It should be underscored that this system does not include infant homes (*dom rebenka*) which provide for children from birth to age three who have no parents. Such children's homes, under the control of the Ministry of Health, have virtually no special programs to facilitate child development, as a result of which the general and psychological growth of such children often lags behind; subsequently, such children need to undergo intensive remedial programs in orphanages.

Orphanages and Boarding Homes

The network of institutions responsible for children bereft of parents includes orphanages, boarding schools, and foster homes or "family-run children's homes" (*semeinye detskie doma*) (see Table 19.10). Between 1976 and 1985 the number of orphanages fell by 38 percent (from 890 to 553); since then the decline has halted. In the meantime, the number of boarding schools has risen: from 136 in 1985 to 185 in 1990. These trends reflect changes in official policy (Decree Number 85 of the Central Committee of the Communist Party and the Council of Ministers of the USSR, dated January 24, 1985: "On Measures to Upgrade the Education, Upbringing and Material Provisioning of Orphans and Children Deprived of Parental Care, in Homes for Children, Children's Homes, and Boarding Schools") designed to improve the status of such children. However, implementation of such policies was contrary to the real educational needs of these children, since it led to the rapid expansion of the number of

TABLE 19.10

Number of Orphanages and
Boarding Schools for Wards of the State

	1975	1985	1990
Orphanages	890	545	542
Boarding Schools	---	136	185
Family-Run[a]	---	---	163

[a]The first were established in 1987; the number rose to 34 in 1988, and 90 in 1989.

boarding schools, which tend to isolate children from their environment, rendering more difficult their adaptation and socialization. It should be emphasized that the plan to build more boarding schools was based less on calculations of the educational worth of such institutions than upon the needs of contractors. For example, the cost of one place in a boarding school is from 1.5 to 2.5 times more expensive than of a place in a children's home (in absolute figures, from 11,500 to 14,400 rubles and from 6,700 to 9,200 rubles respectively). Today, with the realization of the unjustifiability of such policies has come a reversal, and boarding schools are being converted back into children's homes (the number of boarding schools dropped from 195 to 184 between 1989 and 1990). In addition, in the past three or four years a new type of educational institution more in line with established practice throughout the world has come into being: family-run children's homes in which the child's upbringing approximates the conditions of family life, and socio-psychological rehabilitation as well as child development. The number of such children's homes rose from two in 1987 to 90 in 1989 and 163 in 1990; the number of orphans being raised in these homes now is approximately 1,000. But a number of factors are limiting the further spread of children's homes: among them are the absence of legal status, the gap between official per capita allocations and actual expenditures on children, the difficulties of providing for children given the prevailing goods shortages today, and the dearth of medical, psychological and educational training for "parent-upbringers" who staff these institutions.

The policies and changes discussed above are reflected in the number of wards in the various institutions. Thus, in children's homes there were 60,500 orphans in 1985. Since then, the number has gradually declined, reaching 43,500 in 1990. In boarding schools, the number jumped from 39,600 in 1985 to 48,200 in 1986. It stayed relatively stable until 1990, when it dropped to 45,800.

The contingent of children in these institutions differs from students in general education schools in that among the former a higher proportion of children with developmental problems and anomalies can be observed. Over the past six years, this proportion has been growing: thus, between 1985 and 1990 in boarding schools it rose from 52.9 percent to 65.5 percent of all children (in absolute numbers, from 53,000 to 58,500 children).

The development of children's institutions of this type is linked to the more general processes by which such children are detected and declared orphans and, on the other hand, put in foster homes (see Table 19.11).

TABLE 19.11

Children Decreed Orphans or Wards of the State,
and Placed in Families or Boarding Homes
(in thousands)

	1971	1975	1980	1985	1990
Decreed Wards	48.2	52.0	60.6	69.3	49.1
Placed in families	33.2	36.6	39.2	45.4	38.0
Placed in institutions	13.4	14.8	20.4	23.0	10.2

The table indicates that in the last decade the proportion of children for whom families have been found has risen significantly, from 64.7 percent in 1980 to 77.4 percent in 1989. The overall number of children who were wards of the state rose from 96,300 in 1980 to 173,000 in 1990, and the overall number of adopted children rose from 96,300 to 125,100 in the same interval. This process could be considerably accelerated if the existing inadequacies in the Instructions on Adoption approved by the Ministry of Health and Ministry of Education of the USSR were removed. Foster care is also handicapped by the miserly scale of the subventions provided by the state to foster families. At present in the RSFSR a family agreeing to take a foster child receives only thirty rubles a month; a decree of the Council of Ministers of the USSR raising this monthly sum to seventy-five rubles has yet to be approved by the Supreme Soviet of the RSFSR. It is instructive that in Moldavia, where in 1989 the monthly sum allocated to foster parents was raised to 100 rubles, the number of children in orphanages dropped 20 percent. Thus, an increase in support could facilitate a high-priority development--the placing of children presently in state institutions into family environments--which in general are more propitious for their education and development.

The number and educational qualifications of personnel employed in orphanages and boarding schools for orphaned children are presented in Table 19.12.

TABLE 19.12

Personnel at Orphanages and Boarding Schools for
Orphans and Wards of the State (Jan. 1, 1990)

Education	Orphanages		Boarding Schools	
	number	percentage	number	percentage
Higher	3,127	37.1	2,352	57.4
Incomplete Higher	448	5.3	241	5.9
Specialized Secondary	4,586	54.4	1,340	32.7
General Secondary	270	3.2	167	4.0

We can calculate from this table as well as the numbers presented above on children in such institutions that the ratio of staff to children is 5:1 in orphanages and 12:1 in boarding schools. The low percentage of teaching staff with a higher education is noteworthy; in addition, upbringers in orphanage and boarding schools do not undergo professional training to prepare them to work with children without families, among whom a significant proportion have physical or mental handicaps. Furthermore, teacher training institutes and IUUs do not have special divisions or offer courses for specialists in this area. Consequently, the organizational of daily life in such institutions is directly borrowed from the general education school, which takes no account of the highly distinctive psychological and educational features of development and schooling for such children. At present the diagnostic facilities and psychological services for such institutions are primitive.

Boarding Schools: General and Specialized

Boarding schools were first established in 1956. It was assumed that they would serve as educational institutions providing a comprehensive and multifaceted schooling, would promote physical and aesthetic growth, and provide practical training for the various sectors of the economy. Initially the boarding schools expanded rapidly in the RSFSR: in 1956 184 boarding schools were established with an enrollment of 35,000 children, and by 1960 the number of schools had risen to 1,000 with an enrollment of 350,000. The Seven-year Plan for 1959-1965 called for further increases of enrollment to 2,500,000. But such plans proved unworkable, answering the needs neither of society nor of pedagogy. Beginning in the 1970s the number of boarding schools declined markedly falling from 989 in 1975 to 666 in 1989; the number of pupils also plummeted, from 331,000 to 161,500. The decline was especially precipitous after 1984, when a decree of the Council of Ministers of the USSR (Jan. 1, 1984: No. 25) fundamentally redefined the basic mission of boarding schools, changing them "from model educational institutions for the comprehensive development of the child" into general education institutions for children from children of deficient family circumstances. In addition to these general-type boarding schools (which include schools for peoples of the North and for nomadic peoples), the system now came to include rehabilitation centers of various types and rehabilitation orphanages, but also special boarding schools providing advanced instruction in the sciences, sports, arts or Russian language.

The Decree stipulated that priority in admission to general boarding schools be given to children whose family circumstances were rendered difficult because of work, health or other conditions, including foster children or wards of the state, children from impoverished (the Soviet euphemism used in official studies was "insufficiently provided for") families, from single-parent families, or large families.

This reorientation of goals for the boarding school led to a massive reorganization of general boarding schools into specialized institutions for the learning-disabled, into orphanages, and to the transfer of numerous institutions to different branches of the bureaucracy. In all, between 1985 and 1990 some 146 general boarding schools were converted: into auxiliary schools providing special services for the learning-disabled--53; into orphanages--66; into special-profile boarding schools--15. The transfer to other sectors of the bureaucracy began in 1988, and was particularly marked for general education schools providing accelerated training in various subjects, which were turned over to leading universities (Moscow, Leningrad, Kranoiarsk, Novosibirsk). We can anticipate more such transfers in the future. Finally, a number of sports boarding schools have been turned over to the State Committee of Sports of the USSR, which used them to found new Olympic Preparatory Schools (*Shkoly olimpiskogo rezerva*).

Thus, an analysis of the network of general boarding schools demonstrates that this network is undergoing a massive transformation, the basic aspects of which include:

- a fundamental reorientation of goals for the general boarding school towards greater specialization, including, but not restricted to, intensi-fied work with mentally and physically retarded children;
- transfer of a number of these schools to other branches of the bureau-

cracy, which is removing from this network schools working with the gifted and talented;
- emphasis upon orphanages as institutions better suited to properly socialize children than the boarding schools.

These changes are transforming the network of general education boarding schools into a base for the education of children from disadvantaged family backgrounds. The preponderant majority of children in such institutions today (70-80 percent) come from such disadvantaged families. Ten percent have a parent who is incarcerated or from whom the child has been legally removed; 8-10 percent are children of group 1 or group 2 invalids. Of course, this circumstance has a negative impact on the moral climate in these institutions, and contributes to the increased crime rate (among such youths).

At present boarding schools employ 17,100 teachers and 11,100 upbringers. The work routine in general boarding schools includes twenty-four hour shifts and year round schedules for these employees, as well as evening, late-night, and holiday and vacation-time shifts. Regardless of this, such employees receive the same salary as teachers in regular schools; as a result teachers are seldom motivated and turnover is high.

The inadequacies of staffing policies for boarding schools becomes evident upon comparison of such institutions with orphanages. Boarding schools, which work with children with numerous difficult problems, need the same staff as do orphanages, but they do not have a staff of psychologists, social workers or other specialists to ensure the normal functioning of the institution. Moreover, the training policies for preparing personnel for boarding schools are inadequate; there are virtually no developed methodologies for working with educationally deprived children.

Special Institutions for Children with Mental and Physical Handicaps

Specialized rehabilitative institutions exist for children whose developmental difficulties or psycho-physiological problems inhibit their ability to learn in the standard classroom. Such children include the visually and hearing impaired, the mentally retarded, children with cerebral palsy or with psychological impairments. Such institutions aim to provide an instructional environment which compensates for such impairments, to rehabilitate students and help prepare them for life and work, to adapt and ultimately to integrate children and adolescents into a dynamic society. Rehabilitation takes place in a variety of types of institutions, including boarding schools and mainstream schools with special classes. Over the past twenty to thirty years this network has seen its greatest period of expansion. Every five years during this period, on the average thirty to sixty new boarding schools were opened and the number of children enrolled continued to grow. Thus, in 1970 there were 1,271 institutions with 204,800 children enrolled; in 1990 this had risen to 1,791 schools and 315,300 children.

The education and upbringing of children with developmental anomalies takes places both in specialized institutions and in mainstream schools. Special classes in the mass school were first established in the early 1980s and received their most intense development in the last five years. The number of children enrolled in special classes in the mass school has increased tenfold in the last decade, from 3,600 in 1980 to 6,300 in 1985, 19,500 in 1989 and 35,500 in 1990.

Nevertheless, the majority of children with developmental difficulties are enrolled in boarding schools or special schools; only about 10 percent study in special classes attached to mainstream schools. Yet, specialized research indicates that between 30 and 50 percent of this contingent of psychological impaired children (*ZPR--zaderzhka psikhologicheskoi razvitiia*) have the potential to function in the mass school after receiving special attention in the primary grades. Therefore, the proper approach is to continue to increase the number of special education classes in the mass school, especially for developmentally handicapped children with normal family conditions. It is worthy of note that the process of setting up boarding school institutions for the various categories of special needs children (*anomal'nye deti*) proceeded unevenly. For example, over the past two decade the number of institutions for the visually impaired has remained virtually the same (72 boarding schools with 11,500 children in 1970, and 72 schools with 11,700 children in 1990). The situation is analogous for children with hearing impairments: in 1970 there were 142 institutions serving 23,000 children; in 1990 there were 149 institutions and 24,100 children. As for those afflicted with cerebral palsy, in 1970 there were 29 schools serving 5,200 children with dysfunctions of the gross motor system; in 1990 there were 34 institutions with 6,100 children. As for children with severe speech impairments, in 1970 there were 28 institutions enrolling 4,800 children; by 1990 these number had risen to 60 and 10,900 respectively. Finally, in 1975 there was one institution with 400 children labelled psychological impaired (*ZPR*); by 1990 this had risen to 39 institutions with 7,600 children. In sum the number of institutions for children with intellectual impairments has risen: from 999 institutions with 160,200 children in 1970 to 1,437 institutions with 254,700 children in 1990. Children with intellectual impairments (*narushenie intellekta*) make up 80.8 percent of the total of school-children with developmental problems. Finally, in 1988 a new type of institution was established for orphaned children with mental defects--the **auxiliary** boarding school or orphanage.

The number of children diagnosed with ZPR has significantly increased. In 1985 the number of such children in special boarding schools or in compensatory classes in the mass school was 3,500; by 1990 it had risen to 33,700.

Providing a special course of instruction for ZPR children at the level of the primary school helps reduce the unjustified practice of sending those with the most severe disabilities to the auxiliary schools. This is particularly urgent in the case of parentless children, the diagnosis of whom is complicated by their precarious environment.

Despite some encouraging tendencies in the evolution of the network of specialized support institutions for children with various developmental problems, only half of them, according to the estimate of the Scientific Research Institute of Defectology of the APN of the USSR, are provided with an adequate educational environment. Thus, there is a significant gap between need and provision, and approximately 300,000 to 500,000, if not more children lack access to professional support. The majority of such children are studying (without the needed auxiliary support) in the general classes of the mass school, and this not only complicates their "condition," but also condemns them to failure in life.

A number of factors contribute to this situation, among them: the absence of a precise system of detection and registration; a lack of coordination between the educational and health bureaucracies; and **the extremely negative image (i.e., stigma) society has of children with physical and mental disabilities** (emphasis added).

Particularly disturbing is the shortage of staff with professional training in special education for these compensatory institutions. Of 75,164 teachers and upbringers working with special children, two-thirds have a tertiary education, but only 10 percent have specialized training. Moreover, in recent years this proportion has declined (from 10.9 percent in 1986). A primary reason for the continuing, even growing gap between supply and demand in this area is the lack of material incentives; teachers in the field of special education are paid no more than teachers in the general schools.

At present special education teachers are trained at eleven teacher training institutes in the RSFSR: at the Leningrad Herzen Pedagogical Institute, at MGZPI (external study teacher training) institutes in Sverdlovsk (Ekaterinaburg), Irkutsk, Saransk, Khabarovsk, Saratov, Kuibyshev (Samara), Kursk, Stavropol, and Cherepovets. The majority of such institutes provide training in only one designated field, for example, speech defects in children or cognitive disabilities. Until recently, no training was provided for working with children with ZPR, with disorders of the gross motor system, or with multiple disabilities; to this date there is no program to train teachers or psychologists for specialized compensatory institutions. And only five pedagogical institutes provide the opportunity for teachers in such institutions to receive a second degree in special education.

The system of inservice training is also in unsatisfactory condition. Only one-third of all institutes for teacher retraining have methodologists in the field of defectology (i.e., special education). The majority of such institutes take no responsibility for personnel training in the area of special education on the grounds that they themselves have no qualified personnel in this field.

Personnel shortages and lack of training in psychology in many ways prevent compensatory educational institutions from successfully carrying out their mission, namely, preparing developmentally disadvantaged children to cope successfully in the larger world.

The effectiveness of specialized compensatory educational institutions for children with learning handicaps depends also largely upon issues of structure, content and the mix of students admitted (i.e., admissions policies).

In the area of admissions there is a special need for attention to the medical-pedagogical commissions for selection purposes. At present, the work of such commissions is doomed to failure. They do not have permanent staff, and often lack qualified specialists or methodologists capable of carrying out a differentiated diagnosis. A high degree of overcrowding (exceeding by a factor of 1.5 or 2 staff-inmate ratios in the developed countries) leads to exhaustion, nervous stress, difficulties in mastering the curriculum, which in turn hinder achieving the compensatory goals of the program.

The content of special education needs fundamental revision. With the exception of the primary grades and the auxiliary schools, it is hardly distinguishable from the curriculum offered to normally developing children, and takes little account of the real capabilities of children with different types and degrees of articulation of developmental anomalies. Despite the fact that many special education institutions deal with children with multiple disorders; i.e., visual impairment, mental retardation or psychological problems, in addition to the fundamental impairment, no corresponding programs, textbooks or teachers' manuals have been created for such children. Institutions serving children with serious speech impairments or with ZPR do have special curricula, but lack the accompanying classroom material necessary for instruction. All compensatory schools experience shortages of instructional materials and teachers' handbooks.

At present the Russian Federation has no research center prepared to undertake the task of drawing up such materials, of carrying out systematic research on the proper learning environment, or of developing a program as a whole for the education and upbringing of children with developmental disabilities.

Special General and Vocational Schools for Children Needing a Distinctive Learning Environment

Speical general and vocational schools for children needing a distinctive learning environment were first created in the RSFSR in 1964. Their primary goal is to provide a comprehensive program of social and psychological rehabilitation and adaptation to society and work for deviant adolescents and juvenile violators of the law. Children aged eleven to fourteen are sent to special schools, children aged fourteen to eighteen to special vocational schools (PTUs).

Between 1984 and 1990 the number of special general schools increased from thirty to thirty two (of which two were for girls, the remainder for boys); total enrollment fell from 6,600 to 6,320. In the same period the number of special PTUs increased from thirteen to fourteen (of which first five, then four were for girls), while enrollment fell slightly, from 4,550 to 4,521. Thus, there has been little change in recent years. A Decree of the Council of Ministers dated December 6, 1984 (No. 251) calling for construction of 11 new special PTUs was not implemented. Two special schools and three special PTUs are closed for major repairs, seven special schools and eight special PTUs are located in buildings in need of renovation, and twenty-two buildings have exhausted 60-90 percent of their designated life-cycle. In sum, we can speak of the virtual collapse of the system. To make matters worse, a number of regions (Leningrad, Irkutsk and Khabarovsk regions) are entertaining the question of closing down special schools and special PTUs.

It is estimated that the shortfall in supply of such rehabilitative (correctional) institutions equals 90 percent of demand. Data on the degree of criminality of the adolescent milieu provides confirmation of this assertion. In 1989 alone, pupils in the general secondary schools and PTUs of the RSFSR committed 80,982 crimes; in the first quarter of 1990 28,720 youths (of whom 21.5 percent were girls) were brought to preliminary detention centers. In 1989 3,493 school youths were charged with using narcotics, and of this number 538 were found to be addicted. Another 5,548 were charged with using prescription drugs or intoxicants, among whom 1,033 were diagnosed as addicted (*toksikomaniia*). The age at which young people begin to use alcohol has declined significantly. Flight from home and homelessness begins at age ten to eleven, is accompanied by theft, extortion, hooliganism (a catch-all terms with a notorious history in the Soviet Union, meaning roughly: rowdyism, vandalism, disturbing the peace) and acts of wanton cruelty.

If we consider the student bodies of special institutions, over sixty percent have committed theft, robbery or acts of hooliganism; ten percent have been brought in for murder or rape; 35 percent of the students in special general schools and 87 percent in special PTUs systematically abuse(d) alcohol, and more than 70 percent of the girls can be described as sexually promiscuous. The presence in these institutions of so many students (more than 40 percent) convicted of criminally liable acts but freed from penalties, exerts a powerfully negative influence on the student body as a whole.

When children are routed to special educational institutions of this sort little account is taken of the nature of their psychological abnormalities or distinctiveness. As a result, passive, withdrawn, defenseless children are thrown together with those who have committed serious crimes and have vicious, vindictive personality traits.

Research carried out over two years has demonstrated that 70 percent of students in special (rehabilitative) educational institutions suffer from one or another psychiatric disorder of the nervous system, including: organic dysfunctionings of the central nervous system--20 percent; pathological personality traits--29.5 percent; protracted and acute neurotic reactions--21 percent. Longitudinal studies reveal a relative and absolute increase in the number of juvenile infractions by adolescents with early organic dysfunctions of the central nervous system. In conditions of enforced isolation and strict-regime confinement such children are emotionally aggressive, and prone to depression.

A central aspect of special rehabilitative educational institutions is their mission of helping adolescents adapt to work and to society. Despite the fact that in the schools of this system 43.2 percent of the equipment at work stations has been in operation more than twenty years and that there is a shortage of equipment, raw materials, and other supplies amounting to roughly 50 percent of norms, such institutions yearly produce more than 8.5 million rubles' worth of usable output. This fact might be a source of pride for the leaders of this system of social and labor rehabilitation, if it did not conceal the scale of child exploitation taking place here: the volume of output produced by 11,000 adolescents, accounts for 10 percent (!) of the total output produced by all the general education schools and PTUs of the Russian Federation, that is by 15,000,000 adolescents .

In considering the general features of admissions policy and curriculum of these special educational institutions, it must be emphasized that from the beginning the system was set up not to reeducate but as a place for serving time. In practice, this has led to the formation, on the basis of these institutions, of special "children's transit prisons" and "children's corrective colonies (*zony*), where adolescents create and maintain the traditions and codes of the criminal world. This situation was engendered by the drive to punish (deviant) children, as well as by another set of factors, including: the absence of criteria to differentiate children by the scale of criminality, the nature of the infraction committed, or by distinctive personality traits; the failure to conduct detailed medical and psychological evaluations of such children when routing them to such institutions; the failure to provide psychiatric therapy and individualized treatment for such children; the absence of conditions conducive to social, labor, and psychological rehabilitation for those released to places of work, study and residence; inadequate research and methodological underpinning for such special institutions; planning schedules without any account taken of the need to individualize correctional programs on the basis of professional psychological diagnosis.

The above analysis demonstrates the urgent need to differentiate the various correctional educational institutions according to the type of violator sent there, and to change the routing patterns accordingly. Moreover, the ongoing practice of extra-judicial compulsory assignment of adolescents to special general schools and special PTUs (in reality, the deprivation of freedom for two to three years), according to the decision of public (i.e., non-state) organizations such as the juvenile affairs commissions of the executive boards of local soviets, is in direct contradiction with principles of legality and a law-governed state, and with the Conventions on the Rights of the Child adopted by the United Nations General Assembly and ratified by the Supreme Soviet of the USSR, and must be firmly repudiated. The existing Statute on the Special (Corrective) School and PTU must be altered, and the size of the scale of operations of these institutions reduced.

As for personnel in these institutions, a shortage exists of teachers amounting to 8.3 percent in schools and 3.9 percent in PTUs, of upbringers--9.3 percent and 21.8 percent respectively; of shop teachers--4.3 percent and 29.3 percent. The low salaries (the supplement for working in such conditions amounts to only 20 percent) and the lack of housing provide little inducement to work in these institutions, which call for highly specialized training. Turnover is high: during the past five years 32.3 percent of the directors of special schools and 44.4 percent of the directors of special PTUs have left their positions. In terms of level of education, only 56.5 percent of upbringers in PTUs have a higher education; in special schools the proportion is 84 percent. Among shop instructors, 77.7 percent have a specialized secondary education, and 7.7 percent have completed a higher education.

According to selective (scattered) research findings, 15 percent of personnel in special PTUs suffer from nervous disorders or display pathological psychiatric tendencies indisposing them to work; 33 percent are in need of special training to work with a criminal contingent, and virtually all need instruction in methods for working with disturbed youth. Again, present there is no program preparing personnel for work with at-risk youth (*s vysokokriminogennym podrostkovym kontingentom*); the very methodology itself has not been worked out.

Physical Facilities

Boarding schools of all types are in extremely poor condition. Of the 12,800 buildings belonging to boarding schools 1,500 (12 percent) are in need of a major renovation and 317 need to be torn down. More than 780 have no running water or sewage disposal, 69 are without central heating. Year after year, construction plans for boarding schools are only fulfilled by 10 percent to 30 percent of projections. In order fully to meet demand, over the next five to seven years the following number of places must be created each year, either through renovation or through new construction: in orphanages and boarding schools for orphanages--one to five thousand places; in general education boarding schools--twenty to thirty thousand places; in schools (both boarding and day) for developmentally handicapped children--seventy to eighty thousand places; in special schools and special PTUs--3,500 places. . . . In more than 700 institutions there are no sports facilities. . . . More than one-third of all boarding schools fail to meet minimum space requirements (four square meters per pupil). . . . In special PTUs the shortfall of equipment needed for production training is in excess of 50 percent. . . . Health-care facilities in such institutions are in need of an addition 80,500 square meters of space. Institutions for children with mental and physical disabilities are in critical shape; more than twenty thousand such children are in overcrowded facilities; over 60 percent of these institutions are housed in buildings adapted from other uses. . . . Many lack hot water, indoor plumbing or other amenities. Despite the efforts made in recent years to draw up blueprints of specially designed buildings for developmentally handicapped children, there has been virtually no new construction in this area. . . . Specially designed equipment and furniture for handicapped children are lacking, largely because there is no system in place for the design and production of such vital equipment. . . . More than 300 boarding schools have no buses for transportation, and fuel needs are met only to 30 percent. Each year some 200 to 300 new buses are needed for boarding schools.

The State of Vocational-Technical Education

In the Russian Federation, vocational-technical education is an important component of the system of lifelong education, promoting both the professional and the civic identity of the individual worker. Annually, the Russian professional school turns out more than 1,300,000 trained workers and provides refresher courses for roughly 400,000 adult workers.

It is the graduates of vocational-technical *uchilishcha* who in the present world shape the structure of the working class and make up its most flexible and mobile component. The vocational school continues to carry out a long-established role of helping thousands of adolescents from broken families, orphans and problem youth (juvenile infractors) gain their bearings in life.

Today the professional and vocational school is experiencing difficult times. A sharp rift has occurred between the workings of the system of professional and technical education and the perestroika of the republic's economy, between this system and the requirements called forth by the transition to market relations. As enterprises have moved to cost-accounting and self-financing, regular subsidies to the schools have shrunk, and coordination of efforts to plan the training of workers and professionals, to organize workplace (on-site) training as well as job placement have been far more problematic. The articles on base enterprises for professional and technical education included in the Law on Enterprises (1987) are, for all practical purposes, a dead letter. Many enterprise managers have evinced little interest in manpower training.

The system of planning as it has evolved for the vocational-technical schools takes little account of the real capacities (both material and academic) of these schools, of regional manpower needs and resources, and produces too many poorly qualified workers and machine operators. It is ill-prepared to adjust to the long-term structural changes taking place in the workplace, the workforce and the economy as a whole.

From year to year the admissions targets for PTUs remained unmet. In the current year (1990) the target was to admit 1,200,000 students; instead slightly more than 1,000,000 enrolled, a shortfall of 10.5 percent. The overall enrollments in PTUs have been steadily shrinking. At present, in the 4,326 such schools in the RSFSR roughly 2,000,000 students are enrolled, which is 200,000 fewer than last year, and 8 percent fewer than in 1985.

The intended system of contractual relations in training qualified workers is not working out. Training on the basis of direct *khozraschet* contracts with individual enterprises involves only 27,700 individuals, or 3.4 percent of enrollments.

The student cohort in professional-technical institutions is, from a pedagogical and a societal point of view, extremely difficult. Roughly 80 percent of those who matriculate in a PTU have demonstrated criminal tendencies, unlawful (hooligan) behavior and are educationally deprived. In 1989, 45,500 PTU students were brought before the law for criminal infractions--1.2 times the figure for general education schools (despite the vast difference in enrollments). In the same year, 43,300 individuals from PTUs were given administrative penalties for abuse of alcoholic beverages--2.7 times the number of general education schools.

The system of vocational education is unpopular among youth. Its efforts to provide a professional orientation for youth are generally unsuccessful. Thus, despite certain gains in prestige achieved by these schools in the 1980s, according to sociological surveys only 10 percent of graduates (of the eighth grade) of the secondary school intend to enroll in a PTU.

A Description of the Network of Vocational Education

By the early 1990s an extensive network of vocational education was in place in the Russian Federation. On January 1, 1990, there were 4,346 institutions of professional-technical education under the Ministry of Education of the RSFSR, of which 3,853 were day-time vocational schools. During the Eleventh Five Year Plan 151 new schools were opened, and during the first four years of the Twelfth Five Year Plan another 150 were opened. Of these new schools, 114 and 108 were daytime institutions.

Despite this, we have no systematic plan for rationally locating these schools; as a result some 360 smaller and medium size cities in the RSFSR have no vocational education, and of the 1,813 rural districts in the Russian Federation only 62.4 percent can boast of such schools.

In the republic roughly a third of the vocational-technical schools are in need of major repairs; every sixteenth PTU is in such dilapidated shape it should be condemned and torn down. Such conditions are not conducive to a quality education. To make matters worse the rate of forced closings virtually equals the new number of student places being created: between 1986 and 1990 246,120 places were created by the construction of new schools; during the same time 246,100 places were lost to closings. . . .

No system of ranking (lit: differentiation) exists for the various types of schools within the system according to the type and level of professional or vocational education provided. This works against efforts to improve the quality of education.

The present expansion of the system, the organization of training for new specialties, the establishment of new types of educational institutions, such as VPTUs, technical and agricultural lycées and colleges (*kolledzhi*) is taking place in haphazard fashion and without the necessary preliminary analysis or preparatory work to ensure that quality is maintained or enhanced. Efforts in scattered regions to arbitrarily close down existing PTUs, to turn their facilities over to cultural, health, cooperative or joint enterprise institutions have not been halted. During 1990 more than 100 PTUs were closed down; the facilities of a third of these institutions were converted to non-educational purposes. The "dismantling" of the vocational and technical schools, the utilization of facilities for non-designated purposes or their transformation into boarding schools, is a temporary phenomenon connected with delays (footdragging) in renewing the system of vocational education.

The professional profiles by which students are educated with the vocational network no longer corresponding with the structure of the economy. For example, the relative weight of training afforded to future employees in the service sector is entirely inadequate, comprising only about 10 percent of all graduates. At the same time, in the economy the demand for trained workers in the service spheres, trade network and catering industries is constantly growing. The vocational network can meet demand in these areas only by 10 percent to 15 percent.

The present system of administering vocational schools is not conducive to its independence.

In recent years the issue of quality has come to the fore. The technological complexity of work is increasing far faster than the skills provided by the schools. (In the Soviet Union, all workers are provided with skill rankings (*razriady*) on a scale of one to five.) In the construction industry in 1960 the skills levels of workers on the average lagged between the estimated complexity of tasks by .3 of one ranking, in 1987 this had jumped to .88 and today the gap equals one full rank (i.e., 20 percent of the entire scale of skills rankings). It is estimated that the tempo of growing complexity of workplace occupations exceeds by twofold ongoing gains in training. Inadequacies of training of the majority of the workforce is already beginning to impede further technological progress, rendering more difficult the mastery of new equipment.

The state of instruction in the republic's PTUs has become a serious problem for the country's economy. We have singled out the service industries, but the demand for qualified workers remains unmet also in the machine-building, metal-working, construction, mining, chemical, oil and gas industries. There are acute shortages of tool-makers, fitters, engine-fitters, assembly-fitters; comparable deficits exist in agriculture and construction. At many machine-building enterprises there are not enough operators and adjustors. As a result much new machinery stands idle or is inefficiently used, the state does not receive expect returns on outlays for technical upgrading of equipment, and the new equipment does not have the anticipated impact on labor productivity, nor does it result in savings in energy, material or labor inputs.

Teaching Personnel

Despite the fact that the vocational-technical schools work with the most difficult contingent of students from the pedagogical point of view, it has the least well-trained staff of the entire secondary school system. As of January 1, 1990 there were 183,750 personnel in the vocational schools, including 4,380 directors, 55,900 teachers, 94,500 production instructors, 6,000 upbringers and 5,300 physical education instructors.

The most poorly trained group of instructors in the vocational-technical schools are the engineering cadres in the PTUs, that is those most instrumental in defining the professional qualifications of future workers. Specifically, we have in mind production instructors (*mastera proizvodstvennogo obucheniia*), of whom only one-fifth have a higher education, and only 3.4 percent specialized teacher training in the field of engineering. Two thirds are graduates of technical schools and only 20 percent graduated with a teaching degree in the industrial arts. As for production instructors one in three have a skills qualification lower than that received by the graduates they have trained.

Among teachers in the PTUs the percentage with a degree from a higher education institution is quite high--95.1 percent. However, even here the situation is not entirely satisfactory, because those teaching both general technology and specialized industrial disciplines--that is, those subjects most important in defining the professional skills of graduates--are less well trained (89.3 percent have a higher education). Moreover, the majority of these teachers are inadequately prepared in psychology and teaching methods.

In the RSFSR the number of teachers in these areas is rapidly shrinking. In 1989 the number of production instructors fell by 12 percent (more than 13,000 left the PTUs), the number of teachers by 8.9 percent. Although turnover has always been high in recent years--hovering at 10 percent to 12 percent, what is different now is that the exodus from the PTUs is not being balanced by the arrival of new personnel. Moreover, the republic has no balanced system of training, retooling or periodically enhancing the skills of engineering teaching personnel, a system which should be based on the principles of voluntary choice of type and place of work, of contractual relations between schools higher and specialized secondary institutions.

The existing situation described above has resulted in a quite palpable decline in the quality of vocational training of young workers.

Financing Vocational Education

The overall sum of expenditures on the vocational educational system in the RSFSR stands at roughly 2,000,000 rubles a year, among which outlays on students make up 1,800,000 rubles, on purchasing equipment, 70,000 rubles, on capital repairs, 800,000 rubles. The average outlay per student amounts to 1,089 rubles per annum.

Financing vocational education can be characterized by a lack of autonomy and by the prevalence of the residual principle. On the whole the evolving situation is a complicated one. The absence of clear funding guidelines norms, the cost increases of equipment and basic goods, food and uniforms, the refusal by many enterprises to contribute to the funding of vocational schools has engendered instability and uncertainty about the future. Further complicating the situation in some areas has been the transfer of vocational schools from the republican level to local budgets. This has complicated attempts at interregional manpower planning, inter-school cooperative production efforts and endeavors to purchase expensive equipment. . . .

In the prevailing conditions, especially rampant inflation, present budget outlays are entirely inadequate to feed and clothe the student population of the PTUs. Outlays are calculated on the basis of 1.31 rubles per student each day for food, and 83.24 rubles per student each year for outfitting. Because this is inadequate to ensure proper diet, an increase has occurred in student morbidity and items of clothing are difficult to obtain. Because the majority of students in these schools come from disadvantaged families, the lack of adequate clothing is particularly disturbing. In order to redress this situation, an increase of three- to five-fold of outlays on food and clothing must take place.

The proper organization of production instruction, the core of which must be practical workshop training, must be at the core of any attempt to enhance vocational education. Vocational schools must be prepared to provide instruction in technologically complicated areas of production, including metal-working, consumer goods, educational goods, furniture, etc. An increase of 35 percent in output in these areas has been achieved in the past two years, bringing the total to 82,500,000 rubles for 1989 alone. The overall output of vocational and technical institutions stands at over a billion rubles a year. . . .

However more than half of the equipment in use is obsolete, and less than 2 percent can be described as fully up-to-date. The capital funding of equipment (measured in per capita terms) for students in vocational schools is only one-third the figure for workers in industry. At the same time, this production capacity is utilized only 40 percent to 55 percent of potential. With the transition from central distribution to wholesale trading, obtaining equipment, instrumentation, raw materials, and fuel for workshop operations will be immeasurably complicated.

Instructional workshop facilities provide a good base for producing both new and more traditional goods, and for testing experimental product designs produced by enterprises, universities and research institutes. Such cooperative endeavors are mutually fruitful, and examples of such mutually-profitable operations can be found in a large number of schools in the Leningrad, Cheliabinsk, Sverdlovsk, Novosibirsk and Riazan regions.

The Role of Vocational-Technical Education

. . .No systematic effort has been made to plot optimal manpower needs in the various sectors of the economy and regions of the republic; this has resulted in extensive growth, manifested in the continued preparing of specialists in areas where there is little need, and failure to train professionals in new areas where the need is great.

There is no science-based approach in place for providing accreditation for PTUs. The republican-level officially set training standards do not provide the tools for assessing the performance of individual institutions, nor are such standards useful for setting criteria of quality improvements in educational achievement, to which teachers' salaries could be pegged.

Moreover, granting to the vocational-technical schools the status of VPU (technical lycée), of commercial school, or some other new designation, without first providing a system of accreditation, only serves to discredit the system of vocational education. The extensive growth of the network of vocational and technical schools, the pointless increase in the stream of graduates, and endless expansion, without the necessary preliminary research and preparation of curricula, has led to a situation, wherein even the 300 most heavily subscribed and highly important job areas where training is provided in these schools find their need for textbooks and classroom materials met by only 50-60 percent and over 400 areas have no centralized provision whatsoever in this area. . . .

The fact that along with skills training in their profession graduates receive a general secondary education has served to discredit the entire system, since the quality of general secondary education provided by the PTU in reality is quite dismal. The gap between prescription and reality exists just as well for the vocational skills and abilities provided by the PTUs. . . .

At present a legal framework is lacking to regulate the functions of the vocational and technical school network. This makes the system unresponsive to ongoing economic changes and leaves students, graduates and employees of the system without the necessary social guarantees. Furthermore, without such a framework, individual enterprises lack the incentive to invest in personnel training, which in turn undercuts the financial base of these schools. . . . Curricula and training programs are highly diverse, as a result of which there exist substantial differences between products of one school and the next.

The overwhelming majority of graduates of PTUs, immediately after, and sometimes before, graduation enter the Soviet army. As a result, graduates seldom become attached to a specific work collective and, in return, individual factories, seeing little prospect for returns on their investment, are seldom interested in promoting vocational training in the schools.

There is no legal foundation in place for the new types of schools that have sprung up, such as higher vocational schools, technical lycées, commercial schools and colleges. Correspondingly, no legal status has been accorded to the degrees granted by such institutions. . . .

The State of Extramural Education

Extra-mural education is an inseparable component of a system of lifelong education. It aims to provide the child with additional opportunities for spiritual, intellectual and physical growth and to satisfy the child's creative and educational need in the sphere of recreation. However the true societal and educative potentialities of extramural education are not fully appreciated today by state or society.

The importance of extramural education in the career choices made by youth is indicated by selected sociological surveys which indicate that up to 70 percent of youth belonging to young technicians' clubs and stations and 65 percent belonging to young naturalists' stations choose a profession corresponding with their club affiliation. Up to 90 percent of creative youth get started in their careers in creative arts organizations for the young (Palaces and Homes for Pioneers and Schoolchildren, studios, music and art schools).

The newspaper *Pionerskaia pravda* carried out a survey of 22,000 schoolchildren (grades 1-10) in 1990, and concluded that one in every three schoolchildren in the Russian Federation would like to enroll in an extramural institution but cannot because "there are none in the vicinity." Of those enrolled in circles, sections, or clubs 14 percent are dissatisfied with the nature of activities, and 42 percent with the degree of autonomy offered. Only 1 percent reported that they had established governing boards (*sovety*); 81 percent noted that they had never taken part in planning activities for their institution. Until recently the growth of the system of extramural education has been **extensive** in nature (focusing on quantitative indicators), and failed to reflect the genuine aspirations of youth.

Like the school, extramural education institutions were afflicted with the ills of the administrative-command system: bureaucratization, levelling, enforced uniformity, and imitation (*reproduktivnost'*). Numerous extramural institutions, particularly at the level of the republic, region and *oblast*, began to practice a "pedagogy without children" (*bezdetnaia pedagogika*) aimed at reducing the number of children's organizations (i.e., consolidating into ever-larger units) and emphasizing a "frontal" or top-down instructional approach. One of the most disturbing results of the bureaucratization and impoverishment of extramural institutions was to alienate the family, parental associations, older adolescents young adults as well as highly competent professional staff from extramural education. In turn, such a state of alienation seriously diminished the content, quality and effectiveness of extramural institutions, and vitiated the processes of self-initiative, autonomy and self-government, both among youth and in society as a whole.

The Network of Extramural Education Institutions

At present, the network of extramural institutions sponsored by a variety of ministries, is entrusted to the executive committees of local soviets of people's deputies (the departments of education, culture, municipal services, physical culture and sport), to trade unions, the Komsomol and other public organizations, voluntary associations, enterprises and businesses. This ensures that extramural institutions will be of a combined public and governmental nature.

Until 1985 the list of types of extramural education institutions comprised only nineteen names; today a comparable listing produces fifty-two different types. Some nineteenth thousand permanently functioning extramural education institutions (excluding children's recuperative facilities as well as libraries) cater to approximately ten million children, or about one-half the school-age cohort. Even after taking into account the tendency to exaggeration in our statistics, this is an impressive figure; nevertheless it is clear that the cultural, educational and recreational needs of children and youth are not fully met by the system.

The Ministry of Education includes in its network of extramural education institutions some 7,276 units of twenty-one different types. Here some 6.5 million children engage in activities ranging from the arts to biology and ecology, sports, local history and hiking.

From Table 19.13 it is evident that over the past twenty years the network of extramural education institutions has grown by 60.4 percent, and the number of children participating in this network has increased 250 percent.

TABLE 19.13

The Network of Extramural Institutions

Types of Extramural Institutions	1970	1980	1985	1989
Pioneer and School Palaces	2025	2678	2849	2933
Youth Sports Schools	1919	2214	2232	2558
Young Technician Stations	254	622	723	840
Young Naturalist Stations	151	369	454	530
Young Explorer Stations	84	90	97	205
Children's Parks	106	97	94	81
Children's Stadiums	--	--	20	25
Young Sailor's Clubs	--	--	--	52
Young Aviators and Astronauts' clubs	--	--	--	3
Children's Choir Studies	--	--	--	3
Other	--	--	49	46
Total	4539	6070	6518	7276

Sources: Narodnoe obrazovanie i kul'tura v RSFSR (Moscow, 1989) pp. 7, 109-110; *Narodnoe obrazovane v RSFSR v 1989 g.*, Part 2 (Moscow, 1990), and an unpublished census of extramural institutions conducted by the State Committee of Education of the USSR on October 2, 1989.

The increase in enrollments has significantly outpaced the capacity of the system to meet demand, which has resulted in a marked decline in the quality of the services provided. Today every second child enrolled in a program in this network pursues his or her activities off the premises of the institution. Even on these terms the network cannot keep up with demand, particularly because of the shortage of institutions specializing in given areas such as hiking, technology or nature studies.

Up until 1990 the growth of extramural education institutions was tightly regulated by an interministerial listing (*nomenklatura*), a procedure dictated by the nature of central financing. This *nomenklatura* dictated where and when institutions could be opened. For example, pioneers' and schoolchildren's homes could be opened by municipalities, regions or republics, while young naturalists' stations could only be sponsored by municipalities and union republics with no regional administrative divisions. As a result, in all of Russia there are only 530 stations for young naturalists, of which a mere 170 are located in rural district centers. Limitations on stations and bases for young hikers as well as on stations for naturalists and young scientists were even more restrictive. Now such restrictions have been listed and the results are already evident: in 1990 alone the number of stations and bases for young hikers increased by ten percent.

Of 4,634 extramural education institutions covered by a census carried out in 1989 (the first in sixty years), 49.8 percent were located in cities and 50.2 percent in rural areas. The average number of enrolled was 1,263 and 786 respectively. According to the census, 20.7 percent of demand for places in extramural education institutions is satisfied in urban locations, and 32 percent in rural locations. In urban areas this gap in developing the infrastructure of extramural education is partly filled by institutions under other authorities. But the need for enhanced attention and even radical measures to develop the network is great, especially in the larger cities where the additional problem of distance between home and site arises. According to selected surveys conducted in Moscow, Leningrad, Sverdlovsk and elsewhere children spend from forty minutes to two hours just to get to and from the location of their activities. This drastically limits the appeal and effectiveness of such institutions, particularly for children in primary schools. The entire system of extramural education institutions needs, in addition, a new set of regulations and norms to guide their activities, whether in the countryside, small towns, or large cities.

Physical Plant

The 1989 census demonstrated that local soviets of people's deputies, while rapidly expanding the network of extramural education institutions, lacked the means to provide adequate physical space or even to underwrite the cost of programs. Surveys show that some forty percent of children feel the need for expanded facilities, contemporary equipment and adequate supplies of materials. . . . Between 1970 and 1989 only 1,484 buildings were erected for extramural education activities, or 54.1 percent of the total number of institutions opened. The 1989 census showed that 57 percent of extramural education institutions were housed in facilities randomly acquired rather than specially built. Half of all youth sporting schools had no facilities of their own; for other types of extramural education institutions the proportion was 31 percent. Of all institutions surveyed 46 percent had no indoor plumbing or central heating; 74 percent had no hot water; 10.4 percent were heated by Russian stoves; 8 percent had no heating whatsoever; 7.2 percent were housed in condemned facilities; and a third failed to meet minimal hygienic standards.

In the Russian Federation the norm for children in general education schools is 7.2 square meters of space per child. There are no set norms of extramural education institutions, but the census shows that it ranges from .51 square meters to 1.03 meters. Only children's stadiums offered more--7 square meters per child.

The languid growth of science and technology clubs as well as of arts-oriented clubs can be explained primarily by the absence of appropriate facilities. Furthermore, only .4 percent of all extramural education institutions have swimming pools; 1 percent have *kartodromy*; 2.7 percent have *kordodromy* (areas for go-carts and remote-control model airplanes). There are only two observatories for children; roughly only one in ten institutions have exhibition halls, assembly halls, or sports facilities.

The average sum spent on extramural education for children in the Russian Federation comes to 120 rubles per capita per year (390 rubles is spent for each pupil in the general education school). But even this miserly sum gets partially diverted or vitiated because of a thicket of financial or other limitations or restrictions, because of the chaos of the internal market, and the soaring costs of technology, equipment and materials.

In some areas of extramural activity the situation is particularly grim. For example, young naturalists' stations as well as the fifty thousand experimental garden plots attached to schools have virtually no access to equipment, whether mechanized or hand tools. Special clothing of appropriate sizes is unavailable. Instruments and materials to practice folk crafts (leather and woodworking, etc.) are in short supply. It is practically impossible to obtain offset type or rebinding presses. Sewing machines, tailor's dummies. . . the list could be extended. Through conventional bookkeeping procedures it is hopeless trying to put together wind orchestras, combined vocal and instrumental groups, or folk music ensembles.

Outdoor activities groups find their needs met roughly thirty percent of the time. Inventory and equipment is produced for these groups with little or no allowance for size or age. There is an acute shortage of nylon rope and other special safety equipment for expeditions. The cheapest tent made of tarpaulin costs 70 rubles; light-weight, comfortable tents made of cambric muslim cost over 100 rubles. Inflation has made many items unaffordable, when available: for a boy or girl to be outfitted for ballroom dancing the cost has increased from 280 to 470 rubles; ballet slippers have increased from 1.60 rubles to six rubles; skis, from 20 to 150 rubles, etc.

No systematic studies are carried out of the supply and material needs of extramural education institutions; there are no prototypes in existence of equipment, tools, clothing etc. needed for such institutions. Nor is there a systematic way of placing orders, purchasing and actually obtaining such goods. This has significantly lowered the quality and effectiveness of extramural education in the past two years. In general, the existing administrative structure of education concentrates upon formal schooling and pre-school institutions; extramural education institutions are stepchildren. Such a situation cannot be allowed to continue.

If we wish to renew the content and improve the quality of extramural education, we must fundamentally alter the provisioning of such institutions. They must be given access to the most advanced contemporary technology, electronic and other equipment designed specifically to meet the needs of the school-age cohort. Expansion of the system must be the domain of district-level decision making bodies. The existing system must be fundamentally modernized and reconstructed with funds from the central budget as well as from local soviets. Priority in design and construction must be given to smaller facilities located close to the place of residence. New designs must be created for integrated sports and cultural centers, functionally adapted to meet simultaneously academic and recreational needs. Priority must be given to developing careful designed summer recreational camps appropriate for various age groups, a diversity of activities, as well as for family recreation and even recuperation.

Teachers of Extramural Education

Conditions in this area reflect the generally dismal state of affairs in extramural education. Despite the constant growth over the past twenty years in the number of teachers in this area, specialized training is inadequate and turnover high. (Many directors of clubs, circles, etc., were amateur volunteers or teachers moonlighting from other jobs.)

Teachers in extramural education institutions are the lowest paid professionals in the sphere of education. Between 1970 and 1990 for the economy as a whole per capita income rose from 126.1 rubles to 277 rubles. In education, salaries rose from 109 rubles to 204 rubles, and in extramural education the increase was from 81.5 to 170 rubles. This miserly salary is further reduced by the administrative practice of fines imposed when students fail to attend. . . a procedure which does little to enhance the prestige of the profession. There are no incentives in the system to encourage the teacher to work harder or more effectively.

Within the system of extramural education institutions so-called circle leaders (or group leaders: *rukovoditeli kruzhkov*) play an especially important role, and comprise up to 80 percent of all employees in this sphere. Most (76 percent) work in children's palaces or homes where, accordingly, the opportunities are best for providing a diversity of activities and the best professional conditions. In more specialized organizations such as clubs for young naturalists or scientists, there is a dearth of trained group leaders, since the low pay is a disincentive to trained engineers and scientists. Thus, most circle leaders in such groups are moonlighting from other jobs. Another disincentive here is that such group leaders must themselves think up ways to make sure their clubs are provided with the necessary equipment and supplies.

We need to consider the motivations of those who serve as circle directors; this occupation enjoys very low prestige among professionals in the economy, in the worlds of culture and art whence they come. The low pay and absence of merit incentives virtually guarantee that there will always be vacancies and that virtually anyone can take the job. Even today there is no scale of job rankings or skill qualifications in the sphere of extramural education that would allow for differentiated salary scales. Few measures have been taken (exhibitions, competitions, displays) to enhance the prestige of this work. Group leaders are not accorded the social benefits offered to teachers (preferential access to housing, the right to a full pension for teachers willing to work as group directors, extended vacations). Honorary titles such as Merited Education Employee of the Russian Federation or Merited Teacher of the RSFSR are not awarded to them. Currently one in three circle directors has no training in education. However, no systematic effort is underway to retrain or enhance their qualifications.

The other major category of extramural education employees is that of methodologist. Currently there is no standard training for this position, though more is being done in the area of retraining than for circle directors. Methodologists are generally former teachers or employees of pedagogical research institutes working on a contract basis, or recent graduates of pedagogical institutes whose last year of schooling was devoted to specialized training in methods. . . .

At present employees in the sphere of extramural education show little interest in leadership roles. The high turnover, shortage of qualified candidates, and unsystematic recruitment procedures mean that administrative positions are often filled by people with little experience or interest in the field. The roots of this problem can be seen in: the extensive professional training involved with no certainty of rewards; the high degree of responsibility combined with low prospects of advancement or of increased rewards; the long work day and absence of compensation for overtime; the absence of firm legal protections and the low social status of the position.

In sum, a review of the situation points to the low status of those working in extramural education in comparison to general education teachers, and indifference to their plight on the part of local soviets, trade unions and the educational bureaucracy.

Today we must focus our efforts on training professionals in this sphere with a broad and sound fundamental background, and certainly not narrow subject specialists. We need to avoid the extremes of narrow overspecialization and total unpreparedness (subject specialists dragooned into the position of "class leader"). The contemporary *vospitatel'* is poorly prepared in the methodology of upbringing and in child psychology, and lacks the ability to infuse the learning process with an element of play or creativity.

The problem is that there is no systematic effort underway to train specialists to work with children outside the classroom, both during and after the schoolday. The state must intervene to establish an inter-ministerial program to train or retrain specialists in this area.

A Description of Curricula and Methods

In the area of curricula and methods, systematic scholarly research is lacking, and programs have been constructed haphazardly. Out of these haphazard programs, mostly developed in early seventies, came, at the end of that decade, a number of anthologies (at present there are fifteen such), unifying the curricula according to type of extramural activity. Such recommended curricula provide for a course of varying length: from 144 hours a year, to 216 hours, and to 360 hours (based on a school year of thirty six weeks, with a load of four, six and ten hours respectively). Of 366 curricula, twenty percent are based on a program lasting four to five years, fifty percent on a program lasting three to four years, and twenty percent on a program lasting only one to two years. There are eighty seven different curricula providing for short-term activities (summer camps, recuperative camps, etc.) based on an eighteen-hour (weekly) schedule.

The curriculum of extramural education is in need of a fundamental overhead based upon systematic research. Such efforts were earlier sponsored by the Ministry of Education and later by the State Committee of Education, and must now be financed by the Ministry of Education of the RSFSR.

Teacher Training in the RSFSR

Supply and Demand

The most urgent task facing teacher training institutions up to the present has been to remedy the deficit of teachers available to the schools. The remedy has been the *extensive* approach; i.e., to open wide the doors of admission to teachers' institutes and schools. The system of teacher training today comprises ninety-four pedagogical institutes with three branch campuses, 350 teacher training colleges (*uchilishcha*), and eighty-nine inservice institutions for teachers. At present virtually every *oblast'* in the republic has its own institute offering training in virtually every speciality required by the school.

For the 1990 school year the admissions quota (plan) for teacher training colleges was set at 79,450. As for pedagogical institutes, the plan called for 67,200 new students. Over the past twenty years, the number of pedagogical institutes has declined from ninety seven to ninety four, yet admissions quotas have risen 145 percent. This fact testifies to the strains imposed upon the system of teacher training at the college level. To worsen matters, in recent years a tendency has emerged to convert pedagogical institutes into universities. Between 1968 and 1975 alone, ten such pedagogical institutes were converted. So, just as the demand was sharply increasing for specialists for the schools, for the pre-school system and for extramural education institutions, the supply was being cut back. Thus, in a number of regions, such as Tver and Tiumen *oblasts*, the Iakutsk and Kalmyk autonomous republics and Krasnodar *krai*, there is a new need for pedagogical institutions and branch campuses.

Despite the increase in absolute terms of the number of specialists to be produced by pedagogical institutes, the projected proportion of such specialists to the total number of teachers with a higher education remained unchanged--that is, most teachers remained generalists. In fact, recently the proportion has actually declined, from 5.2 percent in 1985 to 4.8 percent in 1990. To make matters worse, the real output of such institutions is considerably lower than called for by state planning (the gap can be explained by the declining prestige of the profession, low wages, long hours and conditions at work in general). In short, we can conclude that the existing system of teacher training at the university level is not meeting the needs of the schools. Thus, the shortage of qualified teachers increased from 126,300 in 1982 to 147,600 in 1990. And recently, the growing deficit stems largely from the outflow of the most qualified teachers to work in joint enterprises, cooperatives or to leave the country entirely. Activist teachers are leaving to work in alternative schools.

As a result, the primary school today--that most vital rung in the ladder of lifelong education--employs 178,000 teachers (62 percent of the total) without a higher education. In rural areas the situation is even worse; there 75.2 percent of all elementary school teachers and 4.6 percent of secondary school teachers do not have a university level education. Worst of all are the villages of Tver, Perm, and Orel regions, where 17 percent, 12 percent and 11.2 percent respectively of all secondary school teachers are underqualified. And of the 208,800 thousand graduates of pedagogical institutes during the Eleventh Five Year Plan only 180,900 took teacher positions, while no fewer than 155,500 teachers left the schools during the same time. We are thus talking about a chronic shortage of teachers, a shortage which has been worsening in recent years.

Teacher training institutes provide training in all the subject disciplines, as well as in pre-school, elementary and special education. In 1987 a number ofpedagogical institutes began to train school psychologists as well. Accordingly, the intake was increased in the various disciplines as demonstrated by Table 19.14. The table shows that between 1985 and 1990 the planned intake for pedagogical institutes rose by 11.5 percent. The greatest increases were for specialists in *vospitanie*, in psychology, special education, elementary military training (eliminated in the schools in 1991) and physical culture, and production

TABLE 19.14

Changes in the Plan Targets for Admissions to Pedagogical Institutes, by Speciality

	1985	1990	Increase
Mathematics	8,706	8,737	.3
Physics	4,793	4,989	4.0
Chemistry	744	1,113	49.5
Biology	3,482	3,810	9.4
Geography	2,199	3,004	36.7
History	3,719	4,446	19.5
Russian Language and Literature	8,260	8,866	7.3
Russian Language and Literature in Minority Schools	1,463	854	-41.7
Foreign Languages and Literature	7,153	7,763	8.5
Labor	2,744	3,272	19.2
Physical Culture	2,845	3,840	34.9
Military Drill	752	1,381	83.6
Music	734	697	-5.1
Draftsmanship and Fine Arts	1,027	1,137	10.7
Pedagogy and Psychology	1,635	3,668	124.3
Pedagogy and Methods (primary schools)	7,252	7,929	9.3
Pedagogy and Methods of *Vospitanie*	50	300	500
Defectology	739	974	31.8
Total	58,297	67,231	11.5

(labor training). Such growth can be explained by the introduction in the schools of new permanent positions, especially extramural activities organizers and school psychologists; by the growing demand for special education-- reflecting the growing numbers of special needs children in our country, and by the special situation of physical education, basic military training and labor instructors in our schools. The planned increase in admissions of students specializing in certain specialities such as chemistry and geography can be explained by the chronic shortages in such subjects and by the disproportionate attention given them in the curriculum despite the inadequate recompense offered. We should also take note of the decline in numbers of specialists in the area of "Russian language and literature in the minority school" (by 41.7 percent) and in music (5.1 percent), caused by repeated changes in the plan in these areas and by the introduction of new curricula in the native as well as Russian language in the minority school.

Beginning in 1984 a number of the country's pedagogical institutes began to address the issue of shortages of trained personnel by experimenting with or actually introducing new specializations such as: specialists in teaching in boarding homes and children's homes; specialists for small rural schools, competent to teach four or five subjects; teachers of foreign languages for pre-school institutions; early childhood crafts specialists, etc.

The State of Teacher Training

According to sociological surveys, eighty three percent of teachers are dissatisfied with the training they received. Most graduates of pedagogical institutions emphasize the inferior quality of education there, and believe that they were not adequately trained for their profession. The existing shortage of qualified faculty at teacher training institutions can be explained largely by the content of instruction at pedagogical institutes and schools.

A key problem in this area is the primitive nature of the curriculum at teacher training institutions. At present most work being done in this area consists primarily of meaningless phraseology where, for example, it is stated that the graduate of the pedagogical institute should be characterized by "a love for children, the ability and need to give one's all to them," (*Concept Paper on Pedagogical Education*, published by the State Committee of Education, 1990), or of a variety of model curricula listing, according to whatever plan, the names of courses, and how many hours to devote to each. Most such new curricula do not have the detailed course plans to back them up. It must be noted that there is little relationship between the general principles purportedly shaping teacher training, the actual course content of the training program, the curricula and the approaches employed. Moreover, as a result of what actually takes place within the walls of such institutions, the kind of teachers we produce are capable only of turning out conformist "living tools" of the production system.

As for local arms of the educational bureaucracy, they show no interest in the type of training prospective teachers receive, for they are preoccupied with finding replacements for vacant spots. All pedagogical schools (*uchilishcha*) are under the control of the deputy directors of personnel of the UNO (local education office).

As a result the situation is distinctly worsening in the realm of teacher training; certain negative tendencies have acquired the force of tradition and blot out all individual strengths and interests among the student body in pedagogical institutions. The result is a decline in motivation and indifference to genuine learning among the majority of students. Massive surveys have uncovered disturbing conditions among the student body: a growing dissatisfaction with or indifference to their studies, to scholarly research, to public service, to self-government, to social interaction. In recent years anxiety about careers and about society in general has mounted. The absence of differentiated approaches to teacher training, manifested in the uniformity of the degrees issued, presents a serious obstacle to instruction. This derives from the unified, but also uniform, system of higher teacher training, which offers only one type of institution at the tertiary level: the pedagogical institute. The present pedagogical institute takes no account of the present day proliferation of a diversity of levels and types of general and specialized education secondary schools; in fact it stands in the way of this diversity. The system of inservice training for faculty at pedagogical institutions is also highly outdated.

According to sociological research 93.6 percent of teachers are dissatisfied with existing types of inservice training. The system now in place of inservice training does not adequately account for previous levels and training of the individual teacher, does not provide for the timely inclusion of advances in pedagogy, whether foreign or our own, and leaves little room for creativity on the part of the individual teacher. There is little material incentive for enhancement of skills levels. In this area there is little or no cooperation between in service training institutions or university level retraining and skills enhancement programs for faculty at pedagogical institutes.

The lack of coordination between schools, pedagogical institutes, inservice institutions, and the educational bureaucracy has produced a situation wherein virtually no institution takes responsibility for helping young teachers adapt to their new and changing environment. The process of training teachers has turned into a set of ritualistic exercises at so-called experimental schools attached to pedagogical institutions. There is no sustained effort to incorporate or implement fundamentally new technologies or content in education. It is revealing that a great variety of cooperative enterprises set up to retrain teachers and introduce them to modern psychology have enjoyed considerable success.

An analysis of the scholarship underlying teacher training demonstrates that there is a gap between practice and the theoretical discourse among scholars in the area of pedagogy. Most works by scholars conceptualizing teacher training are obscure, pedantic and vapid.

A study of officially sanctioned research projects (*goszakaz NIR*) for pedagogical institutes for the period 1986-1990 shows that one quarter of the themes listed reflect an ideological formulation: for example, themes such as "Increasing the Effectiveness of Ideological Upbringing in the Schools" or "Perfecting the Forms and Methods of Communist Upbringing." Sixty five percent begin with the words "Perfecting. . ." or "The Path to Intensifying. . ." etc. We look in vain for a single theme devoted to analysis of new processes or content, whether in the school itself or in the pedagogical institutes.

With the percentage of gross national product devoted to education holding steady (at 4.9 percent for the Soviet Union, compared to 6.5 percent for the USA and 5.8 percent for Africa as a whole), the number of students at pedagogical institutes has doubled over the past thirty years, while faculty at these institutions has aged considerably and undergone a marked feminization. The percentage of faculty over 60 has doubled; the proportion of males has declined to 17.3 percent.

At a time when each pedagogical institution is confronted with the need to train teachers in a broad range of profiles, the general faculty level of professional mastery has declined and the course load increased. In the 1989 school year the yearly course load for senior and middle level faculty was 750 to 800 hours of instruction; for junior faculty and assistants, 950 to 1,050 hours. Such a course load leaves no time for scholarly activity or for skills upgrading.

At the same we must not overlook the expanding movement for innovation within the pedagogical institutes. This movement can be divided into two branches. On the one hand, this includes "common sense" attempts to improve existing practice. Here we see initiative groups of teachers using empirical methods to introduce new content and processes into practice. On the other hand, the movement for innovation includes attempts to create alternative systems of teacher training. New technologies and new content are drawn up based upon fundamentally new approaches to learning and instruction. Nevertheless, official pedagogy keeps clear of these developments, and for all practical purposes today there exists no serious scholarship in this area. Nor is there, in reality, differentiated training to prepare teachers for the variety of secondary schools (now emerging), for rural schools or for nationality schools.

A major shortcoming in the administration of higher pedagogical institutions is the absence of juridical autonomy, whether in terms of academic or of financial self-management. For example, pedagogical institutes have the right to alter only fifteen percent of the set curriculum, and they received this right only two years ago. They do not have the right to use the revenues generated by fees from various services offered to create a supplementary wage fund. Salaries are tightly regulated, which results, as noted above, in the feminization and aging of the profession: the salary of a new teacher with a degree from a

TABLE 19.15

Financing Pedagogical Education

	1985	1986	1987	1988	1989
Annual expenditures on pedagogical education (thousands of rubles)	271	284	319.3	354.7	391.4
Basic capital fund (millions of Rubles)	606	622	647	670	697
Cost of educating one student (per year) (Rubles)	1,069	1,090	1,292.8	1,383.1	1,527

universal level teacher training institution is set at 160 rubles a month. Table 19.15 provides an overview of changes in recent years in the level of financing of pedagogical education.

. . . The resources allocated to pedagogical institutes are calculated according to patently antiquated schedules which take no account of inflation. . . . As the number of students in *pedvuzy* has expanded, the residual principle of financing has led to a deterioration in physical plant, and a chronic shortage of qualified teaching personnel. Only one quarter of *pedvuzy* have buildings more or less suited to their mission; the vast majority are housed in buildings dating from the eighteenth and nineteenth centuries. . . . The space available each student has declined from 7.9 sqaure meters in 1985 to 7.2 square meters in 1990--this despite statutory norms of fifteen to eighteen square meters. Dormitories are also cramped, average space there having declined to 4.4 square meters per resident. In Western Siberia only 65-70 percent of those needing space in a dormitory can find a place. If one keeps in mind that the greatest demand for dormitory space comes from students whose homes are in the village, then it follows that in the future the shortage of teachers in the countryside will only worsen.

The backwardness evident in terms of classroom space and living quarters, of catering and health services (forty percent of students in *pedvuzy* suffer from chronic illnesses), the general lack of social benefits both for teachers and for students, as well as the persistence of conditions rendering normal instruction virtually impossible, present a real threat of outbreaks of disorders in this system. There have already been student strikes in pedvuzy in Orekhovo-Zuevo, Tomsk, Michurinsk, Vladimir, and Piatigorsk.

Study of the teacher training system shows that it is incapable of overcoming the shortage of teachers in the schools, it lacks modern instructional technologies, it has a grossly inadequate material base, it has no way to attract enough qualified personnel, and it is hampered by a maze of regulations. In consequence, the system is capable only of producing teachers able to work only according to set routines.

The existing state of affairs is such that the system of *pedvuzy* is unprepared for the transition to a market economy, and especially to train future teachers on a large scale who are ready to live and work in a market environment, to contribute to this environment.

The Production System for
the Schools of the RSFSR

A study of the material and technological underpinnings of the republic's school system permits us to conclude that a serious crisis exists in providing for the needs of our schools.

The basic deficiency in our planning system is that in the attempt to equalize the resources available to the various educational institutions, the need to differentiate was lost sight of, for example, between rural and urban schools, between dwarf schools and large consolidated schools. For example, at present (vocational) work stations at rural and urban schools are provided with precisely the same equipment, despite the obvious differences between life in the village and in the city. Rural vocational schools, school garden plots, etc., do not have available the necessary mini-technology or equipment. Today some sixty percent of urban and seventy percent of rural schools do not have workshop facilities. Inadequate school design, the absence of necessary equipment, and egregious shortcomings in manufacturing that equipment which is available, have resulted in quite unsatisfactory conditions in subject-area laboratories. Measures adopted some years ago in order to ensure timely repair of equipment have not been implemented in any region of the republic. Spare parts necessary for such repair are not being produced by the industries under the purview of the ministry nor by other enterprises in the republic.

We must also call attention to serious deficiencies in the training of teachers and the lack of the skills necessary to properly use equipment, instruments and other classroom aids. Here the most salient example is the program to computerize the schools, which took no account of teacher training in this area nor of the extreme unreliability of locally built computers, or of the absence of appropriate software. In recent years, no fewer than a billion rubles have been spent on computerizing education. It was assumed that the existing system of training teachers to work with computers and to teach a course on the "Basics of Informatics and Computers" would initially suffice for the introduction of computers into the schools. However, even the first results of these efforts demonstrate that the lack of a systematic approach to implementing computer technologies has resulted in considerable waste. The republic's schools at present have more than eleven thousand instructional computer stations which are not backed up by trained teaching personnel, software or maintenance provisioning. The diversity and incompatibility of models, the absence of reliable ways or channels to compile, analyze or communicate information on instructional approaches in this area means that we cannot talk even of the establishment of local computer networks in the school system.

The existing categories for instructional aids and equipment make attempts to diversify instruction or to allow for alternative approaches very difficult. That equipment which is produced is inadequate to allow integrated use in the classroom. At the same time, output of elementary types of equipment is sorely inadequate: of metal and wood-working tools, for example. In addition, only fifty percent of the sewing machines or film projectors, and ten percent of the televisions needed for the classroom are produced annually.

If we consider the pedagogical or didactic functions of the classroom equipment produced today, we see that much of it is unchanged from designs drawn up decades ago. A check of the approximately 2,500 types of instrumentation or equipment produced for the schools shows that more than half are antiquated in terms both of design and of classroom use. At the same time, the kind of equipment or instrumentation needed to demonstrate modern technological processes is simply not being produced. Instruction takes place exclusively with the aid of traditional tools: the book, the test tube, and in rare cases, the film projector. For all practical purposes our schools are devoid of intra- or inter-school telecasting facilities, video machines, microfilm readers, etc. In especially lamentable shape are rehabilitative institutions, where extreme shortages exist, for example, of Braille typewriters, opticons and of equipment for the hearing-impaired.

The design and production of school equipment takes place in two ways, including specializing enterprises under the ministry and those under contract from other branches of the economy. Since 1985 the proportion of output generated by ministry-controlled enterprises has declined from 17 percent to 6.7 percent. Since 1986 the list of items produced by in-house factories has declined from 420 to 338. A basic cause has been the removal from production of outdated items as well as the lack of incentive for enterprises to undertake new types of production. In addition, the weak economic condition and poor quality of the workforce make it difficult for such ministry-run enterprises to make the necessary adjustments. The attempts made over the past five years to modernize and reorganize existing plants or to introduce new capacity were done in line with the old scheme of organization of production, which did not provide the flexibility necessary to assimilate new technologies or to design new outputs. . . . The overall increase in output for the last five-year plan was only 9.8 percent (compared with 19.9 percent during the previous five-year plan). The total increase amounted to 1,069 billion rubles, which is simply inadequate for the needs of the schools for equipment, and does not provide a stable environment for these enterprises.

The actual productive potential of these ministry-run factories, the absence of a systematic approach to design of new equipment, the entirely inadequate level of capital investment in such enterprises, the lack of legally enforceable contractual guarantees that the schools will be supplied with the necessary equipment, and the genuine instability existing in this production sphere, mean in practice that upon entering into a market environment the specialized enterprises operating under the ministry are inevitability forced to cut back on production (in the present year, original production goals had to be reduced by more than 2.3 million rubles, for example).

Analysis of the basic production equipment available to such factories demonstrates that of 3,620 pieces of equipment more than a third (1,360) have been in operation more than twenty years. Moreover, the proportion of work done by hand rather than machine is more than thirty nine percent.

Another major obstacle to increasing production and improving quality is related to personnel: a high level of turnover and a shortage of skilled technicians and workers. . . .

It must be emphasized that virtually the entire increase in obtaining instruments, equipment or classroom aids has come from outside enterprises producing by contract with the ministry. If we compare the sum of such production in 1986 and 1990, we see it has risen from 162.3 to 420 million rubles; orders from rural schools have increased from 80 to 166 million rubles. Thus, the relative share of production for rural schools has declined from 49.3 percent to 39.5 percent, which speaks to a decline in the provisioning of schools in the countryside.

In previous years the basis stimulus to the production of school supplies and equipment was in special incentives regulated by the government (linked with categorizing such output as consumer goods). With the ongoing changes in the economic situation, the only way to maintain, and eventually to bolster production is through direct material incentives (to such factories producing under contract). In this connection, delays in producing the appropriate regulations (*normativnye akty*) as well as the failure to take into account the needs of education in such regulations, will lead to the exacerbation of an already difficult situation, in terms both of the provisioning and organization of the educational system.

The schools of the Russian Federation at present are not adequately protected from arbitrary re-allocation by the State Committee of Education of resources earmarked as capital resources for education.

Despite the fact that over the past five years measures have been taken to increase the delivery to schools of equipment and instructional aids, and that over this period such deliveries have totalled 1.2 billion rubles, the unmet demand for equipment (using even the existing, outdated listings) amounts to forty percent.

Production of pre-school and school furniture is an area of special concern. Even in terms of existing prices and categories of furniture the annual shortfall in production amounts to two hundred million rubles. This, despite the fact that ninety percent of all specialized enterprises for the production of school furniture in the USSR are located within the territory of the Russian Federation. Moreover, the designs long in use, the age categories for which furniture is produced, the materials and technology used in production, do not live up to health and sanitary standards appropriate for children. The republic has no facilities for repairing school furniture, and the occasional attempts made my teachers and pupils themselves to make up for this gap have been of little account. To the general problem of school furniture must be added that of school desks. No other developed country has resorted to using plywood for desk tops, an approach resorted to in several areas of the republic.

A look at the actual state of affairs in the area of sports facilities demonstrates that conditions are genuinely catastrophic at both the pre-school and school level. In actuality, there is no production of sports equipment for the small village school or for pre-school institutions.

In sum, our analysis shows that it will be necessary to fundamentally restructure the practices by which we plan, design and produce school equipment. A new nomenclature of items needed by the schools must be drawn up taking into account the diversity of ways of organizing instruction (now emerging) and paying heed also to differences in way of life of the various nationalities and regions of the RSFSR.

Education in the Russian Federation
In the Transition Period:
A Program of Stabilization and Development
ed. by E. D. Dneprov, V. S. Lazarev and V. S. Sobkin
(Moscow, 1991)

Notes

1. A table accompanying this text shows that the print run of *Doshkol'noe Vospitanie* was 409,100; it rose to 747,900 in 1985, then to 997,000 in 1989, and fell to 948,300 in 1990. The reason for the discrepancy between the texts and these figures is not clear.

2. *Materialy o sostoianii narodnogo obrazovaniia v RSFSR za 1985-1986 god* (Moscow, 1987), p. 56; *Narodnoe obrazovanie RSFSR v 1989 godu.* Part II: *Obshcheobrazovatel'nye shkoly* (Moscow, 1990), p. 10.

3. This increase occurred exclusively in the cities, while in the countryside the ratio has remained virtually unchanged (1.11 in 1980, 1.12 in 1990).

4. This was achieved in 1991: a Federal Council on Nationality Education as well as an Institute of National Problems in Education were established: see *Vestnik obrazovaniia*, No. 3 (March), 1991, pp. 25-35; see also an article describing recent changes by the director of the Institute, Michael Kuzmin, "The Rebirth of the National School," in *Soviet Education Study Bulletin*, Vol. 10, No. 1 (Spring, 1992) pp. 17-23.

20

The Educational System
of the Russian Federation

The system of education of the Russian Federation is of a state-public character (this implies that public organizations and institutions as well as state structures are involved in governance). It is organized as an uninterrupted continuity of levels or stages of education, realized through educational institutions of different types.

The state system of education includes:

- pre-school education;
- general secondary education;
- secondary vocational training;
- specialized secondary education;
- higher education;
- post-graduate education and improvement of professional skills;
- courses for training, retraining and improving professional skills of personnel.

Today a non-state system of educational institutions (parallel to the state one) is being created with the support of the Ministry of Education of Russia. To date this system consists mostly of pre-school institutions and general secondary schools of different types. By the beginning of 1992 there were more than 500 such institutions.

The structure of the system of education of Russia, types of educational institutions and the stages of continuous education are represented in figure 19.1.

Pre-School Education

According to vital statistics, 2.0-2.5 million children are born in Russia every year. Before entering school most (about 70%) are educated not only in the family but also at pre-school educational institutions.

The main goal of pre-school institutions is to assist families in providing appropriate conditions for educating children of pre-school age (under 6-7 years) with due regard for parental interests as well as for the distinctive cultural, national, ethnic, religious, social and economic features of a region. Such institutions are to nurture the child's health and promote his or her normal physical, mental, intellectual and personality development; they are to provide for the emotional well-being of every child, and establish close ties with parents so as to promote harmonious individual growth.

In terms of goals to be achieved pre-school educational institutions can be divided into the following types:

- providing for the child's general development;
- compensating for deficiencies in the child's psychic or physical development;
- serving a custodial (creche) function;
- combined functions.

The network of pre-school institutions can be presented in quantitative terms as follows: children first entering pre-school under three years old--30%; after completing their third birthday--40%; and not enrolling in pre-school institutions--30%; children departing from the pre-school system at the age of six--15%; at the age of seven--45%; children six years old beginning the equivalent of first-grade instruction while still enrolled at a pre-school institution--10%; children enrolled at special health facilities or special education institutions--0.5%.

According to statistics for 1991, there are 87,800 pre-school educational institutions, enrolling 9,634,700 children, with the total number of personnel equal to 968,300.

The basic problems confronting the system of pre-school education are as follows:

- a shortage of pre-school institutions (about 10% of children cannot be admitted);
- many institutions are overloaded (there are on the average 108 children for every 100 places);
- a shortage of skilled personnel staff (only 75% of educators have a degree in education, and only 17% of this group have graduated from institutions of higher learning);

- only 2% of children have the opportunity to spend the summer in the countryside.
- the nutrition of children in pre-school educational institutions is unsatisfactory.

General Secondary Education

General (secondary) education is the core of the Russian school system. It includes:

- general (secondary) schools;
- schools specializing in accelerated study of selected subjects, gymnasiums, lyceums;
- evening schools;
- boarding schools;
- schools for children with special needs (for mentally and physically handicapped children);
- extra-mural educational institutions.

The main goals of schools offering a general education are as follows:

- providing favorable conditions for intellectual, moral, emotional and physical growth;
- promoting a scientific world outlook;
- enabling students to master systematic knowledge about nature, society, man and his activities and to acquire necessary skills.

General secondary education includes:

- primary school (1st level of general secondary education, 3-4 years);
- basic school (2nd level - basic secondary education, 5 years);
- high school (3rd level of general secondary education, 2-3 years).

Most children receive their education in comprehensive secondary schools. The central features of this system are given below:

1. The number of children entering school every year is from 2.0 to 2.5 million (2.159.689 children in 1991).

   - about 70% enter school at the age of 7 to take the 10-year course of studying.
   - about 20% enter school at the age of 6 and take the 11-year course.

- about 10% enter school at age 7, their schooling lasting for 11 years.

Children of the latter group take the 1st year of study while at pre-school institutions and enter the second grade of primary school.

2. At the start of the 1991/92 school year there were 66,679 comprehensive secondary schools in Russia, enrolling 19,929,693 children and employing 1,464,829 teachers. These institutions included:

    - 17.1 thousand primary schools (25%),
    - 14.6 thousand basic schools (23%),
    - 33.0 thousand complete secondary schools (52%).

Basic secondary schools provide primary and basic secondary education. Complete secondary schools provide primary, basic secondary, and a full secondary education. The proportion of those enrolled in the full program is growing steadily. In contrast about 30 years ago it constituted only 12% while the corresponding figure for primary schools was 62%.

3. Virtually all students (close to 100%) receive their primary and secondary education at secondary schools. After finishing basic secondary school 55% of students continue studying at high schools, 35% enroll in vocational training institutions and 10% of students combine work and study in the evening and by other inservice (e.g. by-correspondence) educational programs.
    After finishing (complete) secondary school:

    - 30% enter higher educational institutions;
    - 55% enter institutions of vocational training;
    - 15% combine work and study in evening and other inservice educational institutions.

Up to 20% of students receive their education in secondary schools specializing in accelerated study of selected subjects, lyceums and gymnasiums (the number who would like to study in such institutions is 1.5 greater than the number of places). By the start of the 1991-1992 school year there were:

- 7,398 schools specializing in accelerated study of selected subjects enrolling a total of 1,107,917 children:
- 195 lyceums enrolling 114,535 children;
- 303 gymnasiums with a total enrollment of 228,835.

4. The non-Russian share of the population of the Russian Federation is

about 19%. There are about 120 nations and ethnic groups with their own national language. Study of the native language is conducted in so-called national schools in order to give non-Russian students the opportunity to improve their command of their native language. Recently the number of students attending national schools has increased almost twofold; the number of native languages studied in schools has gone up by 20%. In 1990 as many as 66 native languages were taught in various different schools to 1,700,000 students.

5. Besides traditional secondary schools there are educational institutions of the boarding type for children deprived of parental care. In 1990 Russia had 1,007 such institutions with a total enrollment of 91,100 thousand, including:

   - 43,500 children receiving an education in 542 orphanages;
   - 45,800 children enrolled in 185 boarding schools;
   - 1,800 children being educated in 280 family-run orphanages [foster homes].

6. Physically or mentally handicapped children can be educated either at specialized rehabilitative educational institutions or in specialized classes attached to public schools. According to data from the beginning of the 1991-92 school year, there were 1,843,000 specialized institutions enrolling 374,475 children with special needs, whereas 76,902 children were taught in special classes.

7. The main problems facing the contemporary secondary school can be singled out as follows:

   - a shortage of accommodations: in 21,531 schools children study in 2 (22% of schoolchildren) or 3 (0.4%) shifts; the number studying in multiple shifts is 4,696,626;
   - a shortage (over 10%) of teachers;
   - most curriculum materials have become obsolete;
   - inadequate provision of equipment (e.g., only 12,000 schools have computers).

Vocational and Professional Education

Secondary vocational education is the first stage of a professional education which has as its mission training qualified specialists for all branches of national economy. Individuals can train for their profession through a network of technical secondary schools, "vocational" *technicums* providing technical education, or offering a humanities and arts profile, as well as *uchilishche* providing comprehensive professional training.

The principal task of vocational educational institutions is to create favorable conditions for trainees in obtaining a working profession or specialty along with a general education.

Vocational educational institutions enable students to gain a profession through day-time or evening study, as well as at extramural faculties combining work with study. Students can choose among 117 professions. The duration of the training course is from 2 to 4 years. (The main types of educational institutions include vocational schools and vocational technical *technicums*).

Vocational schools generally provide a secondary education and training in a manual occupation. According to data for December 31, 1990, the following figures obtain:

TABLE 20.1

Vocational Education
(Secondary Level)

- number of schools	4,300
- number of teachers	184,000
- number of students	2 million
- annual intake	1.2 million
- at day-time faculties	0.3 million
- at evening faculties	0.4 million

The number of students entering day-time faculties:

- immediately after completing basic secondary school	0.4 million (20% of all school-children)
- with a basic secondary education as well as work experience	0.2 million
- immediately after graduating from complete secondary school	0.2 million (10% of all school-children)

Vocational-technical colleges (technicums) prepare specialists (technicians, foremen, etc.) with a secondary education. According to the statistics, in 1991 there were:

TABLE 20.2

Vocational Education
(Advanced Level)

- technicums	2,600
- students, total enrollment	2,300,000
- Annual intake	750,000
- at day-time faculties	500,000
- at extramural faculties	250,000

In 1990 the entrance statistics were as follows:

Number of students entering vocational technical colleges:

- after basic secondary school	280,000 (15% of all school-children)
- after completing secondary school	420,000 (20% of all school-children)
- after secondary vocational school	50,000

Vocational institutions are also to solve the problem of re-training personnel. Today they provide annual re-training of about 400,000 adult workers; according to estimates this figure could be tripled.

The main problems facing institutions of vocational training are as follows:

- the inadequate state of the material and technical base (e.g., about 60% of the machine-tools used in the schools are obsolete);
- as enterprises to which vocational training institutions are attached fail, it is necessary to find additional support in order to ensure the survival of these institutions;

TABLE 20.3

The System of Higher Education

- institutions of higher learning	514
- annual student enrollment	2.8 million
- annual number of students entering higher schools	580,000
of these:	
- at day-time faculties (without work experience)	310,000
- at day-time faculties (with work experience)	50,000
- at evening faculties	60,000
- at extramural faculties	160,000
- number of universities	42
- number of students	328,000
- annual number of students entering universities	68,000

- the number of students entering institutions of vocational training is consistently less than planned for (in 1991 the proportion was only 89.5%);
- the low social standing of students and the high level of crime (every third student belongs to a family of inadequate means; as many as 70,000 students (from the total number of 800,000 day-time students) were detained for all sorts of infringements of the law in 1990).

Higher Education

Higher education aims at training specialists with advanced qualifications and is offered by universities, institutes, academies, factory colleges, training centers and other scientific and training complexes.

With the exception of teacher training, higher education is beyond the jurisdiction of the Ministry of Education. A brief description of the state of the system of higher education (data for December 31, 1990) is given in table 20.3.

In 1991, about 400,000 people enrolled at VUZy. The corresponding figure for universities alone was 50,000.

The System of Teacher Training

The system of pedagogical education includes pedagogical universities, teacher training (or pedagogical) institutes and their affiliates (providing in-depth professional training), teacher (or pedagogical) *uchilishcha* (preparing teachers for primary schools) and the so-called institutes for *improving teachers' qualifications* (offering inservice training). At the outset of the 1991-92 school year the system looked as shown in Table 20.4.

TABLE 20.4

Teacher Training Institutions

- number of pedagogical universities	2
- number of students	21,000
- number of teacher training institutes	93
- number of students	437,000
- number of students who entered institutions of higher learning in 1991	105,000
- number of students who graduated from institutions of higher learning in 1991	74,000
- number of teacher-training *uchilishcha*	363
- number of students	295,000
- number of students who entered *uchilishcha* in 1991	105,000
- number of students graduated from *uchilishcha* in 1991	79,000
- number of teacher inservice institutes	89
- total enrollment in 1991	60,000

The main problems facing the teacher training system are as follows:

- inadequate facilities (there are a mere 7 square meters of floor space per student, that is 40% of the prescribed norm);
- a shortage of dormitories for students (only about 75% of can be

accommodated);
- inadequate provision of modern training equipment;
- inadequate students' stipends (lower than the subsistence wage);
- a 20% shortage of teachers;
- a 50% shortage of service staff;
- a decline in the number of teachers awarded a degree at teacher-training institutes, by 5% over the past 3 years and now constituting 45% of the total number of teachers.

The System of Postgraduate and Continuing Education

The system of education of the Russian Federation includes in addition to the types and structures described above:

- Post-graduate education: The highest level of continuous education. Post-graduate education can be obtained in the form of *improving professional skills* through a network of programs, institutes and refresher courses. Post-graduate education can also be obtained through full-time pursuit of an advanced degree (*kandidat* or *doktor*).
- Other structures of continuous education have been established to meet the diverse interests and abilities of children and youth and the individual educational demands of the adult population. These structures include: children's musical, artistic, dancing and sports schools, "centers of aesthetic education", "students' houses" [*doma shkol'nikov*], young technician's stations, naturalists' and outdoor clubs (*stantsii*), centers to promote interest in technology, ensembles and houses of vocational culture, "people's universities," various institutions attached to amateur sports societies, centers of adult education, lecture agencies, diverse forms of parental education and support, sports sections and clubs at enterprises, organizations and trade unions as well as other ways of disseminating scientific and technological, public-interest and political, arts-related and other sorts of information.

According to the data from 1990 the Ministry of Education supervises 7,275 extra-school institutions of various types, with 6,500,000 students (32% of all students) participating.

The Educational Industry and Publishing Houses

The Ministry of Education of Russia has under its authority:

- 15 industrial enterprises manufacturing products needed by educational institutions;
- a developed system of distribution [*kollektory*], including 110 commutators for distributing equipment to schools;
- publishing houses which produce teaching and methodological aids, curriculum materials, fiction, as well as 25 newspapers and magazines.

A significant proportion of the equipment needed by the school is produced by vocational schools: in 1991 such schools produced goods valued at 1,500 million rubles.

Governance in Education

The system of state managemental bodies supervising education in the Russian Federation has the following structure (see figure 20.1):

- the Ministry of Education of the Russian Federation;
- local ministries of education (of the republics constituting the Russian Federation);
- local boards of education, main administrations, committees and departments of education at the *oblast'* and *krai* level as well as local structures of governance for the autonomous republics;
- committees (departments) of education of the cities of Moscow and St. Petersburg.

Education management bodies of *raion*, municipal or city districts can be established at the discretion of local governmental bodies.

The above-mentioned governing bodies carry out the *unified* supervision of the system of state institutions of pre-school, secondary, vocational and technical, specialized secondary, teacher-training and extra-mural education at the federal, republican, regional territorial level.

At present the structure of educational governance is not strictly hierarchical, as republican, regional and territorial managemental bodies are not subordinate to the Ministry of Education of the Russian Federation. Nevertheless, educational policy is worked out at all levels with due account of the opinion of the Ministry of Education of Russia or with the ministry performing the coordinating functions. (See: The Resolution of the Government of the Russian

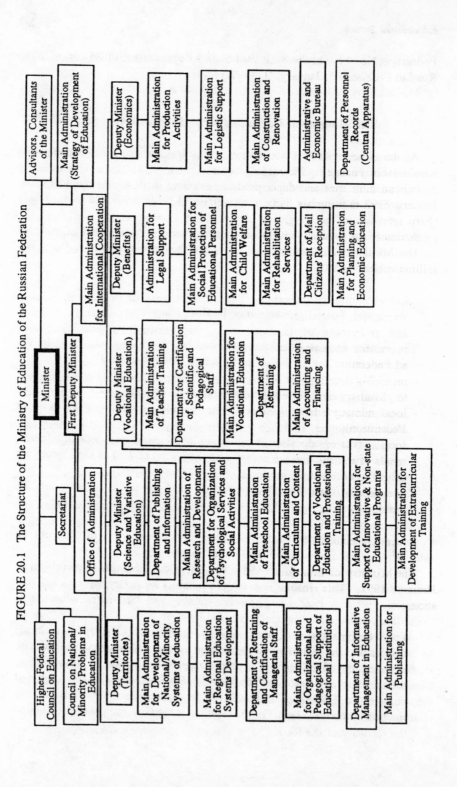

FIGURE 20.1   The Structure of the Ministry of Education of the Russian Federation

Federation No. 21 "On the System of State Administration of Education in the Russian Federation", January, 9, 1992.)

The Ministry of Education of the Russian Federation

At the close of 1991 the structure of the Russian government underwent considerable change. Whereas there were about 100 Union and over 50 republican ministries and departments functioning in Russia in the 1980s, by January 1992 the number had decreased fivefold. In turn, this resulted in a sharp increase in the weight of responsibility resting on the newly created ministries of the Russian Government, the Ministry of Education included.

The Ministry of Education of the Russian Federation is entrusted with the following basic tasks:

- implementing an integrated policy in the areas of pre-school, school, vocational, specialized secondary and extra-mural education; the training and re-training of teachers; promoting research in education; and promoting industries and services serving the contemporary needs of education;
- providing development of *a new core content* of education corresponding to global standards of education for all types of educational institutions;
- implementing federally-designed personnel policy aimed at the effective training, re-training and employment of qualified workers and specialists, from the pool of the young and unemployed population;
- representing the interests of the Russian Federation in the field of education within the Commonwealth of Independent States as well as at the international level;
- providing expert evaluation of federal and local projects and programs (in accordance with the Resolution of the Government of Russian Federation from December, 28, 1991, No. 79).

The Ministry of Education of the Russian Federation was reorganized in January, 1992. This reorganization was prompted by the following considerations:

- since termination of the activities of the USSR State Committee on Education, the Ministry of Education of the Russian Federation has assumed the functions of 20 out of 22 State Committee of Education departments and has assumed responsibility for the implementation of numerous ongoing programs in the field of education;
- the educational, academic and production institutions deployed throughout the territory of the Russian Federation and were previously subordinated

to the State Committee of Education have been transferred to the Ministry of Education of Russia;
- the composition and functions of the ministries of the Russian Federation have been altered; as a result, the Ministry of Education now supervises many training, academic and production institutions (and notably the entire system of specialized secondary education);
- the activity of the ministry needs to be brought into alignment with the social, economic and political transformation underway in Russia.

Structure of the Ministry of Education

Five major directions can be singled out in the new structure of the Ministry of Education:

Work with Territories

As democratization of society and decentralization of governance is implemented the ministry is altering its principles of interaction with regional structures of educational governance. Purely administrative relations are being replaced by advisory and coordinating ones. This determines the missions of the departments of the ministry included in this group:

- advisory services and coordination of regional activities in the field of education development;
- assisting local administrative structures in working out national and regional strategies and programs of education development; re-training administrative staff and acquainting them with innovative techniques to be introduced into educational practice through regional programs of education development.

Science and Variative Education

The units of this group are responsible for working out a strategy for renewing educational content through applications-oriented research in this field. The central mission is to provide scholarly back-up for experimental programs offering long term promise, that is:

- differentiation, individualization and humanization of education, new educational technologies, *new models of schools*, educational standards evaluation, extra-mural education, etc. This group is to provide support for innovative and unofficial educational programs, in particular for the development of lyceums, gymnasia and private schools.

Vocational Training

The departments of this group are expected to provide guidance and coordination for activities in the field of vocational, specialized secondary and teacher education as well as *re-training of teacher staff*. The priorities here are:

- restructuring the system of vocational training in line with structural changes in the national economy;
- integrating vocational schools and vocational technical colleges while providing the greatest possible variety of professional choice;
- organizing staff re-training at all levels appropriate for employment under new economic conditions; the reform of teachers training in line with future challenges; and intensive teacher re-training to stimulate new ways of thinking and innovative classroom approaches.

The content of higher and secondary pedagogical education, as well as the methods and forms of teacher training and re-training are closely integrated with general approaches to education worked out by the units of this and other groups.

Social Protection

The departments of this group are to provide legal support for educational development, for the social and health needs of children and educators, and for special-needs children, etc. These departments, under unstable economic conditions, must provide children a normal environment of study and leisure, and work to retrain teachers at school.

Economy

The mission of the departments of this group is to promote the material well-being of the school system, both through the traditional activities of school supply and construction as well as direct production, and through working out new relationships between education and the economy.

At the official level this implies developing more flexible taxation policies to stimulate investments in education, establishing a system by which schools can be diversely sponsored, and encouraging financing by local school authorities.

The departments of this unit are also to assist educational institutions in organizing their commercial activities which would not damage the process of training.

21

The Law of the Russian Federation on Education (Draft)

Explanatory Note

The current socio-economic and political situation of our society calls for fundamental changes in the legal relations, principles of economic organization, and socio-psychological perspectives which have arisen in the sphere of education.

In the immediate future it is imperative that the education system be readied for market relations and that the opportunities now unfolding in the new socio-economic circumstances be exploited. The educational system must be reconstructed so that enhanced efficiency becomes a vital concern of all types of educational institutions and those educators working in them.

Decentralization of the administration is called for in education, in order to reduce excessive regulation and to substantially empower the agents (lit., subjects) of education at all levels.

The draft Law assumes the enactment of the statutes (*polozheniia*) approved by the RSFSR government on a variety of types of educational institutions and the right of educational institutions to establish their own charters (*ustavy*). Thus, the Law "On Education" should regulate only the most general aspects of educational relations and provide an environment for the conduct of official policy in this area.

In contrast to the RSFSR Law on Public Education now in force, the draft Law "On Education" calls for a humane approach to instruction, for democratic foundations to the educational process, and for economy-minded practices.

During the transition period to a market economy educational institutions need particular nurturing and support from the state as well as reinforcement of their legal and economic base.

The draft Law fixes on paper ideas and principles which today have won their place in the public consciousness and the world of education, and brings the legal norms regulating education into alignment with the emerging legal system of the RSFSR.

The bill takes into account the structure and composition of the educational system as it now exists and creates the legal underpinnings for its further growth.

When contrasted with the law now in force, the bill implements the following conceptually novel elements:

In the area of human rights:

- giving priority to individual rights and interests, and creating favorable conditions for their realization;
- providing for individual adaptation to life in society;
- granting the right to establish private (lit.: "non-state") educational institutions to enterprises, societal organizations and individuals.

In the area of societal needs:

- giving priority to educational development as a factor of utmost importance in the development of society;
- giving priority to the formation of a civic spirit;
- aiming at enhancing the level of general and professional culture, at producing (a highly competent) professional and intellectual leadership;

In the political sphere:

- providing for the sovereignty of the RSFSR in educational matters;
- developing cooperation between republics and peoples of different nationalities;
- pursuing an anti-militaristic orientation in education;
- (encouraging) ideological pluralism in terms of the content of education, and protecting educational institutions from ideological pressure from political parties or societal political movements;

In the area of nationality politics:

- enhancing the nationality component in education;
- broadening the autonomy of nations, peoples and ethnic groupings in terms of educational organization;

In the economic sphere:

- changing the principles by which the government finances education, and namely:
- establishing financial norms based upon per capita calculations of the student population;
- indexing for inflation;
- increasing/fixing the share of national income devoted to education;
- establishing universal norms and principles of financing all licensed educational institutions regardless of the form of education;
- changing the method of financing higher education by instituting a system of individual government loans for students;
- recognizing the right of educational institutions to undertake commercial operations in education;
- introducing components of policies pertaining to taxation, financing and land (use) aimed at accelerating the growth of the education system;

In the sphere of governance and administration of education;

- strengthening the autonomy of educational units, decentralizing administrative functions, broadening the independence and accountability of founders of educational institutions;
- changing the principles of governmental supervision (*kontrol'*) over the activities of educational institutions;
- introducing the notion of "state educational standards" as the basis for regulating education;
- introducing parallel, non-state, educational structures;
- (providing) the right of educational institutions to unite;
- introducing the notion of "educational programs" and regulating, on this basis, the level of education as well as the types of educational institutions established;
- (promoting) a diversity of forms of instruction within educational programs and educational institutions;
- introducing new forms of education (home instruction, external education);
- securing the right of individuals to select their own type of instruction or school;

In the sphere of improving the living standards of teachers;

- providing that teachers' salaries be at the level of the average wage in the productive sphere;
- permitting employment based upon contractual agreements;

- offering partial compensation by the government for expenditures made by teachers to maintain or enhance their general level of culture;
- offering materials incentives for teachers working in remote areas, especially in the countryside.

The drafters of this bill took their cue not only from the recognition of the urgent need for renewal of the educational system, but also from estimates of real opportunities existing now or in the near future.

The need for timely adoption of this law stems from the direct causal link in the modern world between science, technology and the potential available to any state on the one hand, and the relationship between science, technology and the general level of education of a country's citizens, on the other.

The bill at hand is based upon a draft law drawn up by the Ministry of Education of the RSFSR and discussed at the Committee of Science and Higher Education of the RSFSR, with the participation of both the Ministry of Education and the State Committee of the RSFSR on Science and Higher Education. Comments and suggestions were also incorporated in the final stages of deliberation from members of the Presidium of the Supreme Soviet of the RSFSR, and from the commissions, chambers and committees of that body.

The Committee on Science and Public Education of the Supreme Soviet of the RSFSR recommends that the proposed Law of the RSFSR "On Education" be considered for adoption and that the draft of this law be published to encourage public discussion. Unfettered public discussion will allow more precise formulation of the underlying norms both of the law itself and the constitutional principles as well as civic values (*normy*) pertaining to education in general.

The Law of the Russian Federation
on Education (Draft)

Education includes instruction and *vospitanie* and has as its goal fostering the independent, free, cultured and moral individual who willing to assume responsibility before family, society and the state, and to respect the rights and freedoms of other citizens, the Constitution and laws, who is disposed to mutual understanding and cooperation among people, nations, as well as various racial, national, ethnic, religious and social groups.

Education is a fundamental right of the citizens of the Russian Federation.

Education in the Russian Federation is realized in compliance with international law, the Declaration on the State Sovereignty of the Russian Federation and the Constitution of the Russian Federation.

Part I: General Provisions

ARTICLE 1. The State Policy of the Russian Federation in the Sphere of Education

The Russian Federation pursues a sovereign state policy in the field of education and proclaims the sphere of education as a priority one.

ARTICLE 2. Legislation of the Russian Federation on Education

1. Legislation on education includes: the present Decree, other legislative acts of the Russian Federation issued in conformity with the former, decrees and other legislative acts of the constituent republics of the Russian Federation on education adopted on the basis of the present Decree and functioning in their territory.

2. Officials and citizens who have violated legislation of the Russian Federation on education are held responsible in accordance with the laws of the Russian Federation.

ARTICLE 3. The Tasks of Russian Federation Legislation on Education

The tasks of the legislation of the Russian Federation are as follows:

1. Ensuring and protecting the constitutional rights of the citizens of the Russian Federation to education.

2. Establishing legal guarantees for the free functioning and development of education in the Russian Federation.

3. Determining rights and commitments, the competence and responsibility of physical and legal entities in the field of education.

4. Determining the principles of state policy in the field of education.

ARTICLE 4. Principles of State Policy in the Sphere of Education

State policy in the field of education is based on the following principles:

1. The humanistic nature of education, the priority of human values, of human life and health and of the free development of the individual.

2. Links with national and regional cultural traditions.

3. The general accessibility of education within the limits of the state educational standard.

4. The secular nature of the state system of education.

5. The democratic, joint state-society nature of educational governance, and the autonomous functioning of educational institutions.

6. Freedom and pluralism of education, independence of state institutions from ideological directives and decisions of political parties, public movements and organizations.

ARTICLE 5. *The Rights of Citizens in the Sphere of Education*

1. Citizens of the Russian Federation within its territories are guaranteed the right to education regardless of race, nationality, language, sex, age, state of health, social or property status, occupation, social origin, domicile, attitude to religion, beliefs, party membership, or affiliations.

The law may specify cases of limitation of citizens's right to vocational training in respect of sex, age, state of health and previous convictions.

2. A citizen's right to education is ensured by the state through the provision of appropriate socio-economic conditions for obtaining education.

3. A citizen's freedom to choose educational institutions and language of instruction is guaranteed.

4. To promote implementation of the right to education of citizens in need of social protection and assistance, the state bears partial or full responsibility for expenses incurred for their upkeep during the term of education. Categories of citizens receiving such assistance as well as its type and dimension are to be determined in a manner established by the Government of the Russian Federation.

5. The state guarantees that citizens of the Russian Federation receive a free education at state educational institutions within the limits of the state educational standard (see Article 7). Expenses incurred for instruction provided at tuition-charging non-state educational institutions which offer a level of education no less than that mandated by state standards are to be reimbursed to citizens by the state at the same rates allocated for training at an equivalent state educational institution.

6. The state will provide special scholarships for exceptionally gifted individuals with demonstrable financial need, for study at home or abroad.

7. Citizens of the Russian Federation have the right to complete the course of studies at a given educational institution in the form of self-education, to sit for examinations without attending lectures, and (after so doing) to receive a graduation certificate.

8. Graduates of state and non-state educational institutions have equal rights to enrollment at educational institutions at the subsequent level of training.

9. Citizens of the union (sovereign) republics have the right to schooling at educational institutions of the Russian Federation as determined by inter-republican agreements.

Foreign nationals are entitled to enroll at educational institutions of the Russian Federation in accordance with inter-state treaties and agreements.

ARTICLE 6. *Language of Instruction*

1. The language of instruction at institutions of general education in the RSFSR, whether Russian or other, is to be determined by students and their parents and guardians. At all educational institutions where the native language

is the language of instruction, the study of Russian is to take place in accordance with standards set by the state.

2. The state renders assistance in obtaining education in their native language to people of all nations living on the territory of the Russian Federation as well as to representatives of the peoples of the Russian Federation living outside its territory.

3. Freedom of choice of the language of instruction is ensured by the establishment of the necessary number of appropriate educational institutions, classes and groups, as well as by the creation of conditions necessary for their functioning.

ARTICLE 7. State Educational Standards

1. The Russian Federation establishes state educational standards which determine minimal requirements for graduates of institutions at the various levels. The procedures for establishing and implementing standards are determined by the Government of the Russian Federation.

Part II: The System of Education

ARTICLE 8. The Concept of the System of Education

The system of education in the Russian Federation is a totality of successive educational programs at various levels, a network of educational institutions implementing them, bodies responsible for the management of education and enterprises of the system of education.

ARTICLE 9. Educational Programs

1. The Russian Federation implements educational programs which are subdivided into:
   a. general educational
   b. vocational

2. General educational programs are designed to enhance the level of culture, to facilitate adaptation to society, and to provide the basis for a deliberate choice of vocation as well as for professional training in that designated area.

3. General educational programs include:
   a. pre-school education
   b. primary, basic and secondary general education

4. Vocational and professional educational programs provide training of specialists with the appropriate qualifications as well as a steady enhancement of the level of professionalization in society.

5. Vocational and professional programs include those dealing with:
   a. primary vocational education
   b. secondary vocational and professional education

c. higher professional education

d. post-university professional education (clinical studies, post-graduate study at military academies or colleges, post-graduate courses, etc).

ARTICLE 10. Forms of Education

1. With due account of the needs and capabilities of the individual, educational programs are accessible in the following ways:

a. With or without leave from one's employment;

b. In an institutional setting, at home, or through continuing education programs. Resort to some combination of the above opportunities is also an option.

2. The list of professions and specialities, certification in which shall not be available through external studies, shall be determined by the Government of the Russian Federation.

ARTICLE 11. Educational Institutions

1. Educational institutions include those offering:

a. pre-school education

b. general education

c. education for orphans and wards of the state

c. vocational and professional education (primary, secondary specialized, higher, etc.)

d. continuing education

e. other educational services.

2. Educational institutions may be:

a. state and non-state

b. tuition-charging and free

c. commercial and noncommercial.

3. A state educational institution is a legal entity in its own right, and is set up, reorganized and liquidated in a manner established by the Government of the Russian Federation.

4. Non-state educational institutions acquire the status of legal entity upon registration with the state in a manner set forth by the Government of the Russian Federation.

5. The basic documents regulating the activities of educational institutions are the appropriate statutes ratified by the Government of the Russian Federation, as well as charters drawn up in conformity with these statutes.

6. Educational institutions have the right to conclude agreements among themselves, to unite into teaching and educational (*vospitatel'nye*) complexes and combined teaching-research-production associations with the participation of research, production and other institutions, organizations and enterprises, and to link up as territorial teaching-production amalgamations and associations.

The functions, structure and rights of educational and other institutions included in these complexes and associations are determined by statute.

7. Educational institutions which include units enjoying separate status as legal entities function as a single educational institution.

8. In order to grant educational institutions the status of gymnasium, lycée, academy, university, etc., and to assess the performance of these institutions a certification process will be instituted involving both the government and the public in accordance with statutes drawn up by the appropriate bodies of educational governance of the RSFSR.

9. The state guarantees the observance of the rights of educational institutions.

ARTICLE 12. *Founders of Educational Institutions*

1. Founders of educational institutions may include:

a. governing or administrative units at the local, republic or union level.

b. national and foreign combinations, enterprises, institutions and organizations of all property types.

c. public and religious organizations and combinations.

d. (citizens of the Russian Federation)

e. (citizens of other states.)

2. The relationship between founders and educational institutions is to proceed on a contractual basis unless otherwise stipulated by legislation.

ARTICLE 13. *Pre-School Education*

1. Parents are the first educators. They are called upon to establish the fundamentals of the physical, moral and intellectual development of the child in infancy.

2. The state guarantees the financial and material support of education during the infancy of the child.

3. A network of pre-school institutions will be maintained to support the family in the upbringing of infants and children of pre-school age, in the development of individual abilities, and to compensate for developmental anomalies.

4. The mission and functions of pre-school institutions, as well as organizational details, are to be determined in accordance with *national* (i.e. ethnic) and regional socio-economic, cultural and other conditions, and in accordance with the specific type of pre-school institution.

5. Legal relationships between pre-school institutions and parents (or guardians) are to be regulated by a parental contract, the form of which may differ from one pre-school institution to another.

ARTICLE 14. General Education

1. General education is the core of the system of education and grants all citizens of the Russian Federation equal opportunity to obtain and continue in a timely manner their education in conformity with individual vocations, interests and abilities.

2. General education includes three stages: primary, basic ("incomplete secondary") and ("complete") secondary. The age of entry and length of study at each stage are to be determined by charter for each educational institution.

3. Basic education is compulsory.

First Variant:

4. Entry examinations to the first level of study at state schools are not permitted.

Second Variant:

4. At state educational institutions offering an accelerated course of studies, admission to the first level may take place on a competitive basis.

Third Variant:

4. Entry examinations to the first level of study at state schools may be introduced at the discretion of the governing body of the individual institution.

First Variant:

5. Passage from the first (primary) to the second (basic) level of a general education takes place on the basis of examination results.

Second Variant:

5. Passage from the second (basic) to the third (complete secondary) level of general education takes place on the basis of examination results.

Third Variant:

5. Passage from the first to the second level of a general education can be determined by the governing body of the individual institution on the basis of examination results. Passage from the second to the third level of general education takes place on the basis of examination results.

First Variant:

6. Admission to the third level of schooling at general educational institutions can take place on a competitive basis at the discretion of the local governing body.

Second Variant:

6. Admittance of students to the third stage of education at general educational institutions is carried out on a competitive basis. (In the January version of the draft, this is item 4: all other variants are eliminated).

7. At the decision of the governing body of the school, annual examinations may be conducted as a condition of passage from one grade to the next.

8. Examinations may be replaced by a different type of certification (*attestatsiia*), medical or other, as stipulated by the charter of the school.

9. At general educational institutions supplementary educational services may be provided in addition to those stipulated by the state educational standard:

profiling of education (i.e., giving a distinctive educational "profile" to an entire school), individualized curricula, accelerated subject instruction. The curricula of such programs are approved by the institution.

10. By decision of the governing unit of the state educational institution, students 14 or older may be expelled.

11. Elementary vocational training may be conducted at general educational institutions in the form of supplementary educational services, provided there is an appropriate material base, including tuition fees. Elementary vocational training requires the consent of students and their parents (or guardians).

ARTICLE 15. Elementary Vocational Training

1. Elementary vocational instruction provides training, retraining and qualifications enhancement for workers, including the unemployed. A general basic education is the minimal educational level required to qualify for elementary vocational training.

2. Citizens with a more advanced level of education have the right to study at institutions offering a basic vocational education.

3. Admission to such institutions takes place at the request of the individual citizen. When applications exceed the number of places available, a competitive selection process may be introduced.

4. Elementary vocational education can be offered at the third level of instruction at general secondary education institutions, at vocational and professional colleges (*uchilishche*), at special courses, including temporary courses, organized to train and retrain employees and to provide skills upgrading, at other types of institutions, organizations and enterprises, and at other educational institutions.

5. Citizens, training for their first profession at a state school offering elementary vocational training, and those receiving retraining at the recommendation of an employment service, are to be provided with a free education.

6. The state will ensure that conditions exist at elementary vocational training institutions allowing the citizen to receive a general education as well.

7. The state will ensure that citizens without a basic education are allowed to be trained in a profession.

8. The list of professions and vocations taught at elementary vocational training institutions is certified by the Government of the RSFSR.

ARTICLE 16. Vocational and Professional Training at the Secondary Level

1. Secondary vocational training provides training, retraining and improvement of the qualification of specialists on the foundation of a basic and secondary general education; such training will be available for the unemployed and for workers released from their jobs. Citizens with a basic education will receive a complete secondary education along with secondary-level vocational and professional training.

2. Citizens with a more advanced level of education or professional training are allowed to enroll in institutions offering vocational or professional training at the secondary level.

3. Admissions to state institutions offering a secondary-level vocational or professional education may take place at the request of the individual or on a competitive basis.

4. A secondary-level vocational or professional education may be obtained at vocational *uchilishcha*, lycées, colleges (*kolledzhi*), specialized secondary educational or other educational institutions.

5. Citizens studying to receive their first profession may enroll without cost at state institutions offering a secondary-level vocational or professional education.

ARTICLE 17. *Higher Education*

1. Higher education has as its goals meeting individual needs for an advanced general education, acquiring or enhancing advanced qualifications or professional skills.

2. Higher education is built upon a general secondary or a secondary professional education.

3. A higher education may be received at tertiary-level educational institutions. Admissions procedures are to be regulated by the charter of the institution.

4. The right to receive a higher education within the limits of the state standard is provided through the availability of state-provided loans or grants.

5. Institutions of higher education in the Russian Federation may combine research and teaching, or research, teaching and production.

6. Students at institutions of higher education have the right to select their own focus within the framework of programs offered by that institution.

ARTICLE 18. *Post-University Professional Training*

Post-university education (post-graduate courses, clinical studies or residency, post-graduate studies at military academies or colleges, etc.) enables citizens of the Russian Federation to enhance their professional, scholarly and pedagogical qualifications. Such education is offered at higher educational establishments as well as at research institutions and at organizations specifically established for this mission.

ARTICLE 19. *Institutions of Continuing Education*

Continuing education structures in the RSFSR exist to ensure the availability of a diversity of educational services.

Extra-mural institutions of all types and kinds, centers of nationality culture, people's universities, lecture series, special courses, professional orientation centers, skills enhancement institutes, specialized departments (at institutions), programs for technical studies at enterprises, and other institutions may serve this purpose.

ARTICLE 20. Certificates and Documents of Educational Achievement

1. Educational institutions (with the exception of pre-school institutions) which have received state accreditation, grant graduates an official diploma or certificate specifying the education and level of qualification achieved.

2. A state educational certificate is necessary in order to continue one's education at a state educational institution at the next higher level, unless otherwise stipulated by the charter of that institution.

3. In compliance with licensing procedures vocational institutions of vocational and professional education can issue documents certifying achievement of a given level of skills or education.

4. Upon completion of post-university studies and submission of a qualification work (dissertation) an academic degree is granted and an appropriate document issued.

ARTICLE 21. Employment for Graduates of Vocational and Professional Institutions

The terms of finding employment for graduates of vocational and professional educational institutions as set by labor and employment legislation.

Part III: Educational Governance

ARTICLE 22. The Jurisdiction of the Russian Federation in the Sphere of Education

The following are in the domain of the supreme bodies of state authority and administration of the Russian Federation:

1. Determining and implementing a state policy in education;

2. Establishing regulatory codes for education;

3. Elaborating and implementing republican (Constituent Republics of the Russian Federation) educational programs, including international ones, taking into account distinctive nationality, regional, socio-economic, and demographic features;

4. Setting up the structures for the governance and supervision of education;

5. Establishing procedures for opening, reorganizing and closing educational institutions;

6. Establishing, reorganizing, and closing educational institutions, organizations and enterprises under the jurisdiction of the Russian Federation;

7. Organizing and coordinating the material and technical support of targeted (*tselevye*) republic-level and inter-regional programs for the development of education.

8. Approving charters for educational institutions.

9. Determining the order of attestation, accreditation and licensing of educational institutions, and the order of attestation of personnel in research and teaching.

10. Establishing state educational standards, state minimums, and equivalencies for degrees within the territory of the Russian Federation.

11. Determining the share of national income to be allocated to education, setting the RSFSR budget for expenditures on education, and establishing endowments (*fondy*) to advance education in the RSFSR.

12. Determining:

a. preferential taxes stimulating the development of education in the Russian Federation;

b. state norms for financing education;

c. the order of financing educational institutions and organizations of the system of education;

d. the minimal scale of wage and salary rates for personnel employed by educational institutions;

e. benefits, (types of and norms for) other forms of material support for students, alumni and teaching personnel at educational institutions;

13. Direct financing of educational institutions of the republics (of the Russian Federation), as well as of schools offering vocational and professional training at the elementary and secondary level;

14. Establishing a unified system for gathering statistics on education in the Russian Federation;

15. Meeting the needs of the education system for reliable information;

16. Organizing a system of teacher training (to meet the needs of) educational institutions.

17. Supervising the implementation of Russian Federation legislation on education and ensuring the observance of state educational standards.

18. Establishing and conferring honorary titles and awards of the Russian Federation on educational personnel.

ARTICLE 23. Jurisdiction of the Constituent Republics of the Russian Federation, Territories, Regions, Autonomous Regions and Autonomous Areas (Okrugy) in Education

1. Within the jurisdiction of the supreme authorities within the republics of the Russian Federation are the following:

a. Defining official education policy at the level of the republic;

b. Drawing up legislation on education at the level of the republic;

c. Establishing and conferring honorary titles and awards on educational personnel.

2. Within the authority of the supreme authorities of the Russian Federation's constituent republics, territories, regions, autonomous regions and autonomous areas are the following:

    a. Implementing official policy in education;

    b. Drawing up and implementing territorial-level programs, including international programs, for educational development, with due account of *national* and regional, socio-economic, cultural, demographic and other distinctive features;

    c. Establishing and supervising the appropriate territorial-level bodies to administer education;

    d. setting up, reorganizing or closing educational institutions of the system of education subordinated to these authorities;

    e. Formulating a *national* and regional component of state educational standards;

    f. drawing up a territorial budget and establishing endowments for educational development;

    g. Levying local taxes and dues for educational purposes;

    h. Introducing regional norms of financing education;

    i. Financing and rendering services providing material and technical support for educational institutions and organizations within the educational system;

    j. Establishing kinds and norms of material support for students, alumni, and teaching personnel at educational institutions, to supplement those provided by the Russian Federation;

    k. Making available on a regular basis reliable information on education to educational institutions;

    l. Organizing training, retraining and upgrading of qualifications for teaching personnel;

    m. Supervising the implementation of the Russian Federation's legislation on education and ensuring the observance of state educational standards.

ARTICLE 24. *Local Jurisdiction in Education*

The jurisdiction of bodies of local self-government in the field of education is determined on the basis of the Russian Federation's Law "On Local Self-Government" and of the Russian Federation's legislation on education.

ARTICLE 25. *Governance of Individual Educational Institutions*

1. Governance over state educational institutions is carried out in conformity with the legislation of the Russian Federation and with the charter of a given educational institution.

2. Overall governance of state educational institutions is carried out by the elective representative body--the Council (*Sovet*) of the Educational Institution.

Direct supervision (*rukovodstvo*) of state educational institutions is carried out by the head, director, rector or another administrator.

3. The relationships between individual educational institutions and local authorities proceed in conformity with the legislation of the Russian Federation and the constituent republics of the Russian Federation. Such legislation defines the jurisdiction of these bodies.

4. Intervention by the state in the academic, research, economic or other affairs of state educational institutions is permitted only in the case of violations of the law of the RSFSR.

5. Political parties and movements shall not establish organizations, nor shall such organizations function at state educational institutions or within the system of administrative governance of education.

ARTICLE 26. *The State Administrative Structure for Education*

1. The following official units of administration in education function in the Russian Federation:

    a. State administrative units supervising education in the Russian Federation;

    b. State administrative units supervising education in the constituent republics of the Russian Federation;

    c. State administrative units supervising education in regions, territories, autonomous regions and autonomous areas.

2. Administrative units supervising education in districts, cities and municipal districts can be set up by decision of local self-government bodies.

3. State administrative units supervising education ensure the implementation of state educational standards and norms at educational institutions in conformity with legislation of the Russian Federation.

4. (In the event that an educational institution violates the legislation of the Russian Federation on education and/or its own charter, state authorities supervising education have the right to terminate its activities in respect of a possible violation of the legislation pending a court decision on the matter.

5. The state may raise before the governing unit of a given educational institution and/or the sponsor of an educational institution the issue of whether the personnel or administrators of that institution are fulfilling their obligations.

ARTICLE 27. *Public Governance in Education*

At the initiative of the public or of individual citizens, (non-state) organizations providing for public governance of education can be established.

ARTICLE 28. *Mutual Relations Between the State and Non-State Educational Institutions*

1. Non-state educational institutions are registered by the local administration, which is expected to file an application for the purpose. These institutions

obtain the right to pursue educational activities after licensing has been effected by state bodies supervising education.

2. At the request of non-state educational institutions state authorities exercising supervision over education carry out their attestation and accreditation according to established procedures.

3. State educational authorities are empowered to intervene in the affairs of non-state educational institutions only in the event of violations of the laws of the Russian Federation on education or violations of the internal charters of those institutions.

ARTICLE 29. The Relationship Between State Educational Authorities and Educational Institutions under the Authority of other Branches of Government

State educational authorities supervise the observance of the Russian Federation's legislation on education at educational institutions belonging to enterprises or other branches of government.

Part IV: Economics of the System of Education

ARTICLE 30. Property Rights in Education

1. The property of educational institutions, organizations and enterprises belong to their founders, who have the right to cede such property to the usage or direct ownership of the institutions.

2. Land plots granted to educational institutions, organizations and enterprises by local government authorities are to be held in perpetuity without compensation, but must not be alienated (*variant: or can be transferred or sold only in the event that the institution is liquidated*).   The allocation of plots of land for the construction of new educational institutions will take place on a priority basis, effected by local Soviets of People's Deputies and regulated by the land Code of the Russian Federation.

3. State educational institutions, may be privatized according to procedures established by legislation of the Russian Federation.

4. The Russian Federation recognizes the right to ownership of intellectual property in the sphere of education, including educational technology. The procedures for establishing patents over intellectual property are regulated by the laws of the Russian Federation.

ARTICLE 31. Financing Education

1. State financing of education serves as a fundamental guarantee of the citizen's right to an education in the RSFSR.

2. Financing educational institutions takes place on the basis of state norms of financing calculated in terms of numbers of pupils, wards, or students for

each type and kind of educational institution, and with the assumption that real outlays per student will regularly increase over time. The absolute sum of per-capita outlays will be indexed to keep pace with inflation.

3. The state guarantees the annual allocation of funds for educational purposes to the sum of at least 10 per cent of the GNP, as well as protection of corresponding expenditure items of the budget in conditions of inflation.

4. Educational institutions, regardless of property type, have the right to attract additional financial resources, including hard currency, by providing educational and other services. Attraction of additional sources of funds does not entail reduction of norms or of the absolute sum of funds allocated to a given educational institution from the state budget.

ARTICLE 32. State Measures to Stimulate Education

1. Educational institutions are exempt from all manner of duties, taxations or exactions.

2. Enterprises and organizations, at least thirty five percent of whose assets (*ustavnoi fond*) are dedicated to education, belong to the system of education. Such enterprises and organizations are not subject to taxation on output destined for use within the system of education;

3. Producers of goods for education will enjoy the same privileges accorded producers of consumer goods;

4. Enterprises, organizations, institutions and individuals working to promote educational growth will enjoy privileges stipulated by existing legislation.

5. Enterprises will be allowed to deduct from taxable income that proportion of the goods and services produced which are sold to educational institutions or governing structures in education;

6. That proportion of the income of enterprises invested in educational development, including scholarly research, design and experimentation, is exempt from all taxes, exactions or duties of the Russian Federation;

7. Enterprises taking part in implementing republican, regional, or municipal-level educational development programs are eligible for tax exemptions stipulated in the laws of the Russian Federation;

8. Enterprises and organizations engaged in producing or delivering those material resources needed by educational enterprises and for the production of textbooks, instructional aids and equipment for the schools, are eligible for a tax reduction of fifty percent on the profit earned in such transactions;

9. Publishing houses and printing firms which receive government orders for textbooks and instructional materials amounting to no less than five percent of their output are eligible for a tax reduction of twenty-five percent on profit earned from such activities;

10. Firms engaged in school construction and housing for personnel in education are eligible for:

a. salary and wage supplements of twenty-five percent for work completed on schedule;

b. bonus supplements of up to five percent of the budgeted costs for work completed on schedule;

11. Newly established firms and enterprises of the educational system are exempt from all taxation and payments for the first two years of their existence;

12. Individual income not subject to taxation will include the equivalent of those sums spent for instruction or training in educational institutions or those fees paid by parents to pre-school institutions;

13. The state will remunerate parents of children receiving home instruction the average sum spent per capita on state educational institutions at the corresponding level in a given region, through the level of secondary education.

ARTICLE 33. *The Material and Technical Foundations of Educational Institutions*

1. Growth of the material and technical base of education will take place on a priority basis according to state-set norms.

2. State property turned over to educational institutions is not subject to confiscation or to exploitation for goals or purposes contrary to the fundamental mission or goals of the educational institution.

ARTICLE 34. *Rights of Educational Institutions to Utilize Financial Resources*

1. The financial and economic activities of state educational institutions will follow procedures set down in statutes confirmed by the Government of the Russian Federation;

2. Financial resources will be used in accordance with regulations set down by the charter of the educational institution;

3. Resources not expended during the current fiscal year are not subject to confiscation, but may be utilized subsequently by the institution;

4. Unexpended resources originally designated to supplement the well being of students or wards of institutions will be dedicated to the same purpose in the following fiscal year;

ARTICLE 35. *Fees for Educational Services*

1. Educational institutions may render the following or other supplementary fee-bearing services to the population, to enterprises and organizations: instruction in specific courses or disciplines, advanced subject study. Such services must not be in place of budget-financed activities.

2. Budget allocations to finance educational institutions may not be reduced through the imposition of fees for services previously provided without charge.

ARTICLE 36. The Commercial Activities of Educational Institutions

1. Educational institutions are entitled to engage in commercial activities other than rendering educational services to the population. Such activities must not violate the law of the Russian Federation nor interfere with the basic mission of the institution.

Part VI: Social Protection of Education

ARTICLE 37. The Rights and Social Protection of Students

1. The rights and duties of students at educational institutions are determined by institutional charter as well as by the laws of the Russian Federation.

2. Students of all educational institutions have the right to obtain education in compliance with a definite state educational standard; to have their human dignity respected; to enjoy freedom of conscience and information; to possess their own views and convictions and to express them freely. Institutional charters shall define the rights of students to participate in governance, to select individualized programs or curricula and shall set the length and pace of study.

3. Students of educational institutions are provided in prescribed manner with scholarship grants, allowances, accommodation at hostels and boarding houses, subsidized or free meals and transportation, and with other types of material aid.

4. Those studying at educational institutions, both state and non-state, during their working hours and maintaining a satisfactory record have the right to an additional paid holiday from their place of work, to a reduced work week and to other benefits provided in a manner fixed by the legislation of the Russian Federation.

5. At state educational institutions and at non-state ones possessing a license the cost of educating orphans and wards of the state will be assumed by the state.

6. Children and adolescents with special needs (physical or mental) will be entitled to an education at specialized educational institutions capable of providing them an adequate education as well as compensatory training or rehabilitation. Children and adolescents shall be sent to these educational institutions only with the consent of their parents or guardians and by decision of a psychological-medical-pedagogical commission. Certain designated categories of those enrolled at such educational institutions shall be fully maintained by the state.

7. For children and adolescents needing highly structured learning environments, specialized institutions are set up to provide for their education, vocational training and medical-social rehabilitation. (The January version of this draft adds: *Students are sent to these institutions only by court decision*

taken on the basis of recommendations by the governing structures of education-
al institutions.

    8. Individuals held at corrective-labor institutions shall be allowed to pursue
their own education or self-education.

    10. Governing institutions, state or otherwise, can set up elite educational
institutions for gifted children, adolescents and young people. Above-norm
funding of such educational institutions is provided by the budget of the sponsor.
The criteria for selecting students for such educational institutions are
determined by the sponsor and made available to the public.

    11. Once the schedule and curriculum of an educational institution have been
adopted they become mandatory for all official bodies and personnel.
Responsible authorities who violate the schedule or curriculum shall be fined
1,000 to 5,000 rubles by the court.

    12. Students shall not be coerced to join political organizations, movements
and parties or to participate in the activities of such organizations, in political·
activities or campaigns. [Individuals or groups] guilty of such coercion shall be
fined 1,000 to 3,000 rubles by the court.)

ARTICLE 38. *Measures to Protect the Health of Students*

    1. Educational institutions will provide a healthy environment for students.
The burden of the academic and work load imposed upon students and their
regimen of studies are determined by the charter of the educational institution
on the basis of guidelines set down by official bodies supervising education by
mutual agreement with health organizations.

    2. For children in need of prolonged medical treatment special institutions,
including those of sanatorium type, will be available. Classes can also be held
at medical institutions or at home.

    3. The inflationary growth of expenditure on children's meals and health
protection are fully compensated by the state.

    4. The responsibility for non-observance of established conditions of studies,
labor and leisure for alumni and students at institutions of general education is
borne by the sponsor and/or directors of educational institutions in accordance
with legislation and jurisdiction.

ARTICLE 39. *Rights and Obligations of Parents and Guardians*

    1. Parents or guardians of children have the right to select the forms of
instruction and types of educational institutions their children receive, to insist
that their children be treated with respect, that their legal rights and interests be
observed, and that conditions be maintained ensuring that their children receive
an adequate education. They shall have the right to file complaints, both
through administrative channels and through the judiciary, against educators,
administrators, or founders of educational institutions.

2. Parents or guardians have the right to provide their child with an education, up to and including the secondary level, at home. In such cases an agreement is to be concluded between parents or guardians, a school selected by the parents or guardians, and the appropriate educational authority, setting forth the legal, economic, and others commitments of the parties with due account of the interests of the child, family and society. (Added in January draft: *This agreement may be nullified at the initiative of the proper educational authorities, only upon evaluation of the child and through judgement of the court.*) Children have the right to continue their education at any level of schooling after receiving the appropriate *attestatsiia*.

3. (Added in January draft: *Parents or guardians are liable for all additional expenses incurred for the education or training of their children in the event that they repeat a class or are transferred to classes (schools) of a correctional nature or to specialized education institutions.*)

ARTICLE 40. *Hiring Procedures for Teaching Personnel*

1. Classroom instruction in state educational institutions shall not be engaged in by individuals forbidden to do so by court order or restricted on medical grounds according to a list verified by the Government of the Russian Federation.

2. Hiring procedures at educational institutions are regulated by their internal charters. Labor relations are determined by contracts concluded between employees and the given educational institution.

ARTICLE 41. *Salaries and Wages of Personnel in Educational Institutions*

1. The minimum wage and salary rates set for teaching personnel at educational institutions are to exceed the average industrial wage rates prevailing in the Russian Federation.

2. (Added in January draft: *The size of the average salary rate for personnel at educational institutions is fixed at the following levels:*

for professors and lecturers at higher educational establishments--twice that obtaining for industrial workers in the Russian Federation;

for teachers and other educational personnel--not less than the average wage rates of industrial workers in the Russian Federation;

for auxiliary and service personnel--not less than the average wage paid similar categories of industrial workers in the Russian Federation.)

3. Instructional or other activities carried out above and beyond those functionally related to the teacher's obligations are to be remunerated in accordance with existing legislation.

4. Employees are not to be compelled to carry out tasks not directly related to their contractual obligations without their explicit consent, except in circumstances stipulated by law.

5. Educational institutions can fix, within the limits of available funds intended to be used as wages and salaries, differentiated increments to wage and salary rates specified in contracts, and can employ various progressive approaches to setting wages and stimulating efforts.

(*Added in January draft: It is forbidden to seek funds for these purposes by surpassing the admissible teaching loads.*)

ARTICLE 42. Rights, Social Guarantees and Privileges of Personnel at Educational Institutions

1. Personnel at educational institutions are entitled to freedom of instruction (*na svobodu prepodovaniia*), to their professional honor and dignity, to fair conditions conductive to their professional duties, to the opportunity to improve their qualifications, to (the opportunity for) classroom initiatives (*pedagogicheskoi initsiativ)* and to participate in running the school.

2. Educational personnel have the right, after ten years of uninterrupted service, to a sabbatical (of up to one year); the appropriate procedures being determined by the charter of the given educational institution.

3. Employees in education enjoy pension rights, the right to extended paid vacations, a reduced work week, special dispensation to receive apartments and other household services, free medical care and other privileges (modified in successive drafts).

4. Employees in education will have special benefits in obtaining printed materials, including periodical publications. This will include compensation by the state of up to ten percent of salary.

5. Employees in education at state educational institutions located in workers' settlements and small towns are offered the same privileges provided specialists in agriculture, including priority access to housing and food.

6. Graduates of teacher training institutions (higher and secondary) as well as other specialists taking up employment in rural schools will be eligible to receive the same living adjustments offered graduates of higher agricultural institutions and technicums.

7. Employees of (instructional) workshops or enterprises and training facilities connected with educational institutions will receive the same privileges and benefits provided to employees in analogous institutions.

8. State and local authorities, enterprises and organizations may offer educational personnel supplementary social benefits not stipulated in existing legislation.

Part IV: Joint International Activities in Education

ARTICLE 43. Cooperation Between Republics

In the field of education cooperation between the Russian Federation and the sovereign republics takes place on the basis of treaties and agreements among the respective republics.

ARTICLE 44. International Cooperation

1. Education authorities at all levels and individual educational institutions have the right to establish direct ties with foreign and international institutions, organizations and enterprises in the implementation of international education, scientific and research programs according to procedures determined by legislation of the Russian Federation.

2. The training, retraining and upgrading of qualifications of foreign nationals are carried out in accordance with agreements concluded by educational institutions and organizations with foreign institutions and organizations or with individual foreigners.

ARTICLE 45. International Economic Activities

1. Educational authorities and individual educational institutions, organizations and enterprises connected with education have the right to carry out foreign economic activities on their own in a manner stipulated by legislation of the Russian Federation.

2. Institutions, organizations and enterprises of the system of education retain no less than seventy percent (*later drafts changed wording to "all"*) of hard currency earnings gained through their foreign economic activities. These earnings are to be reinvested in education to enhance its material and technical base.

Teachers' Gazette
July, 1991 (No. 29)

About the Book
and Editors

Framed by an introductory essay by Ben Eklof, the translated documents in this volume are crucial to understanding Russian educational reform efforts. These primary sources, based on previously unpublished statistical data and public opinion surveys, depict current conditions in Russia's schools. Reflecting the approach of the leading historian of education Edward Dneprov—now the powerful minister of education serving under Boris Yeltsin—the documents describe the radical reform philosophy and program first published in *Teachers' Gazette* in 1988, which now serve as the operative legislation for all secondary schools.

The VNIK (Temporary Scientific Research Collective on the Schools) reform movement is a fascinating microcosm of perestroika in terms of goals, mobilization, and the complicated, painful process of implementation. This unique glimpse into Russian education in a period of turmoil will interest all those who follow Russian politics and society.

A specialist on nineteenth-century Russian education and culture who has spent many years in the Soviet Union, **Ben Eklof** is associate professor of history at Indiana University. **Edward Dneprov** is minister of education in Russia.

Index

Framed by an introductory essay by Ben Eklof, the translated documents in this volume are crucial to understanding Russian educational reform efforts. These primary sources, based on previously unpublished statistical data and public opinion surveys, depict current conditions in Russia's schools. Reflecting the approach of the leading historian of education Edward Dneprov—now the powerful minister of education serving under Boris Yeltsin—the documents describe the radical reform philosophy and program first published in *Teachers' Gazette* in 1988, which now serves as the operative legislation for all secondary schools.

The VNIK (Temporary Scientific Research Collective on the Schools) reform movement is a fascinating microcosm of perestroika in terms of goals, mobilization, and the complicated, painful process of implementation. This unique glimpse into Russian education in a period of turmoil will interest all those who follow Russian politics and society.

Ben Eklof is associate professor of history and codirector of the Institute for the Study of